CREATING WAVES

By the same author:

Single Fin

CREATING WAVES

How surfing inspires our most
creative New Zealanders

AARON TOPP

HarperCollins*Publishers*

To Ian,
mate, mentor, surfer

National Library of New Zealand Cataloguing-in-Publication Data

Topp, Aaron, 1975-
Creating waves : how surfing inspires our most creative
New Zealanders / Aaron Topp.
ISBN 978-1-86950-748-0
1. Surfers—New Zealand. 2. Surfing—New Zealand.
I. Title.
797.32092293—dc 22

First published 2009
HarperCollins*Publishers (New Zealand) Limited*
PO Box 1, Shortland Street, Auckland 1140
Copyright © Aaron Topp 2009

Aaron Topp asserts the moral right to be identified as the
author of this work.

ISBN 978 1 86950 748 0

Cover design by Natalie Winter
Cover image: *Rising Swell Raglan* by Tony Ogle
Typesetting by Pauline Whimp, PawPrints Design and Illustration

Printed by Griffin Press, Australia

70gsm Classic used by HarperCollinsPublishers is a natural, recyclable
product made from wood grown in sustainable forests. The manufacturing
processes conform to the environmental regulations in the country of origin, Finland.

CONTENTS

Preface

Surfers are a fascinating bunch. They may function in a normal society, but in reality, they're a few steps removed from it. Sometimes they're unashamed about it and openly fit the stereotype, other times they're hidden behind business attire and briefcase. Underneath either exterior is a soul with a physical and emotional affinity with our environment that the rest of the world often struggles to understand, yet I suspect, deeply admires. To put yourself at the mercy of something as awe-inspiring as the ocean is to accept your place in the world. While there's great risk and skill required in doing so, at the same time, the reward is such that these children of the sea will do it again and again, and for hours at a time. It is their sanctuary, a time to meditate, a place to share with like-minded souls, to be free of constraints. To feel the highs of life. At times, it seems land for them is just a place to hang until the next swell arrives. Kinda like evolution in reverse.

New Zealand's future is at a tipping point. Our untouched environment has been compromised and some of our resources exploited unsustainably. While we like to think we are a small oasis at the bottom of the world, in reality we are a small cork bobbing on the waves left by the bows of much bigger ships. To survive, the business world is throwing the bean counters out of the CEO's chair, and ushering in creative people. Creative people see things outside the square. They, too, are often one or more steps removed from mainstream society.

Creative people have traditionally articulated their thoughts and experiences of the world for the rest of society to feed upon. They're the storytellers, the movie makers, the artists, the sculptors, the photographers, the musicians, the philanthropists. The visionaries. They're where inspiration radiates from and information is shared. Where a less creative person simply sees a wave, the creative individual sees energy in motion, inspiration, a moment in time as unique as a fingerprint. This distinction formed the basis of this book; my challenge was to gather a collection of highly imaginative people from a diverse range of disciplines who could explain the world from a surfer's perspective. A group of people with nothing in common but a love of the ocean and the exhilaration of standing upon it.

Well, that was the initial pitch. But this journey around the following 19 New Zealanders delivers so much more. Sure, they talk of their creative talents — their journeys to becoming successful in their chosen field — and their love of surfing, but what also follows are stories from the heart, from deep within the creative surfer's life. They have drawn strength and nurture from the ocean to overcome major personal battles from which many in society would fail to recover. These are issues not exclusive to surfers, but what makes these surfers different is that their stories champion outside-the-box solutions. To them, the ocean is as much a healer as it is a source of inspiration.

While some generations may still scowl at the thought of learning something from a surfer, the world is very quickly moving to a place where these people have been living for decades. Keep it simple, stupid. The people featured in this book have found the definition of happiness and proceeded to wrap the rest of their lives around it. After being in the presence of these remarkable people, I came to the conclusion there is a lot to be said for following your bliss. Stick the corporate ladder, the traffic jams, the precious clients! These surfers all peeled the complications of society back from their lives a long time ago and found what made them happy. From where they're sitting, the world makes sense, expectations are met, life is lived. The ocean has been as much a form of guidance for them as it is an entertainer.

Surfers as leaders, now there's a thought. If the ocean takes up 70 per cent of the earth's surface, then it's fair to say surfers understand a good chunk of what makes the world go round. They understand how to capture the concentrated forms of nature as they roll to shore, and to use them for the purpose of empowerment. That's what it's about. That connection with a greater force and how it's used for creativity and personal enlightenment. These are the fundamentals of the following inspiring stories.

Thanks for reading.

Aaron Topp
2009

Introduction

By Bob Harvey

Painting the edges

I don't know why we call this planet we exist on 'Earth'. Clearly, the word we are searching for is 'water', for that is what this spinning orb, flying through space, is really made of. Like us, in fact, for we too are Oceanic.

A few years ago, I was invited to Stockholm to get one of those prizes that the Swedes like to give you for doing good deeds, but I really wanted to go for another reason. In Sweden, they have done the most work on water: its composition, its uses and its reuses. I spent three days with a group of hydrology scientists and researchers who had devoted most of their lives to water and its properties. I was working on my own theory also, and although their obsession was to re-energise and re-charge polluted water, turning it into fresh water again, my idea was more complex and more mystic: does water retain a memory?

The Swedes said it did — that water which has passed over shallow creeks, along rivers, cascaded down waterfalls, through mountain glens and ravines, will retain a memory that can be recalled. Closer to home it's said that the ancient voyaging Polynesians sailing by the great Southern sky, wind and bird flight, also had a blind navigator on board who would taste water from a coconut bowl, not unlike the tea tasters of India. The taster could, with his learned taste buds, analyse where ocean currents were going, the taste of distant Atotoland islands and rivers and coastlines in the mists. He was in fact tasting not just water but the essence of the sea. Sadly, this ancient art has now been lost to us, but not the idea.

Then I asked the hydrologists the really big question: does water have life? Does it somehow have a pulse? If it has memory, does it also have another dimension? The search for a pulse in water has been going on for nearly 50 years, and in the 1960s the team of Swedish researchers claimed they had got very close to breaking down the molecular structure of water. I believe this is possible. The great oceans of the world still hold the secrets of their origin and the people who have sailed on them. It's a tough ask, for even their creation is unknown — the origin of the great oceans is still uncertain to the most enlightened scientists of today. But in the future we will hopefully know more, we will uncover the mystery and secrets of its watery memory and, in doing so, we will possibly find our own destiny as human beings. For now as always the sea enthralls and awes us, and when it touches and comes near land, it draws us closer to it. We feel as one with it, wanting to be part of it, to challenge it, to enjoy its many pleasures, to voyage on its great, vast surfaces, to swim above and below in its depths, and over the past 200 years, to understand its playful possibilities in the ultimate thrill: the joy of surfing.

We can only imagine the wonder that struck the crew of Cook's *Endeavour* to see the surfing kings of Ancient Hawaii, standing proudly on their massive wooden boards, true golden gods of the Pacific Ocean. Later they bore witness to the sight of splendid women surfers. Awesome golden goddesses of Polynesia. For here in the Hawaiian islands at this time, in the home of surfing, are the origins of the world's greatest ocean pastime.

Surfing in the Hawaiian islands and throughout the Pacific is as old as the ancient cultures and traditions. It was given its own name, he'e nalu, and with it came traditions that to mess with would be fatal. Surfing was ritualised by class, by culture, by festivals. It was the sport of the kings, who sometimes surfed wearing their massive feathered headdresses and ceremonial cloaks, for this was never simply about catching waves, this was a mysterious and glorious art. Surfing was noble and commoners would take their rightful place on smaller boards, but never at the same time as their hierarchically chiefly leaders. I guess it was fatal to cut in on a chiefly ride. Certainly, there was a taboo class system and to break it was to invite death.

It is said the surfing ritual around the ancient Makahiki festival had been celebrated for a thousand years in the Hawaiian islands, but in 1819 it fell apart, abandoned due to pressure from the recently arrived missionaries. It was one of the most significant catastrophes in Hawaiian history and, indeed, began the breakdown of integrated Hawaiian society. The Hawaiians loved the water and the rolling, roaring surf that blessed their islands. They celebrated it with their art. Their woven paintings and surfing sculptures carved on ceremonial bowls and other sacred instruments, on weapons of war and death, were the first recorded depictions of surfing. Along with the arrival of missionaries and the end of surfing came restrictions on the sexual freedom of men and women surfers, who could no longer surf naked on the reef swells at Waikiki and throughout the islands. It was simply forbidden by the moral doctrine of the near-fanatical and obsessed missionaries.

The near disappearance of surfing was certainly not restricted to the Hawaiian islands. Tahitian surfing, equally enriched in tradition and ritual and second in celebration to Hawaiian surfing in pre-European times, completely vanished. The New Zealand Maori, by the time of early colonisation, had also seemed to have given up the love of surfing. There is no record of surfboards or early descriptions of Maori taking to the waves, although they were a committed water people. Their pleasures and gains were by then based on tribal warfare training, on hand and body agility. This isolated society had moved from the pleasure of enjoying wave-riding to the art of war.

It is a great cultural tragedy that there are no relics or archaeological finds that have traced this lost art. In the late 1950s, four months of ferocious winter winds stripped the coastal sand on the West Coast. South of Karekare, in an area known by surfers as the wastelands, on the beach lowered almost to bedrock, a group of us on a morning run found an outline of a massive shaped plank. Within the outline was caked dust, fine as powder to the touch. Surfers all, we instantly felt it had once carried a rider. It could not be touched or held, it eluded carbon dating or testing. I have always believed this find held the ancient link. Within days the west wind had blown it skyward.

By the end of the 19th century, there had been no significant attempts to recreate the art of surfing as a modern tradition. The revival of Hawaiian surfing happened by chance in the first years of the 20th century, when Hawaii became a tourist destination. Even in those days, few Hawaiians actually surfed, although a number of young tourists on Waikiki Beach were given demonstrations on the lost art of surfing by local beach boys, riding the easy rolling breakers inside the reef. It relieved the boredom, and suddenly there was an awareness that this sport had a thrill to it, a certain level of skill, and surfing once again became an interesting and popular pastime in Hawaiian culture. By 1911, you could see a hundred surfboards in the water at Waikiki Beach.

It might have stayed that way — a quaint local tradition — if it hadn't been for the extraordinary Duke Kahanamoku, Olympic swimming champion and surfer. He embarked on a world tour, bearing the ancient culture of his ancestors. In Australia, he demonstrated the sport of surfing on Bondi Beach with a hastily cut and shaped board. As clumsy and heavy as it was, the Duke rode it to shore to the amazement of the overdressed onlookers, and surfing was thus introduced to another country and another culture. It is interesting to note that when the Duke came to New Zealand, they were neither awed nor impressed by this amazing man, and nor did they ask him to demonstrate the art of surfing. It's my feeling that racism played a role here. As a native Hawaiian, the Duke was seen as a savage, a second-rate citizen in 1915 New Zealand culture. He had nothing to offer this arrogant country, and Maori were not represented at any of the receptions or swimming demonstrations he attended.

Therefore New Zealand did not catch the surfing wave. In those strict times, with separate bathing beaches for men and women, tight controls by local councils and authorities on costumes and swimming times, the system was as rigid — if not more so — as under the Hawaiian missionaries. There was simply no place for surfing in society.

But New Zealand did have its fledgling surf clubs, founded in 1910 in Sumner in Christchurch, and Lyall Bay in Wellington. They were based upon beach drills for rescues and their members were trained like soldiers and firemen. Their ritual, if it can be called that, was linked to the stringent ritualised rescue procedure for swimming pools, rivers and lakes. All members were tested by instructors.

So surf life saving, the beach culture of New Zealand, had no wish or will to loosen and free the spirit of its members. For this was not a sport. This was a service. And surfing was perceived as a foreign native culture, one which had the stigma of racial inequality. It would stay that way for 50 years.

It took the arrival of cinema and the cult of beauty, bodies, tanning, swimming and diving, to change our attitude and break the chains. New Zealanders finally went to the beach to simply enjoy it. To lie in the sun, to fish, and to swim and play. We bought humble baches on remote beaches, played cricket on the sand, and walked in shorts and sandshoes. We swam in short woollen togs, with women daring to wear two-piece costumes. Although a war would come along and call a short halt to this, the '50s would see us in the best of times, enjoying prosperity, sun and sand.

I remember in 1958 the arrival of two remarkable, out-of-work lifeguards from California, Rick Stoner and Ben Copland, who turned up at Piha Beach. They had with them two surfboards, made of beautifully shaped polystyrene coated with the miracle-of-the-age fibreglass, with a polished wooden stringer and a single fin. They demonstrated with ease surfing for the first time in New Zealand off Camel Rock. Within a fortnight, they had joined the Piha Surf Club, and started to teach a local club member and tomato grower — Peter Byers — the art of shaping boards. The new age of surfing had begun.

The boards owed their success to the recent scientific advances of polystyrene and fibreglass. Over the next winter, boards were skilfully shaped in backyard sheds and garages by clubbies and their dads. They were dream machines, a glorious homage to freedom and to a rebel culture, breaking free of English society in the South Pacific. Surfing cut through society; everyone under 20 could do it. All it took was a little practice and skill. It ruined many New Zealand schoolboys' future academic careers. It was addictive and impossible to regulate or police. It was total and absolute freedom of mind, body and spirit.

At the end of 2008, I stood on the deck of the Piha Surf Club drinking a cold beer with Ben Copland as a great orb of West Coast sun descended into Roaina the surf. We were waiting for the famed green flash. Ben had returned to New Zealand for the first time in 50 years. He'd come back to be honoured by this club and this community. He'd come back without Rick, who he had clearly loved greatly. He spoke affectionately of his lifeguard buddy, of the great times they'd had at Piha. They had been accepted into the club, had competed for the club, and now with his wife, Ben had made this symbolic and very emotional trip back. Rick had died in the late 1980s, but he was very much part of this grand evening and dinner.

Ben had gone on to be one of the most successful board-makers in the United States. His brand and boards, of which he claimed there were 60,000, were out there catching waves and had made his life complete. In his early 70s, Ben was still preaching the gospel of surfing. As I talked with him, we remembered the weekends at Piha in the '50s. It was a different New Zealand, both socially and culturally, tied to a bleak institutional culture; surfing set us all free and gave a generation of young men and women the chance to achieve a personal pleasure that, unless you were an All Black, you would never have experienced. This was the only sport borne of the 20th century which gained a cult following great enough to transcend culture, race and New Zealand society's rigid structure. I credit surfing with giving New Zealand a new future.

As surfing started to influence New Zealanders' lives, a new cult was emerging in California. Freedom had bred a new individual, and the mood was changing, returning to the natural world, the primitive and the wild. With it came a heady mixture of hallucinogenic art. The art of the new came out of the Haight-Ashbury area in San Francisco. Its psychedelic, rhythmic graphics grew out of music and dope, filling concert halls for the new rage of music artists such as The Grateful Dead, Janis Joplin and The Beach Boys. The Beach Boys were the link to the surf through the new invention of the transistor radio, which allowed music to travel to the beach. And travel it did.

Now the threads become a trend. Music was transformed into visual imagery, and music and surfing became intrinsically linked. Yet it was still missing another ingredient: art. Photography always had a place in surfing, but its audience was small. The magnificent surf photographers, probably some of the best of all time, were surfing's great ambassadors. Alfred Richard Gurney Junior, who somehow got his heavy camera into an outrigger in 1914, published 'The Surf Riders of Hawaii', a fantastic mystical photo essay which was first published as a handmade book and later reprinted in an early surfing magazine. His work captures Duke Kahanamoku at his peak, a homage to him. What is astonishing is Gurney's ability to focus from his outrigger, to hold the image of what must have been two fast-moving objects.

There were also, in those days, a few piers and swimming platforms around Waikiki, and a growing interest in postcards and images of Hawaii and surfing. Yet it was still very difficult — the telephoto lens and waterproofed camera were still a long way in the future. A close-proximity photograph of a surfer was nigh-on impossible — they had to come to the camera. Gurney did it first, a pioneer of surf photography. Others would follow: Tom Blake in the '30s, Doc Ball in the '40s and Don James with his magnificent photographs of surfing San Onofre to Point Dune 1936–1942. They were more than just pioneers, they were innovative and competent masters of the lens, and they were advancing surf photography to an art form of beauty, balance and style.

Soon after the late '50s visit of Stoner and Copland, a group of us young clubbies went to hear and see Bruce Brown narrating his home-made movie *Endless Summer* in the Auckland Town Hall. With a 16 mm projector and two turntables, he would spin a stack of small 45 rpm discs in some semblance of a soundtrack, which had no bearing whatsoever on what was on the screen, except that it was absolutely magical. We watched Mickey Dora and Buzzy Trent catching waves, weaving an amazing path to enlightenment. Bruce Brown, an entrepreneur, had also realised that waves, surfing and music were entwined, and that the borrowed interest of the world's most popular music — whether it be The Beach Boys or heavy rock — fitted exactly the moment and the image on the screen. We saw for the first time the beaches of Piha and Raglan on the big screen, and we saw ourselves surfing waves, goofing around in old cars on dirt roads, getting to the beach on time. We were living the music and we were living in our time and the moment. The world belonged to us.

Brown toured New Zealand for a long, hot February with his projector and his turntables, and whenever a big surf meet was on, he would fill the local hall every night. I remember this well as I was chased by the police in Napier for trying to souvenir a massive canvas banner that was strung up over the main street to advertise the New Zealand surf champs. I eluded the cops by getting into the back of a community hall where *Endless Summer* was showing. My big feet somehow pulled out the cables attached to the speakers, the movie ground to a halt, and the cops demanded that the audience reveal who had just run in through the back door. The comradeship of surfing never wavered, and I escaped to live another day.

Brown returned to the USA, cutting his home movie for the big screen and turning it into the most popular surfing film of all time. The cinema release of the hypnotically beautiful film cost Brown around US$50,000 to make, yet it grossed over US$30 million worldwide. What Brown's film did was to take the camera into the waves, inside the tubes, into the mystic essence of the sea and its powerful presence. This was no Hollywood set, this was the ocean and this was surfing.

Hollywood finally got it right in 1978 with the John Milius classic *Big Wednesday* — although it had a line-up of stars that could surf, they couldn't handle the big waves; that was left to Jay Riddle, Billy Hamilton, Jackie Dunn and Mickey Dora. It still stands up today as a classic.

Surfer magazine was the surfer's monthly *Playboy*, the brainchild of surfer John Severson, who played editor and introduced his protégé, Rick Griffin, a 19-year-old surfer from Palos Verdes, California, to the world of surfing omnivores. Griffin understood the new meaning and interpretation of surfing. In 1963, already a surf culture star, his 'Murphy' comic strips were appearing in the cult magazine that, with a worldwide circulation of 50,000, was one of the most popular sporting publications of the time. Griffin's cartoons defined not only the look of surfing graphics, but the very culture itself. 'Murphy' was the surfer, with baggy shorts, bleached hair and big feet. Griffin was, of course, drawing himself, but around him and in his work was the surfing universe, and from it grew the psychedelic art of posters. Not since the Victorian era had posters been so popular. They reflected the generation, its music and its art. Jimi Hendrix, The Rolling Stones and The Grateful Dead all fed off surf culture. With it came clothes and the uniform of a T-shirt illustrated front and back with the latest screen-printed graphics, announcing utopia, the universe and waves. Griffin's prolific life would be cut short, but from his genius came the art of surfing.

Californian in style and feel, *Surfer* magazine ran two or three pages each month on new surf artists. Severson was not a bad painter himself and had an incredibly sharp eye for emerging talent. The magazine was showcasing new phenomena, not only the moment of point break, but also the beach culture of the time. The '60s were alive with newness, with new energy from the freaky to the sublime, from the sophisticated image to the combinations of new lettering, type style and art, which was picked up by the advertising industry and so art imitated nature. The curious became converted. Surf painting and art could do no wrong. Whatever you wanted to put on paper or canvas would work. You could improvise as long as you caught the feel, the heat of the beach and the wave. The big artists were American and they moved surf culture from Laguna Beach in Southern California to major galleries. Their work is still dazzling: Ken Auster, John Comer and Kevin Short were at the forefront. The Hilton bought 200 pieces in 1962. The Hyatt chain accumulated a massive surf and beach collection. The interpretation of the wave became a Californian obsession capturing the energy of not only the blue wave and sea, but the shimmering glare, and the immediacy and blur of the rider and the ride. The paintings were colour drenched. They smelt of the hot Californian sun.

In New Zealand, surf art was basic and slow to ignite. It started on T-shirts screened in garages and print shops, bearing messages that were never profound. A poor imitation of Californian art and culture. For so many years, art in New Zealand had been dominated by a small, self-serving group of self-appointed critics and experts. God, they are a painful lot. It was always substance and little style, and if it wasn't a McCahon or a Rita Angus, it didn't get a look in. So surf paintings, which were often on driftwood and painted planks, were relegated to beachfront coffee-house cafés in Gisborne and Taranaki. Their sale, if it happened, would hardly feed an artist for a week.

In the 1970s, surfing took on the tag of being what you did when you didn't have a job, and so it became the male version of the DPB. If you surfed, you couldn't hold down a job. Surfing never appeared in stylish magazines, or in the lifestyles of New Zealand's rich and famous. The politicians and missionaries still hated anyone who surfed. It was the equivalent to having a 'tat'. It was also only a summer sport. If you wanted to try it in the subtropical North Island, you would wear a football jersey, but in the South Island you would wear two and light a massive fire on the beach to save you from freezing to death.

In the 1980s, a new generation of surfers emerged who were also skilled in graphic art and new technical skills of paint and brush. They knew their subject well, they lived their work, and they started to get their own defined audiences. Surf art is not easy and certainly water — heaving, churning, rolling — is decisively difficult to paint. It needs either a very light touch, an iridescent, translucent veil of colour, or a rugged spume of paint. Less is more or more is less.

Suddenly, the waves became bigger. Out of nowhere, the surf culture changed from easy rideable waves to ocean monsters. Now fear and awe dominated surf society. Every surfing movie finished with gut-wrenching, preternatural scenes of surfers riding virtual walls of water. Nothing was spared to get to the tow-in giants. Surfing became a death wish and as Buzzy Trent, one of Waimea's legends said, surfing was comparable to the art of bull fighting — the surfer the matador and the wave the bull. The closer you are to death, the more brilliant you are with style. Surfing now evokes the spirit of Garcia Lorca's epic essay on the duende, the spirit of life and death, which intrinsically combined the magnificent joyfulness of life with the edgy abyss of death. The two became as one in surfing the giants. Heart pounding and adrenalin pumping, matched with sheer survival instinct, took surfing and its art into a new realm.

The New Zealand coast has a mixture of some of the world's best surfing beaches and some of the wildest surf on the planet. This is a combination that can only foster its art, and this book begins to explore the men and women who have mixed the two in their lives and their creativity. Their talent speaks for itself; their work, like that of any artist, survives and challenges them. Through their eyes, we see the ocean differently. Their art is the window which moves the viewer into the next dimension, through the barriers of our sight and senses. Here, the great oceans and the swells reach the end of their journey, for surf is, in truth, the death of a wave. It is a dying monster or fragile shore break, exerting its final moment. It has come to the end of its existence and on that demise, we travel, moving down its face, playing, celebrating. Exhilarated and fulfilled, we waltz on its watery grave. There will never be another wave quite like it in the history of the world or the universe. We have mastered one of the greatest forces of nature; we have enjoyed its pleasures. It will never come again and nor will we. Will the wave hold that memory? And where does art fit? Does it record a moment that never existed or the billions of waves that we have never seen? If only we knew the secret of creating an ocean swell, like the fabled, legendary conductor in Steven Kotler's book, *West of Jesus*. Kotler hears that there exists a surfing grim reaper who can never be reached, who surfs always outside, who points towards the horizon with an object that resembles a human leg bone, and from nowhere arises the perfect wave. Kotler travels the world seeking the origin of belief and comes face to face with the reality of the mystic, the spiritual and the science of surfing. This tale is about mysticism, and it is at the very heart and essence of surfing and art. This is what makes surf art in its many forms and styles so relevant, more than any other creative discipline for today's generations. They understand with a trust and a belief that this is their art, this is their world in all its cerebral wonders. The artists in this book tell their stories in their words and their work stands alone, speaking in its own voice as ancient and as contemporary as the great seas and their fringe of surf, which speaks its own language only to us.

Bob Harvey
Karekare, 2009

Justin Summerton

Aaron Topp

ARTIST
DUNEDIN

Justin Summerton had a decision to make. He could take his last few dollars, get a taxi to New York's JFK airport, and use his open ticket to fly to London. Or he could spend it down at the local supply store in the Bronx and invest in some paint, a brush and a canvas, and attempt to make money selling art in Central Park. The rest of the hostel laughed at him when he chose the latter. You're nuts, they told him, such the dreamer. But he had no choice, it was about taking a risk, seizing an opportunity, and really, this was all part of the nomadic existence to which he'd committed himself. He expected nothing less from life.

So he sat on the grass in the sunshine and painted a group of rollerbladers cruising around to the popular tunes of 1994 being pumped out of a DJ's sound system. A curious crowd started to gather beside him. By the seventh hour they were bidding with cash — $100, $200, $250. The successful bid came from a woman who handed over $300. She asked where he was staying; he said the Bronx. She said she had a friend over on East 60th, between Madison and Park Avenue, who was looking for someone to move in with her. He accepted the offer. He left the wide-mouthed residents of Spanish Harlem and its gunshot-pierced nights and in one day climbed the social ladder, to the opulence of an area with $30 steak meals.

It's probably some sort of city record, a plot at least for the next feel-good flick to come out of the Big Apple. Justin continued painting in Central Park, selling his work for up to $400 a day, before taking his new-found skill to California and Europe, where he painted street scenes, buildings and architecture to the sound of coins falling into a hat. Come evening he'd sell them to some punter on the street and the next morning he'd start again. Savouring each day as it came, not worrying about tomorrow, leaving all those yesterdays behind.

You could say that Justin was raised a free spirit. The breeze began blowing for him when he was born in the Wirral, across the river from Liverpool, England. His dad travelled extensively by himself before serving as a Royal Engineer in the British Army as it undertook peacekeeping roles in Borneo and Burma. He met Justin's mum at a Beatles concert just before there was such a thing as Beatlemania. By the time John was three, his parents were looking for an adventure and decided to move him and his brother out to New Zealand, Justin's father having been offered a job as a fitter and turner at the Cadbury factory in Dunedin. It was a seed, Justin says, that was planted in his own make up. In recent times, though, Justin has lived a semi-settled life with his Brazilian girlfriend, Gisiele, in their house in St Clair, Dunedin. Semi-settled might not be the right term; they've just come back from a two-month stint in Byron Bay, and a trip to Indonesia before that — merely holidays compared to his previous life of living with an art bag hanging off one arm and surfboard underneath the other.

Justin discovered riding waves before he found art. His parents would take him and his brother to the beach in the weekends. When at the age of seven he first saw surfers he knew the activity was going to play a big part of his life. By the age of 10 he was riding the standard polystyrene board in the whitewater. 'I loved it,' he recalls. 'The speed of the whitewash, that letting go. Being taken by another force as the energy of the sea took me on a ride. That was, and still is, exciting for a kid.' When Justin was 13 his dad came home from work one day with a proper surfboard for him. Surfing was a dirty word in Dunedin at the time, and no parent wanted to see their growing kid participating in such antisocial behaviour. But Justin's parents were liberal folk who could see what something so intimate with the environment could do for their son's personal development. With no friends to surf with, Justin would settle for arriving home each day after school, pulling the secondhand surfboard out from the corner of his bedroom, running his hands over the smooth rails, compression dings, pointed nose and residues of wax; smelling the faint aroma of resin and practising putting on the legrope and being in awe of what this six-foot object stood for. He needed others to experience all of this, so he talked two of his mates, Sarge and Adam, into getting boards too. A year later they took the bus to St Clair Beach and stood looking down on the large swell pounding the shore. They may have turned 14, but they were just three kids from town. They had no idea what they were getting themselves into.

It's fitting that Justin's brought me to a small park bench overlooking the spot where his surfing life was conceived. St Clair is breaking at a very attractive four foot and there are only a couple of guys out. Yesterday, Justin was surfing it by himself at a stormy six foot; he draws a line with his finger across the water below to demonstrate the length of the barrel he got. 'We jumped off those rocks,' he says, pointing a little way up the coastline and taking me back 26 years earlier. 'Sarge went onto one and cracked his fins, Adam scraped the bottom of his board, and I put a ding in the tail of mine. We got out the back and it felt like Hawaii, this deep, dark blue. It was so exotic to us, adventurous, we just sat there floating and watching everything going on around us. We had no business out there with all these older guys, but we became hooked from that session on. None of us three have ever thought about doing anything else. We're now all in our forties, but in every sense we're all living exactly the same way.'

Justin originally aspired to be a novelist. When he arrived home from his travels as a street painter he took an idea and his degree in English literature and set out to write five pages a day. For the next four months he drove his van to various beaches and with a primitive typewriter sitting on a special desk that he'd made to sit over the steering wheel, he tapped away until it was completed. He decided Auckland was where he needed to be. On his travels north he mentioned his plans to a couple of people at a party in Wellington.

'You'll see surfers shutting it down and leaving the mainstream system, you'll see communities becoming self-sufficient.'

'Where ya gonna stay?' He didn't know, he knew no one up there. He was just floating, seeing where the breeze would let him settle. He was given a phone number from a friend of a friend, 'It's the mayor of Waitakeres,' they told Justin. 'Give him a call, he's a good guy, he loves art.'

The next morning Justin found the piece of paper with the scribbled digits in his pocket. He screwed it up; it was just piss talk, he thought; probably some bogus number leading to an embarrassing situation. He went to throw it away, but stopped and unravelled it again. He had no money, but experience so far had taught him to take opportunities when they presented themselves. But the mayor of the country's biggest city? And on a Sunday? Surely a best-case scenario would be a few weeks' wait before scoring an audience with such a busy guy? That's a long time to get cold feet. He had to give it a shot though, have a bit of faith in humanity and take a gamble. So he dialled the number anyway. That afternoon, Justin was walking up the Harveys' driveway with a portfolio of his art in his hands. By that evening he was living in their bach at Karekare.

It's probably some sort of social record for the city. From his newly acquired residence at the West Coast beach, Justin sent his young adult novel, *The Albatross Boy*, to a handful of publishers and waited. He began painting again in the interim; if he was going to fail as a writer, he might as well try to bat in another field. He explored the dynamic features of Karekare, looking for, then painting, original angles of iconic landmarks like The Watchman and Split Pin

Rock. A few weeks later he went to show Dean Buchanan, an accomplished resident artist at Karekare, some of the work he'd been doing. While he was there a couple of agents from a gallery in Ponsonby turned up, wanting to discuss Dean's next exhibition. He didn't have any pieces for them, but suggested they might like to look at what this new talent from Dunedin had been doing lately. Justin gave them his number, the Karekare Surf Life Saving emergency phone line, and a couple of days later they rang him to offer an exhibition in six weeks' time. Justin painted like crazy, living off tinned fruit and two-minute noodles, with one surf a day as a reward. By the time the rejection letters were arriving from the publishing houses, his exhibition in Ponsonby was selling out.

They offered him another exhibition, which was even more successful. He was picked up by a respected agent and his work was suddenly featuring in Parnell at Warwick Henderson, one of the most renowned galleries in the country, with a solid catalogue of contemporary artists. Eight years later and Justin's still stoked to be there. Travelling has also meant he's been able to explore different opportunities abroad. That last stint he had in Bryon Bay in Australia was spent painting and surfing, and when it came time to leave he shared his work between two local galleries. It's kinda like fishing, he says, waiting to see if he gets any bites from distant art lovers. It's a routine that isn't new to him; he's previously sold 10 pieces out of Sydney and he's still got work sitting in London and a couple of pieces in American cafes. His biggest break recently has come from an Australian college textbook that covers the technical aspects of how to paint. He's one of two Kiwi artists featured. Justin finds it amazing how he's progressed to a point where he's now helping Australian kids paint landforms.

Listening to Justin talk of his travels over the last 21 years is like listening to an audio version of a *Lonely Planet* travel guide — the surfer's version. He started on the Gold Coast when he was 17 and never stopped. Drifting from destination to destination, overloading his senses, generating a constant creative charge. As his confidence grew, so did his curiosity for what was off the well-worn sheep track and around that next headland. It's taken him to waves in the Canary Islands, Easter Island, the New York coast, around Australia, Barrier Island, Samoa, Fiji, Tahiti, Mexico, France, Spain, England, Scotland and Indonesia. Mostly he's travelled for personal reasons: it's been time to educate himself, explore a culture, seek a prospective market for art, put another coloured pin on a map at home. Almost every time he's gone with only a surfboard as company. As a graduate he went to California to work, but also to decide what he wanted to do with his life. He did a lot of artwork, but it was merely something to fill in the time while he waited for the swell to arrive. He made friends, surfers too, who introduced him to exotic journeys to secret locations along the untouched North California coast, where only the most hardcore surfers travel, sites reminiscent of something from a Ken Nunn novel.

'Each trip became a different surf adventure. It was hard to separate living and working from surfing. When you wake up you worry about what the swell's doing, and if it's not on, then you worry about how you're going to eat and make a living. When you hang out with serious surfers around the world, that's what they do; they'll throw down tools, they'll throw down commitments and meetings, they'll throw down everything to capture that surf. It's the sort of upbringing and social environment I've lived in, from St Clair to everywhere else in the world.'

While we're talking, Gisiele sits on an area of grass reading a Portuguese copy of the *The Chronicles of Narnia*. It was on Justin's third trip to Brazil that they met, after being introduced through a mutual friend who'd previously holidayed in New Zealand. When Justin stepped off the plane in the South American continent, Gisiele was amongst the small welcoming committee of Brazilian beauties the friend had brought with her. They took him out clubbing while his board and bags still sat in a rental car in the airport car park. He left a few days later and journeyed by himself to Rio and Florianopolis, but found himself making the trip back to see Gisiele again. He left for New Zealand and she arrived at his Piha home six months later. Justin says one of the smartest things he's done is invest the early money from his exhibitions into a house at St Clair — before the real estate market created an inflated fantasy world for itself. Justin had become intimate with the Auckland surf, made a lot of good friends, lived in Karekare, Piha, at friends' places, even in an apartment in the city, but he was a Dunedin boy at heart. His Auckland friends thought he was nuts putting money into a place so far south; the water's cold down there, they pointed out, and up here you can be part of our social scene. But he could see there was always going to be a huge difference between the two cities, and in 2007 he and Gisiele moved into his home in Dunedin.

'This is a magical place, the weather can be a little crazy, but you're guaranteed you're gonna get a wave somewhere. It has that surf town feeling, like Hossegor in France or Santa Cruz.' He continues spouting the benefits of the city, the quality and diversity of its waves and how they're on his doorstep and not an hour's motorway travel away, then suddenly changes tack and talks about how cold it gets and how hardcore it is and the number of sharks roaming around the breaks in their Southern-man sizes. For now, it seems, Auckland can stick to its cellphones and lattes and flamboyant nightclubs on K Road; Justin has had his fill of the place. However, he makes the point of saying he will always be attracted to the surrealism of Auckland's West Coast and its people and powerful landforms.

'I think there's a Peter Pan element to surfing. No guy wants to admit they're getting old and slowing down. We don't want to grow up.'

While the surf is a continuum, and the art will always be there, it all means nothing if the market dries up and Justin can't provide for the home. Lately, some artists have found themselves on the verge of throwing in the towel — the collapse of the world economy has meant playing the art game has got too difficult. 'I think we're on the verge of another hippy revolution. It's like we've just come out of the fifties, some Nixon depression era, and we're going back into the sixties where people are starting to think, what do we actually need to be happy? The answer is, not that much. The telecommunication companies have us noosed,' he says, 'we're now overcommunicating, we're constrained by energy bills, taxes, all tentacles of a giant corporate octopus dragging us down. Give us a breath of fresh air,' he says, his eyes lighting up, Gisiele turning momentarily. 'We just need a bit of food, some shelter and some nice people around, that's all we need to be a human being. It's become way too complicated, we've all become connected to this big outside world, this big machine, this big economy.' He sweeps a hand out towards the waves and beyond. 'We live in a paradise island, we have great soils, greenery, it's a beautiful, free country, yet the economy is going down the plughole because we attached ourselves to something unnecessary. The revolution is going to be a big backlash on this economic connection to the outside world, with clean fuels and cutting back on consumption. You'll see surfers shutting it down and leaving the mainstream system, you'll see communities becoming self-sufficient. The rest of the time you can spend growing vegetables and catching fish. Sounds an extreme and simple idealism, but a lot of people are starting to think that way, cutting ties and freeing themselves up more and more.'

We head back to their vehicle and start donning thick neoprene in preparation for the chilly southern water. This vehicle, an early model SUV, is one big surf storage unit on four wheels. As he's digging through the gear to find his rash vest, he holds up a pair of boardies he never knew were there and asks Gisiele if she knows whose they are. She shrugs her shoulders. A passing Malaysian dance troop, in town for a cultural festival and still in traditional attire, stop to watch Justin putting his hoodie on and start filming him with a camcorder. I stand to the side as they begin asking him questions in broken English about surfing, taking turns to hold his board, pose for photos. It confirms my hunch; Justin looks like the sort of guy you can approach at any time, his thin stature and relaxed demeanour are obviously universally accepted. But Justin is every bit as interested in them too, asking questions back, spending that extra time to make sure his answers are understood, smiling happily in the photos, making the best of the opportunity to get a hit of foreign exchange in its most budget of forms.

Once out in the surf, I look back to the lone park bench where we were sitting beneath the exposed slice of coastal landform, and I can't believe how 20 minutes ago I was in a Justin Summerton painting. The whole scene is intrinsic to his earlier work. His clever technique of using heavy amounts of oil to get a textured appearance works particularly well with rugged landscapes, like the West Coast. It allows him to build colour and texture with every brushstroke, giving an impression that you can see every small rock, every branch, every movement of light, cleverly transferring the sense of stored impetus onto canvas. It's a method that has worked just as well in his contemporary pieces in recent years. Art, he says, is always only in its infancy; like anything creative, it's an endless thing. 'I don't think I've even got close to what I can do. I'd like to do some large museum-scale paintings, incorporate all the things I feel and dream about. It's constant exploration, really.'

It's amazing that for all of Justin's work and achievements, his success over 10 years of exhibiting in Detroit, San Francisco, Sydney and at home, selling pieces for over $10,000 each, and his commission work here and abroad, he's never had any acknowledgment from within the national art media. 'I didn't go to art school, so for me, even operating as an artist and having a full-time career has already exceeded what I should've done. The longer I've been in the industry, the more I understand how it works, the connections that have to be made, the doors you have to bust down first before you do well. In a small place like New Zealand, there's only enough room for the right artists, and they're typically the ones who did go to art school and became earmarked. I guess every artist wants success in society, critical success to be written about, but to be honest, I think for many the reality is a load of bollocks. And that's something you have to accept.'

Painting to someone else's expectation would mean Justin's art would flatline. He has to feel empowered at the easel, in control of the outcome of what he's doing; that way the work is at its purist. In the same vein, without surfing as a creative source, his art would suffer the same fate. 'Surfing in the morning and getting that buzz is essential to channel into your work. If I can get one surf in and I know it's in my system, then I'm happy and I can do more vibrant work. I feel more energy from the ocean and that energy transfers onto the canvas.'

Some of the best work Justin's completed came from a period where he was concentrating on landscapes of surf spots. Each day he'd pack a camera and notebook with his surfing gear and head out somewhere new, surf for four or five hours, then sit down and work out how he was going to paint the scene. He got enough work out of that period to complete two very successful shows. 'My job was my fun, my life, it was so pure. There's a saying: "Follow your bliss and you can't go wrong". If you can identify what it is that makes you blissful and create your work around that feeling, then you've cracked it. That's the secret to life right there.' People are smart, he continues, they could see the work he'd done had no preconceptions. It sounds part mystery, part fantasy, but the subtleties of his state of mind generated from surf stoke were there for everyone in the gallery to see in full colour. Each brush stroke was done with enjoyment, each complete piece a portal to Justin's happiness.

Back out in the line-up at St Clair I watch Justin spend just as much time conversing with other locals as he does riding the swell. A set arrives and brings with it the wave of the day, which peaks in front of him. He paddles into it and rides it for 200 metres or more to the beach, defying each closing section with a smooth flow of speed. It seems the skill of art isn't the only thing he's brought back from his travels. After that first exhibition in Ponsonby, he took the money and bought himself a trip to Hawaii for two months. He began training for the trip while he was still at Karekare, preparing for the task of riding giants. He stepped onto a plane with a couple of new big wave boards and began his pilgrimage. 'When I turned up at Pipeline and saw all the pros out there, and the excitement and buzz being generated, I was like, wow, it's actually a place. It was like Arcadia of the gods.'

> There are guys who surf for a long time, who end up moving to an inland town, and you see them start to die.

He'd been there a month, staying with friends, meeting many more. He'd learnt to surf waves bigger than he'd imagined he could ride. Sunset, that fabled stretch of the North Shore famous for being the paddle-in equivalent to climbing Mt Everest, was breaking with solid 15-foot faces. Justin had already managed to pull into a couple, being rewarded with a massive stand-up barrel on one of them. He was feeling good about himself, the water was warm and clear, the residual effects of surviving this far into the Hawaiian season, both in and out of the water, were keeping him pumped. Even when the first of the bigger sets started rolling in off the horizon he wasn't that concerned. He paddled into one of them, but underestimated the extra size and speed something that big brought with it and was consequently launched with the falling lip of the wave. When he impacted, the thousands of tonnes of water on top of his puny human frame drove him down and gave him the beating of his life. 'I remember thinking, shit, this could be it. I was getting pulled down into the dark, I was being wrenched, I felt like I was going unconscious 'cause it was that powerful. I'm not a Christian, but I said to myself, OK, let me out of this and I promise

I'll be a different person, just give me another chance. I found the surface, half unconscious and gasping for air, when another wave broke in front and I was pushed back down again.' The wave dragged him underwater so far that when it let him go Justin found himself on the inside of the reef. He stood, retrieved his board and began walking. He'd never felt so humble in his life.

Anyone else would've staggered back to the beach, found a quiet bar, had a cold beer and proceeded to convince themselves they're still a hellman for trying. But Justin's intimate relationship with the ocean is much more than just a physical thing, it's a mental battle, and even the might of the ocean is no match for some human spirits. So despite any promises he'd just made to his creator, he found himself paddling back out the channel and into the line-up with the rest of the crew. He sat up on his board and watched a couple of waves come through. 'I suddenly felt my own self again. This other part of me, this hardened voice inside started saying, don't be a pussy, get back out there. There was no contemplation. That's when it dawned on me, this is how severe my addiction is. As long as there is a bit of oomph there, I'll give it another crack. There's a lot of pride involved with wanting to surf big waves, aspiring to conquest the moment and not be outdone. Nobody wants to turn back from Hawaii with their tail between their legs. I wanted to get that one big wave, to feel like I was going forward, to get one over the ocean, at the very least to sleep better that night.'

I ask him how long he expects to keep up such an attitude. He shrugs his shoulders and I notice for the first time he's been wearing his cap backwards since we've been talking, just like he would've back in his uni days 20 years ago, just like he could've the day his dad arrived home with that new surfboard. 'I'm thinking about going down to Papatowai and giving those massive swells at the bottom of the South Island a crack.' He grew up watching some of the local grommets who would go on to make a name for themselves chasing the final frontier of big-wave surfing on a regular basis. Justin watched their progress from the sidelines, but between art commitments and travelling, never organised himself to step onto the playing field, despite a deep desire to get involved. But that's changed in recent times and already he's had a few practice tow-in sessions with Sarge at Allen's Beach. They're now in the process of getting a crew together with another jet ski and gear. Mentally he's prepared, for sure, but he sits forwards, rests his arms on his thighs, and begins rubbing his palms together slowly. At 40 years old, he admits he's not as fit as he used to be, and I can see him questioning the reality in his head. But he's not prepared to concede to anything further than his next comment: 'Eventually I know I'll get a worse beating somewhere.'

Justin still looks like the cool kid at school. His attire — the cap, the worn jeans, the bright yellow T-shirt underneath the casual long-sleeved version — could be a one-off for the day, but I doubt it. They certainly don't help with the comparison. Sure, he's sophisticated in a worldly, casual way. He's incredibly articulate. Can hold a conversation with a huge range of people, I'd imagine. But like so many other mature surfers I've met, he's refusing to let old man age get his bony fingers into him. 'I think there's a Peter Pan element to surfing. No guy wants to admit they're getting old and slowing down. We don't want to grow up. One of the big buzzes of surfing is that it makes you feel vibrant and young. It's like a fountain of youth, totally. It's a huge negative ion field that actually draws positive molecules from your body, so scientifically you do feel better. It pulls ailments, sickness, darkness, even oldness, away from you. Getting the sheer physical aspect of being a surfer has to make you feel younger. If you can get away and feel good for two hours a day, it's bound to translate to a healthier body and healthier spirit. There are guys who surf for a long time, who end up moving to an inland town, and you see them start to die. They get mainstreamed or something. They become this robotic, tax-paying automaton. They sacrifice their heart and their spirit to go off and earn money and become successful.'

Justin recalls almost becoming one of those guys when he went back to New York. He hadn't surfed in weeks when he passed a magazine rack and spied a surf mag. He stopped in his tracks to pick it up. As he flicked through its pages, his heart sank. What was he doing here? This isn't me, he thought. He was meant to be getting his art career off to a start, to become the next big thing or die trying, he had the talent to do it, yet here on some foreign sidewalk he was questioning himself. Is this worth it? Is it ever? Maybe he should shelve the lot and go live by some point break somewhere, get a wind turbine and solar panels and shut himself out from the rest of the world and just surf every day. 'I think there's that idealist attitude to surfers, they live in the contemporary world, but they want no part of it. They want to be fourteen years old and paddling out for the first time, with no worries of bills to pay and job demands, just having fun with their mates.'

And there's a small part of that day as a 14-year-old in every session he has to this day. In many ways, he says, it has never changed. Being immersed in something else, getting away from the things you have on land, a job — what you're stuck on, relationship issues, whatever — as soon as you hit the water it's about stripping away the layers and suddenly it's just you and the ocean and a sense of complete peace. 'I think even if you went out the back, sat there and floated for half an hour then paddled in, you'd have a better day, so when you add to that the peace and tranquillity of being in the vast ocean and the fun and adrenalin of riding waves, you have a winning combination. I've seen guys paddle out in the most rubbish conditions at St Clair, but they're addicted to going out there. They might have been dumped and held down, but you can see when they come in they're buzzing. It's in their eyes, they've put their body out there, it's a cleansing thing, sanctifying. I actually think for a lot of hardcore surfers, paddling out is like going to church. They get their mind into a place where they're at peace with themselves, they need to immerse themselves in that feeling. It's natural because it's all around you, it's covering your body, holding you in, yet you're vulnerable, a shark could take you at any time, but there's definitely a bit of letting go out there. You enter a different realm.'

Justin's latest exhibition was driven by a deep environmental theme; man's ability to overconsume resources, to follow one another like lemmings off a cliff, the desire to control nature, the plight of global warming, the endurance of vegetation and the rising of the oceans. There are no surfers depicted; the themes are bigger than one small segment of society, but he says the surfing population are inherently greenies at heart. 'I think surfers are quite visionary in that sense, they've been ahead of the game for a long time. Not even young guys want to see garbage and sewage in their surf. The world is starting to get green and realise that when you make small changes in nature you're going to get a repercussion, cause and effect. If you throw some sand banks here, it's going to affect the beach over there, so everyone is a lot more in touch with the subtleties of nature.' He cites the desecration of the local environment around the Dunedin coast as an example of poor management and short-term thinking.

Dunedin is perceived to be in the untouched south and it is not uncommon for a surfer to share a session with dolphins, whales, seals, penguins, even the odd albatross or two, yet semi-treated sewage being pumped into the Pacific has meant all those who live or venture into the waters are exposed to some pretty heavy toxins. Just over the last summer Justin witnessed sick and dead seals, penguins throwing up green fluid, and other signs that all isn't well around the southern coastline. 'The devastation of Blackhead Beach by the quarry is another concern. They've turned a glorious, world class beach into rubble. There's also the thousands of tonnes of rock which fall down the cliffs, destroying the sacred Maori bathing pools. I was fortunate enough to see the pools in the mid eighties when they were only half covered, now they're completely gone. The entire headland of Blackhead is only half remaining.' Justin is keen to see an idealist with an ecological spirit step up and take leadership in the Dunedin Council before it's too late. 'I think surfers are already leaders in that way. If everyone was a little more surf ethos orientated, the whole world could be saved.'

The lady who purchased the painting in New York, Bob Harvey, the dance troop, the friends he has in every country, even myself, we all see a piece of ourselves in Justin. He's the free spirit we once dreamt of being, before life got in the way. People want to give a hand and cheer him on in his travels, because they feel like they've played a tiny part in some fantasy. And it's not every day you get to meet someone who's made a life-defining decision to see the world purely through his own eyes and heart. 'I'm looking back over twenty years of irresponsible youthful wandering, and I'm so happy I did it; it's been insane. I wouldn't change a thing about it. I don't have a great career, and it's pretty unstable, but I wake up in the morning and I'm free. I can go for a surf, and when I'm not, I'm painting what I want. We're talking about Bohemian ideals, a guy who sets out and wants to be free. What I was and what I am now, it's still my ideal to live a young and exciting and adventurous life. From as far back as I could remember, identifying things that would constrain people and keep them in the same place — like paying bills and mortgages — was a priority, because as soon as I left uni I didn't want any of those ties, I wanted to get out there, I wanted an adventurous life. I knew it'd involve a lot of trekking and a lot of poverty. But I was prepared for it. I had no money, no backing. I had the support of my family, but definitely not a wealthy family who let me live the life of the young gentleman of England, who would roam off in the countryside for a few years with a stipend and paints. No, I hacked my way around the world, sleeping on sofas, painting and surfing.'

He leans back, nods his head and smiles.

'I still miss the feral beginnings of that lifestyle. Lately I've been thinking about getting back to the start, to the idealist point where I left; a magic time, when I had nothing but ideas and a curiosity for what's out there.'

Ben Galbraith

Brennan Thomas

AUTHOR/ILLUSTRATOR
GISBORNE

In a studio above the main street of Gisborne, Ben Galbraith is about to shoot the latest New Wave Surfboards ad. He's with two others, one of them a professional photographer, and the other, Bobby Hansen, one of the country's best surfers. The room is covered in white sheets and looks a lot like the foyer to the Pearly Gates. Sitting at Bobby's feet is a second-hand 40-inch television; they've managed to score two of them, the other sits near an axe that's leaning against the far wall after Bobby opted for the extra weight of the sledgehammer, which he is busy swinging back and forth like a pendulum while he waits for his instructions.

'We try to set our sponsored guys up in some sort of theme that suits their personality,' Ben says. 'Bobby's known to be a bit of a hothead at times, so we began thinking of what props to use. In the end we thought how cool it'd be if we got a TV and captured him smashing it up like he's throwing a tantrum.'

Welcome to the world of Ben Galbraith — licence to create havoc in the name of surfing.

The photographer, one of Ben's mates, counts down from three. Bobby, with only a pair of boardies and sponsor's T-shirt to protect him, gets ready to do the one thing all us males secretly wish to do. And knowing he's gone in to bat for mankind, Bobby smiles and raises the hammer back. Ben, who's already picturing the end result in print, is standing just out of frame, relaxed, with his hands in pockets — hell, everyone knows that television screens implode when smashed.

'Bobby swung and hit the screen,' Ben recalls in his quiet tone, slipping in a retrospective chuckle. 'Thing is, we were told they implode, but it didn't. It was quite the opposite. There was this huge explosion and everyone in the street below stopped and looked up 'cause they thought a bomb had just gone off. There were thick pieces of glass everywhere, like, lethal inch- or two-inch-sized pieces. Bobby was covered in it. We were too.' He shakes his head. 'Worst thing was, though, the damn camera flash never worked.'

But there was always TV number two. Bobby was keen.

'Brennan [the photographer] and I decided we didn't want to be responsible for ending Bobby's professional career by blinding him, so we ended up having to re-enact the smash instead by getting Bobby to pose. The strangest part about the whole thing was that the TV didn't work beforehand, and was nowhere near a plug, yet there were electrical sparks everywhere when the hammer hit it. Weird, huh?'

The first time I met Ben was back in mid 2007, when we were both nominated as finalists in the NZ Post Book Awards for Children and Young Adults. His book, *The Three Fishing Brothers Gruff*, was getting massive props in the literary world for its revolutionary style of illustrations and timely environmental messages. Here we were, a couple of surfers from the provincial areas, standing in the corners of Parliament, enjoying the free canapés, and surrounded by the hierarchy of the publishing world. Ben was in big demand; everyone wanted to talk to the talent from Gisborne in the black jeans and Chuck Taylors. He rightfully won the 'Best First Book' award that night; as the judges stated in their report, 'the sophistication of the illustrations and design in this book is an example of how much thought needs to go into a picture book production'.

It would be another 12 months before I'd catch up with him again, this time at his beach-front family home in Northern Makorori, Gizzy. I'd arranged to come around quite early, but at eight o'clock that morning I got a phone call from him telling me the weather's packing it in and he's just watched the third car with boards on its roof go past — he ain't waiting any longer. He's going surfing out the front of the house. Meet him there.

I look out my window from my motel at Wainui and see blue sky. But by the time I take the five-minute journey to his place over the hill, my wipers are on full and I can't see shit in front of me. I park up on the grass in front of his house and through the blades doing double time I make out a silhouette on a three-foot wave sending his own spray back up to the heavens. I run around to the back of the vehicle to get my wetsuit, but start cursing as I come to terms with the fact I've left it sitting back at the motel. It's not even half eight, and I've already given myself a 'saturated idiot of the day' award. I look up behind me; only one thing left to do . . .

'He was sitting in your seat this morning watching the waves,' Ben's mum tells me as she hands me a hot cup of tea and freshly baked apple and cinnamon cake. 'He gets a little bit impatient when there's swell.'

I can see why; I'm sitting in front of a large double-framed window, two storeys up and looking straight out to Ben in the surf. The view from this seat in his house is about as soothing as a surfer would get, and I find myself sinking deeper into the chair, mesmerised, like a cat staring into a fireplace. In fact, through the period of my discussion with the two most important women in Ben's world — his mum, Linda, and girlfriend, Simonne — I find I have to force myself to look them in the eyes, otherwise my stare is pulled straight back out to sea again.

I once heard a successful businessman comment that today's Gisborne was a place of underdevelopment and decay, but I couldn't disagree more. Anyone who has ever been to Gisborne knows the place is much more than just a first-to-see-the-sun label it uses to brand itself to the world. There's something powerful happening here on the East Coast that uplifts one's soul, successfully suppressing the inner fire that typically ignites with every traffic jam, or eight-hour shit-fight that ends 12 hours later thanks to uptight clients and changed schedules. Yep, if Auckland is the 'big smoke', then Gisborne is the 'fresh air' we're all looking for. It's a cliché, but it could be the one reason why this small city has such a strong chill-out factor — the community is taking its time to enjoy every breath. Decaying? Pleasantly simmering, perhaps. Add the fact that Gisborne just happens to be situated in the middle of one of the country's premier surf coasts, and it suddenly begs the question: would the 'Gizzy culture' be the same if its isolation was confined to an inland community where the surf culture couldn't fester?

'Out-of-towners say people around here drive a lot slower,' says Ben. 'I suppose Gisborne is cruisy like that, it's just so laid back. I'm not sure whether surfing has got anything to do with it or not. Maybe it's not the surf, maybe it's just being so close to the ocean? I suppose you get that in the islands as well. If you look at the road map, Gisborne is like an island in itself. The CEO of Saatchi and Saatchi moved to New Zealand because creatively it's a lot better to be on the edge of the world looking in, rather than being stuck in the middle looking out. And perhaps that's why so many creative people come from Gisborne, too; we're not affected by trends or influenced as much. Growing up here's good, there's surf most times, and even living in town you're close to the beach. In summer you can get a surf before and after work, and if you're lucky, one during your lunch break. The proximity to quality waves is a big reason why so many great surfers come from the district.'

Ben was six when his dad first pushed him and his polystyrene board into waves down in the lagoon at Makorori. 'I remember those boards were like lying on eighty-grit sandpaper. I started riding them on my knees, then progressed to standing. That first thrilling feeling never really changed. I suppose as long as you're progressing you'll still get that initial thrill.' By eight, though, he'd found a few buddies at Wainui Primary who were eager grommets in the making too, and they'd surf together throughout the year — Ben, the little whippet that he was, wore the same spring-suit for three winters because they didn't make steamers his size. During this time Ben's dad, who grew up surfing in Wairoa before settling down in Gisborne, would take them surfing, all the while passing on his deep appreciation of the surfing ethos to his son. 'He wasn't one of those parents who would stand on the beach and tell me what I was doing was right or wrong. He understood completely what the whole stoke was about and was just happy to see me out there doing it.'

Looking at his dad in family photos on display in their house, there's certainly strong similarities between Ben and his father — scraggy blonde hair, wiry frame. That infectious smile. Tragically, when Ben was a teenager his father suffered a fatal heart attack during a surf in front of the family home. Ben doesn't show it easily, but you can tell a deep scar has been left underneath that pleasant exterior of his.

From my seat, it's obvious the Galbraiths' home is testament to the fact art runs deep in their heritage. There are different paintings by Ben and his brother, sculptures, and collages from a wide range of genres covering the walls or hanging from the ceiling — this isn't a home that insists on everything being in sync; nah, this abode is as far distant to pompous interior fashions as you'd get. It's cool. It oozes creativity. Hell, it could've just been the tea and cake and the comfy chair talking over the top of the rain on the roof, but it felt a hell of a lot like home to me.

> 'There were thick pieces of glass everywhere, like, lethal inch- or two-inch-sized pieces. Bobby was covered in it. We were too.'

Ben was always one those kids who was sought after when it came time for art in class — his peers would get him to draw their horses or a picture of a dinosaur. A tractor. A plane. Whatever they desired, actually. And Ben, with his appeasing nature, would happily oblige. He didn't see it as a gift he possessed, just something he enjoyed doing, certainly nothing he'd make a living from when he grew up. It wouldn't be for another decade that it'd become a realisation, as he studied for a Bachelor of Design at Massey University way down in Wellington. It was on this exclusive course that he discovered a new technique in design that he'd go on to make his own.

'For each particular illustration project we were given a stylistic way to complete it, like dry brush, pen and ink, watercolour and so on. Getting through uni and trying them all I found that the collage and digital style suited me best.'

In his fourth and last year in the programme, Ben had to complete a major project. About the only thing he knew it was going to involve was a strong environmental message around the issues of the sea. So that was the starting point. But it wasn't until a mid-year semester break that things would pick up momentum. He'd been toying around with the idea of using the medium of a picture book, and was looking at how others had taken classic stories and re-invented them. One afternoon he was flicking through his old books in the family bookshelf when he came across *The Billy Goats Gruff*. Suddenly the room lit up with the glowing light bulb above his head.

'That story seemed to fit the theme better than anything else. I sat down and wrote the bones out. By the time I headed back to university, I'd already started designing the illustrations. I'd decided the book was going to be for kids — seven- to eight-year-olds — where they were old enough to understand the message and maybe I could inspire them to start to do the little things, like pick up a bit of rubbish off the beach.'

'. . . maybe I could inspire them to start to do the little things, like pick up a bit of rubbish off the beach.'

While the final story came relatively quickly, it was the illustration process that would become the most challenging, and ultimately rewarding, aspect of the book. Whenever you pick up a book of Ben's, the images on its pages have something unique about them that produces an almost three-dimensional illusion. That's the efforts of painstakingly layering each page with a new scanned image to form an illustration, kinda like building a 50-storey building, then viewing it from above.

'My art work looks very collage-y. I was always fascinated by the raw, tactile look of the eighties punk phase, like the Sex Pistols' album covers. There are some really cool artists from that era that I've looked to, like Gee Voucher, who did the artwork for a punk political band. I find the music is very layered in itself, very edgy, and although it's not pleasing to many people's ears, punk music tugs emotional strings with me, especially the more old-school bands like the Dead Kennedys and Bad Brains. As far as other influences go, my favourite children's artist is the American, Lane Smith, who writes quirky and often dark stories. There's also Sara Fanelli, Oliver Jeffers, and the digital art of J. Otto Sebold.'

Ben uses a hybrid technique of traditional and technological to create his effects. He paints his characters, gets the scissors out, then scans them into the environments he's creating. Simply, he's doing some seriously creative cut and pasting. But it's a commitment that requires some pretty quirky moves of his own.

'We had an old shed out the back of our flat in Newtown. It was falling to pieces. It had some old Formica, fake wooden veneer and old wallpaper that I used to rip off. I'd also find things on the street or on the beach. Down the road from our flat there was a fish shop that I'd buy a couple of herrings from, then take them up to the uni scanner late at night. I'd have to make sure all the scales and gunk was cleaned up before I left, although that weird late-night sort of stuff is pretty much the norm at an art school.' Even back at home, the surroundings that he'd been brought up in played a big factor in how the vessels in the book would look. 'The old wooden fishing boats I used were inspired by the ones in Gisborne. I've always loved their wooden lines, and the contrast between what's manmade and the smooth organics of the ocean.'

At the end of the year the students showcase their work at the Great Hall at Massey. It was here that Ben exhibited his completed work, *The Three Fishing Brothers Gruff*. On the opening night a lot of the public come through to view the latest flair to come out of the prestigious course. Among them, and incognito, were talent scouts and representatives from design companies looking for fresh ideas from the young and gifted. Ben's project well and truly caught the eye of one of them, but it would be 12 months before an email would appear in his inbox, all the way from a major publishing house in the United Kingdom. They were eager to print his book. A few negotiations here, the odd compromise there, one important signature, and one important dedication to his father, and the book was ready for the commercial world. Since then TTFBG has gone on to sell 10,000 copies in England, New Zealand and Australia, as well as a few thousand copies in a Korean edition.

It's a great success story. One that's taken him around the countryside to speak in front of thousands of school kids, featuring in writer festivals, enjoying corporate taxis out of airports, a live spot on the *Good Morning* show and, of course, national book awards. But there's something else to this story that makes it quite remarkable. And it wasn't until he and I had just left Howl, the chic second-hand bookstore in Gisborne, that Ben admitted it to me. He was trying to point out a building in the distance, but I couldn't see it. Was it that green one? You know, that one with the blue roof line? But he couldn't tell me, 'cause he's colour-blind.

'My grandfather's colour-blind too. It can get passed down from a daughter and through to her son. It's hard to see things like red and green, like, I have trouble seeing the pohutukawa flower against the green of the leaves. Because of that I have a unique perception of colours. I was told by a tutor at university to use it as an advantage, which I have. I use colours that I think look right to me, but may challenge the normal perceptions of what it should be, like the colour of the sky. It's really strengthened my appreciation of tone and texture — I've since learnt to use those over colour.'

Ben's work is world class. Even the judges at the book awards suggested he had set a new benchmark in illustrations. And I would've expected his work space to reflect that. That was, until he offered to show me his latest creativity down in the 'dungeon'. He led the way. Outside the house, on the bottom floor, is a slightly ajar door I had to go sideways to get through. Squeeze past the car and the old cabinet, watch your head on the stacked timber, the hanging lifejackets, the protruding foam sheets, then head towards the sliver of light coming through the gap in the far wall, beside the scaffolding frames. Welcome to the 'dungeon' — a burrow of a room with a lone computer on top of a small desk and dozens of inspiring pictures that have been cut out over time and plastered on each wall, all very collage-y, of course. It feels like we're lower than sea level here; even the rain on the plate windows looks like it's perilously close to coming straight through. 'It gets pretty cold down here in winter,' he says, then points to a small bar heater on the ground, 'but I just crank that up.'

Behind the computer is the art direction to the latest book he's working on. We discuss the hours that have gone into each page. 'The artwork takes so much longer than the writing. Traditionally, the author gets more credit for a picture book, which I find strange. So much more blood, sweat and tears go into illustrating. I'll tell people I've finished another book and they'll ask me whether I've written it as well. When I tell them someone else has, they're like, well, when ya gonna write another one? That perception peeves me a bit.'

I note the wooden tray beside us with pieces of litter in each of its compartments. In a house of creations, it doesn't look too out of place, but Ben is quick to point out its relevance. 'I was asked by Trade Aid to design a piece of art out of recycled rubbish they could auction off to raise funds. It's actually an old sewing drawer. All that junk in it I collected from just one walk along the main beach in town.' He points out how many different cigarette lighters he'd picked up, showing me the names of businesses on each one, like a kid with a depressing new hobby.

We drive into town to where he works as a graphic designer for New Wave Surfboards, one of the leading manufacturers of surfing hardware in the country. When he started there Ben's job description was brief — 'be edgy'. His work consists of ad design, T-shirts, some packaging, website design, pretty much everything that requires a logo and marketing. Ben has final say on most things, and his boss is happy to just give an opinion when Ben requires it. 'I'd make a spelling mistake in an advert and the owners didn't care, because that's the New Wave culture. It's meant to be a dirty, dusty, raw factory full of boys with pictures of naked chicks and surfing on the walls. And as long as each ad summed up New Wave and it looked like we were having fun, then they [management] were happy, spelling mistakes and all. Like Keith Richards once said, "Keep the imperfections in, it's what makes it perfect", that's what we're about.'

Ben shows me around the factory, the shapers' bay, the new epoxy oven from Brazil, the computer shaping machine, Ralph Blake's 'office'. The place smells like resin, it has a lacquer of foam dust in every room, plenty of female flesh and good times protruding off every wall. It reeks of history and trendsetting. By the time Ben has shown me where he works — a tiny room in the ceiling cavity that's shared by three others — I'm almost ready to hand in my own CV just to be a part of this culture. It is raw. It is dirty. It's like Scouts for the cool guys. Ironically, the only room that was spotless, with no pictures of breasts or barrels, was the toilet. 'We get the groms to make sure it's cleaned every day. It's in their best interests to; they get bog-washed if they piss us off.' Heh, imagine that sort of work culture in Queen Street.

Ben admits that when the shapers are doing the clear-coats downstairs, and in the right wind, there's a chemical smell that wafts up into their hobbit-home of an office, and that can get a bit headachy. Or some days he'd sit down at his computer and find a thin layer of dust over it. 'Ralph's been here for forty-odd years, so it can't be that bad, although he does get a bit moody.' He laughs. 'But in terms of culture-wise, and the characters you meet and the mood you're trying to create in the ads and so on, it's great. We can go surfing when we want. If there are good waves, eight employees in the building turn into only one or two. We get cheap boards as well, which is handy, 'cause Ralph just chucks our previous dimensions through the shaping machine, so you're constantly refining what you're riding.

The place smells like resin, it has a lacquer of foam dust in every room, plenty of female flesh and good times protruding off every wall.

We'd often have the pro guys come in and hang out, which was good for business. The groms would be downstairs in the shop talking to them or using the Internet to check out surf reports and porn.'

But back to those ads. To me they always stood out on the pages of the country's surf magazines thanks to their clean backgrounds and sharp, original imagery. A combination of smashed TVs and surfboards — who would've thought? But there've been others that have caused even more mess, and not just confined to a white room of sheets . . .

'Probably the most controversial one we did was when we decided to do this mail drop through town. It was just a black print on brown paper. The bottom half of the image was a whole lot of vegetation rooting, and the top was the tree,' he says. 'But . . . the way I'd designed it, the bottom half looked like fishnet stockings and the top half like a woman's pubic area. Above it was the title "You Trippin'? Come in and get your wetsuits, surfboards and bags from us for your trip overseas." It was very New Wave, but in hindsight the market we aimed at was wrong and maybe we shouldn't have dropped it to every house in town. We copped quite a bit of flak in the local newspaper, and from mothers whose daughters surfed. I admit, it was sexist and we knew we were going to get some shit for it, but we wanted to get noticed, which we did. At the end of the day the boss was stoked.'

Then there was that 'Jay Quinn' ad. The New Wave crew decided for this team rider they'd focus on Jay's reputation of being a ladies' man. What did Ben do? He scanned a bunch of open condoms, complete with 'used' effect, and wrote 'New Wave' out of them. Underneath was Jay — who'd only recently come back to riding NW surfboards — with a board viced between his legs. And the caption? 'It feels good to be back between your legs, Jay', of course meaning, it was good to have him back riding the surfboards. Did everyone see the irony? The people at *Curl* magazine didn't and refused to run it. But never one to let a marketing opportunity slide, Ben still paid for the full-page ad and instead wrote in big letters, 'Sorry, our ad has been deemed too inappropriate to run in this magazine. www.newwave.co.nz'. Guess what image appeared when the website was accessed?

Oh yeah, and don't forget that billboard above the shop.

'It was a giant image of a rather large pair of breasts. Across where the nipples should've been were the words, "New Wave, more than a handful since 1980". A lot of people complained about it to the council. So we had them on our case for a couple of weeks telling us to pull it down, but we just ignored them. Eventually the council forgot about it, or got sick of telling us, so it stayed up. We finally changed the billboard to something different, but we have continued to use it at the local campground's bikini jam. That event is part of the popular Rhythm and Vines Festival, so there's around ten thousand people crammed into the premises. The organisers bring in professional bikini models and everyone from the campground is there. The massive image sits proudly as a backdrop to it all.'

The relationship between sexual innuendo, blatant destruction, and giant breasts, to the sale of surfboards may seem a little far-fetched, a little risqué, heck, even a slap in the face to potential customers. But ask anyone involved in modern marketing and they'll tell you about the benefits of positioning yourself at the 'edge'. It's that ballsy, almost mythical place in the market where you flag the conventional path being trod, and start walking the one that distances yourself from your competitors. How do you know if you're there? You're upsetting a few people. So although the work Ben does may seem a little on the rock'n'roll side of the cruisy surfing ethos, his creative ability, savvy marketing skills and understanding of the culture has resulted in the New Wave brand becoming the most recognised in the local market, with sales up, and outlet stores in Napier, as well as in the staunchly hard-core west coast surf city of New Plymouth.

On dusk the rain has stopped and the wind has found a hint of westerly direction. At Gisborne's main beach, 'Gizzy Pipe' ('Nah, no reference to Hawaii, just the sewage pipe sticking out down the beach there,' Ben informs me) is stacked with locals all vying for the glassy four-foot peak coming through. Out the back with the rest of the surfers, Ben makes small talk with many of them; I don't bother to ask him how he knows so many guys, but I suspect it's either through his NW connections, his local upbringing, or becoming somewhat of an identity in town since the success of his book. Likely all of the above, I assume. As the day's stormy weather bows out, the sky turns an intense orange colour. The sets rolling in start to look more like oily claret as the walls of water reflect the sun's exodus in the west. I go to point out to Ben the new thin lines of clouds the weather has left behind, stacked against each other out to sea, like a collage effect, but he's since caught the last wave and is busy demonstrating why he won the surfing competition at the University Games three years in a row. Or why he was a previous Wellington champ. Or third-placed in the National Juniors a few years back (he'd show you all the cups, but he shrugs his shoulders as he admits to not knowing where they are and to not putting much emphasis on them).

To me, it's obvious Ben has that special relationship with the sea only a few lucky surfers in each pack have. You know the ones I'm talking about — quietly going about their business, using minimum effort in their session, set waves uncannily appearing in front of them like they're being waited on by Tangaroa himself . . . that deep, personal affiliation with the environment they're in. It's a connection the rest of us aspire to; one day finding that special invitation in our mail box to join the elite club. But Ben, who admits that he's never been one to openly express his feelings, doesn't see it like that. His perception is a little more realistic. 'I'm not really a spiritual person. I've been through phases though, and looking back I can kind of see I was seeking enlightenment in surfing. From that first sensation of standing up and travelling along a wave, to when I surfed in competitions and tried to progress to the next round, I suppose it will eventually come full circle, so when I'm fifty I'll be empowered by standing up and riding along a wave again. There've been times when surfing's taught me little things in life, like if I ruin a wave, not to worry about it, there'll always be another one behind, which on land equates to not taking myself too seriously. I don't think you can explain it to someone who doesn't surf. It's not just the physical thrill of surfing. There's something quite meditating about it. All your worries and stresses wash away in the surf. When I'm out in the water I honestly don't think about anything at all, apart from the present. I've been surfing for so long I go into automatic pilot and the thinking part of my brain turns off.'

Ben has spent many solo sessions in the surf where he's taken time to learn the sea's personality. He's also taken the time to observe his environment and acknowledge the transformations he's seen. 'I've always been fascinated by the fish and sea — all the previous paintings I'd done were of seascapes. After surfing here for twenty years I've seen changes take place, like the increase in rubbish and the erosion of our coastline. I think as anecdotal evidence, observations from surfers are relevant because we're the ones out there in that environment. People have told me that the *Brothers Gruff* is what's happening around here, with the commercial fishermen overfishing the reefs. I've always rowed out in our dinghy and dived for crays or fished, and found that it's definitely become a lot more depleted. I'm not an activist and

> 'It's not just the physical thrill of surfing. There's something quite meditating about it. All your worries and stresses wash away in the surf.'

I probably won't join Greenpeace or get behind some sort of group, but I think as an individual we can make big changes in the environment by changing the way we live and by doing the little things ourselves.'

When it comes time for me to leave Ben the next day, the rain has returned and with it, has brought a strong onshore. From the 'seat' we sip tea, eat cake and watch as any potential surf is scalped by the strengthening nor'easterly wind. I turn down Linda's offer of seconds of her hospitality and make a move to hit the road. Ben, on the other hand, makes plans to do his own trip — this one down to the main beach with Simonne to go to collect more rubbish, including lighters, to add to the Trade-Aid art.

Daisy Day

Aaron Topp

PHOTOGRAPHER
NEW PLYMOUTH

When Daisy was a little girl she'd lean against the large window at her parents' house and stare out to sea. She'd be silent except for the faint sound of her breath as it formed and dissolved clouds of condensation against the glass. Her eyes would scan the giant green mass, watching the small approaching corduroy lines for the sign of a whale. Any sign; she knew they must be out there somewhere. Her parents had told her stories about whales, but they'd never seen one, either. They'd lived most of their lives land-bound in England and had immigrated to New Zealand only a few years before she was born.

To them the sea was as mysterious as it was overwhelming; on the ship's journey over, her mother spent most of it in their cabin room in fear because she couldn't see land. And this fear had remained, despite settling down in a house a stone's throw away from Wanganui's Castlecliff beach. But this paranoia was lost to their daughter's innocence as she heard the sea across the road call to her each day and lull her to sleep every night. Often she'd venture out the gate to play and dance in the soft sand as the waves sang to her on the shore, until she would once again be led back to the house by her mother's firm grip and warnings of the perilous nature of the ocean. Back to the bay window she would be drawn, where the thin glass would deny Daisy the ocean's call. For now, she would watch for whales from the safety of her parents' house. But it wouldn't always be this way.

'I remember when I was sixteen, coming over the hill to the river mouth, seeing a few guys surfing these beautiful green waves, and thinking how awesome it looked,' a now grown-up Daisy recalls. 'A few months later I went up to Gisborne with some friends and managed to borrow a board while at Wainui. That was like the "wee and wow" factor all in one. I couldn't stand, didn't have a clue, but after that trip I couldn't stop talking about it.'

Daisy's new-found enthusiasm paid off with her first board. Before heading off to art school, she began work at a timberyard inland from Wanganui in the small town of Marton. One of the office guys there heard her non-stop surf ramblings and offered her his single-fin pintail to use. She was so excited to have it when she was back home she took it out on a flat day at Castlecliff. She'd brought along a friend who she was trying to introduce to surfing so she had another female to share the waves with, but to Daisy's despair, her friend just didn't get it — it wouldn't be until Daisy was ready to leave Wanganui that other females discovered what she had already found.

These days, Daisy lives in a terraced property that enjoys a wide vista of the Tasman Sea, and most importantly, an instant surf check of the famous Fitzroy beach break. The house is filled with surfing paraphernalia — surf art and photos share the wall space equally, surf magazines of all descriptions sit in small, reachable piles beside the furniture, a brand new seven-foot fish (retro-shaped surfboard) leans against the wall, bearing down on us like a bodyguard as we sit on the couch and drink our coffee. 'It's my new board,' she tells me, with a sparkle in her eye I totally get, 'just waiting for the conditions to come right.' There's a positive energy here that I struggle to comprehend. Even Scout, the German shepherd she adopted from the SPCA not long ago, won't stop wagging her tail at me. The sea breeze is floating through the double doors like a welcome ghost who's free to come and go, filling the room with a blend of salt and freedom. I sit back in the cushions and inhale it all in.

'At first, surfing was all about being in the ocean,' Daisy tells me, 'but I started thinking more and more about it and found it wasn't just about lying on this board. I needed to look at these waves a little bit more in a technical sense. I was hampered a little because I'm horribly short-sighted, and I had to take the glasses off before I went out. I couldn't see the swell coming until the waves were right on me, so I think the learning process took me a lot longer and there was a bit of frustration starting to set in, but nothing was going to stop me. I still remember my first proper wave and the feeling of my stomach coming up to my throat as I free-fell down the face of the wave. I was so excited that I couldn't sleep that night. I persisted with bad eyesight for a while longer until I swapped the glasses for contacts, but that changed things again because suddenly the waves seemed so much bigger. Some of the guys I would surf with would shake their heads when I'd take off on the waves during the bigger stormy days.' A local kneeboarder, Frank Dowers, took pity on the petite blonde — who the local crew had nicknamed 'Gidget' — getting tossed around by the giant rolling pins of water. He offered her his kneeboard to try, with the theory that she'd be closer to the waves so maybe she'd see more. This, with the help of flippers, did improve her perception of the surf for a while, until she decided that standing up was way more satisfying. She ditched the flippers and extra-wide surf craft and paddled back out on her single fin for good.

'These days the sensations come from when I do something a bit better on a wave. I suppose when you become a little bit older and in tune with things there's more of a fear factor involved. When you're young, the fear isn't there.'

About the only thing more recognisable than Daisy's happy face in the line-up is her silhouette on the beach looking back at the surf through a lens. The surf and her cameras are now intricately linked, to the point where the other day she was the photographer for a wedding at a picturesque vineyard along the Surf Highway, but by late afternoon, just when the newlyweds' smiles were peaking, Daisy admits to becoming more and more distracted by the fresh groundswell calling out to her in the background. Her wedding shots are fantastic, by the way. It's been a long journey with the camera to get this far. Right from an early age she was fascinated with her father's old camera, a Zeiss Ikon, and how he could produce exciting images. He taught her how to use it and before long she wasn't going anywhere without it in her hand. Although her parents recognised her young passion for photography (they bought her a basic plastic automatic camera for her birthday once; she was gutted), it wasn't until Daisy was in camera club at college that she would get her first serious bit of kit. Her skills started to take off and soon after leaving school she scored a job at the *Wanganui Chronicle* as a cadet photographer. Five years later, fuelled by the surfing spirit, she decided to look for greener, glassier and more consistent pastures. After considering a few different wave-related spots around the North Island, Daisy settled on the surf cornucopia of New Plymouth. She packed her boards and belongings into her VW Kombi van, and headed towards the giant snow-capped mountain and into her new job as a journalist with the *Daily News*, a job she would hold on to for the next 19 years. During that time, while her photographic skills were being used capturing the local news, Daisy was also getting inspired by the surf shots of Californian cameraman, Leroy Grannis.

'They begin to understand the whole "being out there" aspect, and how it chills them out . . . you actually see them starting to feel so much better.'

'I ended up with a couple of his books he did back in the fifties and sixties. I just thought his images were amazing. He's about ninety now, but he's still chugging along. I met him in Aussie at a surf festival at Noosa. When I found out he was there I didn't want to leave his side.' She shows me a signed book of his. The book itself is a rare find these days, so to have it signed by the guy puts it right up there as a prized surfing treasure. 'I was also inspired by Peter Bush [the legendary New Zealand sports photographer]. He was a mentor to me, not that he'd know it. I'd just get to talk to him after games and such. He wasn't technical, but he had raw talent and so much experience that when he spoke I'd hang off his every word.'

The 'chick with the big lens' is a phrase Daisy uses as though it's a title with which the surfing community have crowned her. She'll claim it; it's something she's worked hard for. Twenty-four hours before a swell hits, she's studying the information to decide where will be the best surf spot to shoot. Then she's up early to catch that small window of opportunity when the sun's waves of energy first expose the ocean's waves peeling down the coast.

'That's when you have the clean light and the nice offshore. I went down to the Kumara Patch a while ago after the first drop of snow and it was freezing, but there was this big swell hitting the reef. We were the first there and I was sitting on the rocks waiting for all these guys to turn up, but they didn't show until after nine, so I started getting all these shots of an empty line-up. I love getting the people side of things the best though, capturing the local characters, because I think that's important. To help, I recently managed to get hold of a six-hundred millimetre lens that lets me get the shots better, especially down at the reefs. I've tried the water-shot thing using a water-housing, but it was a bit taxing on the body, especially in winter. There's still sometimes, though, when I'm out in the water, particularly when I'm surfing Waisy's [Waiwhakaiho], and I just think, oh, man, why haven't I got the camera now? It'll be a big swell, right direction, the lips chucked, someone's under it, it's all on, and there, in the middle of the shot, framed by the lip, there's the mountain in the distance, sitting perfectly in view! I'm gonna get it, one day. Definitely.'

Asking Daisy which is her favourite place to shoot is about as tactful as asking a parent who is their favourite kid. I guess that's what you get when you're a surf photographer and your 100-kilometre back yard is rich with world-class waves. But when pushed, Daisy admits to liking the heavy beach break of Fitzroy and the Groyne more than most spots because of convenience and because of their barrelling personalities. But she's also quick to state a trip over to Backbeach is always on the cards. Then there's the royalty of the south coast reefs, where Daisy will find little glimpses of the swell between the hills as she approaches the spots. That's when she'll stop the car to wait for the bigger sets, and use the big lens to capture that 'search' essence. That way the photos are always kept different and the uniqueness of the Taranaki coast is explored to its richest.

'There was this one big swell at Rockies where I spent the whole day photographing to capture the mood of the place and watch how it changed. The different smells and the sounds — the rock sounds are phenomenal around the Taranaki — the full tide, then the lulls. The early morning, through to the evening. The wind came up during the middle of the day and you got that crinkling of the wave, then it went back offshore again as the day got on and it began to look like the morning again as the sun set. It was great to be there, great to experience and shoot all its personalities.'

For Daisy, there's a lot that makes an 'ahh' moment. Originally it was about seeing those images in the darkroom, but with the advent of high-quality digital, now it's about seeing them on the computer screen. 'You generally know you've got something there, a hunch, and I still get excited to head back and have a look. That feeling has never faded. You see a lot of different things when you're constantly out there on the coast. Lately I've had these bizarre shots happening where a seagull will swoop into frame with the surfer and I'll capture them together. Seems to be happening so regularly I've named the bird "Johnny",' she says with a laugh.

Of course, all those amazing photos would have been wasted buried in the depths of her computer's hard drive, or at best, given five seconds of fame each 10 minutes as her screensaver. Those images depicted the hardcore surf community's environment in a way the national magazines hadn't captured. That's where her husband, local surf identity, Wayne 'Arch' Arthur, comes into the picture. The story of how they met is pretty understandable — Daisy arrives in New Plymouth, decides she needs a new board. Wayne owns a surf store in town. Daisy leaves with new board, but keeps coming back anyway. Things progress. They get married. In 2002 they open Beachstreet, a unique surf store on the Fitzroy road that focuses on the underground surf labels and their own house brands, 'Lost in the 60s', and the more recent, 'Black Sand'. Daisy tells me that she and Arch really like to use the shop to concentrate on supporting the groms and upskilling them by putting on special competitions that cater just for their ages.

But back to all those photos . . .

With such a large percentage of the Taranaki population drawn to the waves, Daisy and Arch decided that the local crew needed a regular medium to help keep them stoked. 'Wayne and I had always talked about doing something local. We'd go through the Kiwi magazines and hardly ever see any of our crew in them. So we wanted to give the guys here more of a profile and produce something with a heavy emphasis on photos, while keeping the advertising to a minimum, maybe just enough to cover costs. We also wanted to have something where we could talk about environmental issues that were relevant to our coast, while getting our own and readers' views out there. And of course, there was the fact I had thousands of photos that required an outlet.'

The idea of a local paper remained just that for a while, until they produced a small marketing flyer promoting the shop. It featured a few photos from Daisy's collection and that sparked some positive feedback from the surfing community. It was enough to convince them to give it a serious crack. By chance, they met a well-known Australian surf photographer, Paul 'Sarge' Sargeant, who Arch successfully talked into coming over to live in New Plymouth and oversee the first few issues. By 2006 the first edition of the *Daily Surf* hit the bookstores, surf shops and Four Squares. But an issue or so later they lost Sarge back to Australia, and Daisy and Arch were forced to produce it themselves.

'Sometimes ideas come to me between lulls. Or when I get done by a big set and I'm underwater listening to the different sounds . . .'

'We had a goal of getting an issue out every two months. Arch does some of the writing, I do some bits and pieces, and we commission another person down at the reefs, Diana Hall, who writes some colourful pieces. The fifteen hundred copies are bundled up and delivered as far north as Mokau and as far east as Wanganui. I'd love it to be glossy, maybe a few pages at least, but that's an extra cost, and in saying that, the newsprint gives it that 'throw-away' feel [not that anyone would], while making it different to anything else out there. Since we've been producing it we've had so much good feedback from the locals. There's a lot of realism there; I mean, the photos are of surfers living next door to you, so it's real as.'

Since 2004 Daisy has run a surf school with the lively title, 'Learn to Surf with Daisy'. It all started by giving the odd lesson or two in her spare time in the weekends while she was still at the *Daily News*. She began to look at it more seriously after discovering that she got a real buzz introducing people to the ocean on a more intimate level and being a part of their journey into surfing. All kind of ironic when you think about how the rest of her Anglo-Saxon family tree considered the sea. The number of her clients has been growing every year, along with the range of people wanting to learn. So far the youngest she's taught is three, while it's not uncommon for her to be dealing with people in their sixties — despite what the surf industry's marketing material might suggest, it's never too late to start. Typically, many of the pre-teens take it up and want to carry it on, enjoying Daisy's easy-going nature and soft approach. But in typical teenage style, most the learners in that age bracket have one lesson and suddenly think they're the next Maz Quinn or Paige Hareb. Thanks to Daisy they've got their foot in the door and they're off to hound the olds for that new stick and wettie they've found on TradeMe. According to Daisy, the over-thirties aren't that dissimilar, except they have a little more disposable income and are pretty much out in the water with the gear straight away.

Whether they have one lesson or many, it's a huge boost to the local surf community to have Daisy fostering so much stoke at a sand-hopper level. But is it just a matter of rocking up to the beach on a sunny day and sticking up a 'lessons here' sign? 'When I first started out there was no one officially teaching surfing. In fact, it was pretty well unknown in New Zealand. Now I'm finding it's starting to become a legitimate business. In summer I'm out there every day, often in the water for six hours at a time. I try to get my own surfing in early morning, and keep my camera close to me. I've got a couple of coaches I've had to employ to help me out, and I've also had to begin upgrading the gear. We get the mad tourists who are always keen and that's great in summer, but in winter they're trying to drag you out in freezing cold ninety-kilometre winds.'

One thing I've noticed about Daisy is that she always finishes her sentences smiling. Sometimes if she's thinking about an answer, she'll get a little animated, like a teenager, giggling, crossing one leg under the other, apologising in case I think her reply isn't good enough. Has she found a fountain of youth somewhere? Even the house music playing in the background has to be turned down a bit because I'm afraid it'll interfere with my dictaphone. She's like a hybrid of youthfulness and experience, an extremely rare combination. It goes a long way to explaining why Daisy is so well respected among the locals, especially the females, and why her surf school is doing so well. Daisy understands the ocean, the environment, and what it really means to be a surfer, while having the ability to articulate it with the grommet in mind, because, well, it's obvious she's still one herself. 'I was taking some girls for a surf lesson down the coast during a really clean small swell and as we approached the water I stopped and said, "Listen to that." They couldn't hear anything and asked what they were meant to be listening to. I told them to listen again, and for a while the sound wasn't there, but with the surge of the swell came the sound of the rocks underneath rubbing together. They could hear it. Then I asked them to tell me what the sea smells like.

'"Seaweed?"

'"Yeah, exactly," I said, "and tomorrow it will smell completely different." That's something I've become a lot more in tune with as I've grown older. I'd never have appreciated it like that when I was starting out, which is why I try and teach my students to look at all the elements from those first lessons. To see their faces and watch that new awareness is awesome. Even the older people who've had no appreciation of the ocean, apart from it's something they've traditionally swum in, they're understanding it a lot more and coming out with some cool things, things that are making more sense to them now. They begin to understand the whole "being out there" aspect, and how it chills them out, so to speak, and you actually see them starting to feel so much better. It just consumes them. One guy in his forties who's been coming out with us lately has been asking himself why he didn't do this earlier. He's now getting his daughters and partner involved so they can start to understand the effect the surf has on him. They start to observe the sea is always changing, never the same, so it's exciting to get out there. It's interesting taking people from other countries out, watching how they cope and how they look at the ocean. They certainly don't look at it like we do. For Europeans and Asians it's full of trepidation and fear, just different cultures seeing the ocean as something to be scared of.'

Having this intimate relationship with the ocean evolve over time has meant Daisy's enjoyment has become amplified; her senses are now highly tuned to its different frequencies. This has opened many new doors of wonderment to her, but at the same time emphasised that many other people have yet to fully understand the gift that surfing has given the rest of us. The unfortunate thing is, their actions of ignorance also become amplified to her, such as a surfer taking their frustration out on the sea by bashing it with their hand. 'You never win over the ocean, so it's no use taking it on. Sometimes I can feel frustrated during a competition, but I just shrug my shoulders and get on with it, I never take it out on the sea. That's probably the most common thing that comes out of my mouth when I'm seeing someone getting annoyed. I tell them to suck it all in, then get them to think of why it's happening and why they think the ocean is doing that. I let them know the ocean is a big spirit.'

So why does Daisy think so many Kiwis are attracted to surfing? 'It's right outside our doorstep. We're surrounded by it and it draws us in because we're traditionally fisher-folk. What's underneath the ocean, what's above it? I think non-surfers miss out on learning about the ocean's true nature and its changing faces, like being able to watch how it can reflect our own moods as humans, such as stormy one day, then pleasant the next. I also think they lose out on that "chill out" factor.' Daisy had recently come back from a college reunion and was surprised to find a negative vibe amongst some of her old peers, particularly the ones who were supposed to have 'made it' in the real world. Out of the hundreds there, she could count on one hand those who appeared truly content and exhibited a sense of vitality, and one of those fingers was hers. She put that down to surfing and being able to retain that passion over the years. 'When I go out surfing I study everything, like the way the ocean looks at that time, how the clouds look, what birds are going across the sky, and I always look across at the mountain to see what the clouds are doing. Most surfers I know say their baggage and troubles just leave them — I know it certainly does for me. It's so nice out in the water. Sometimes ideas come to me between lulls. Or when I get done by a big set and I'm underwater listening to the different sounds, thinking about the different thoughts going through my head.'

Some of those thoughts are about protecting the natural state of the coast she

> Get up early and get out in the surf by half past five and see how different your day will be.

60

now calls home. Making sure that each generation accepts the responsibility to hand it on to the next, in the same state as they first received it. Like the saying goes, we're merely borrowing it from our children. 'It's about being in the environment and keeping it clean. No one likes to see rubbish in or out of the sea. In saying that, I'm still seeing a tiny faction, barely a handful, of the young ones who can't see much further than the waves they're shredding. It concerns me that their parents are surfers, who are quite environmentally minded people, yet their kids will still toss their rubbish on the sand. But on the other hand, I see a whole lot of other grommets taking time to pick rubbish up and keep their breaks clean. We've got it pretty good right here in New Zealand; we have a beach education programme, where, apart from being taught how to deal with the ocean, it also teaches how to deal with the environmental things as well, things like the plastics that can kill the wildlife.' From their shop's perspective, Daisy and Arch like to help support and promote initiatives like 'Tangaroa Blue', a scheme started by Stephen Sait in Waitara, which encourages youngsters to pick up rubbish off the beach and look after their surf breaks. And Daisy is already seeing those ideas paying off. 'Recently I was walking down the long stretch of coast to the [Kumara] Patch after a massive storm and it occurred to me I'd only come across two plastic things amongst all that washed-up driftwood. I thought that was awesome. Many places overseas don't have the awareness that we do here; you go to some beaches around the world — the "commercially" pristine ones — and it's absolutely chocker with litter. I guess there's this mentality that you chuck something in the ocean, it's going to stay out there — but it always comes back, doesn't it?'

But there's a bigger threat along this stretch of coast that, if implemented, could very well have catastrophic effects on the local marine life, the natural beach structure, and, of course, the quality of waves and the surfing community for which Taranaki is world famous. What could do such destruction? Mining the seabed could. What local would have the cheek to do it? No one. But the fourth largest mining company in the world wouldn't have a problem doing so. Rio Tinto has bought into a small South Island-based company specialising in prospecting for iron. After successfully doing a reconnoitre between Kaipara Harbour and Cape Egmont in a purpose-equipped plane, they discovered an abundance of the stuff two to three kilometres off the coast, and at a handy mining depth. Why would they do it? Because iron is in big demand in developing countries such as China and India. They need the mineral so it can be made into building materials to allow them to carry on supplying the world with more of the goods we use everyday. Ah, yes, the old catch-22 scenario.

In the old days, perhaps. But surely sustainability in this day and age counts for everything? If there's one real positive to come out of our forebears' rip-shit-and-bust ways of the last century, then it's the chance to learn from the lack of sustainability in their practices. If our country's natural resources are all there is, do we need to squander such an irreplaceable (certainly in our time) fortune for the short-term gain of making a quick buck selling it offshore? Are we not quickly becoming a global society of better efficiencies and technologies, with savvy-minded thinkers who actually give a damn about cause and effect? Most of the Taranaki locals think we are and that's where my little tirade comes back to Daisy and Arch. The humble newsletter has played a vital role in the global development of communities for hundreds of years. These small documents have connected and changed societies of all sizes through the simple value of being an excellent vessel for freedom of speech.

The *Daily Surf* is a perfect outlet to keep the local community informed and aware of the developments of this issue (at date of publication no iron has yet been mined). It may not seem much against an army of experienced spin doctors skilled in the art of building public perception, or the massive financial backing behind a company like Rio Tinto, but ask any Kiwi about home-ground advantage they'll tell you at least one story about the role it played in David triumphing over Goliath. The ironic thing is, before the giant nose of the global corporate came sniffing around their back yard, Daisy and Arch were looking for another clothing label to run in their store, one that was synonymous with the ocean but retained its uniqueness compared to everything else out there. 'We decided we had all this West Coast black sand around that's iconic to us, so we came up with the Black Sand label. Then word got out about the mining and we thought it was timely. We're working on designs all the time, developing the "no black sand mining" message. We'll find surfers in every group, especially around here, will talk and make sure the word is spread around the non-surfing community.' And it's obvious that's working, with the amount of 'anti-mining' stickers on the back of cars, on surfboards, in shop windows, on the T-shirt of the person walking past you, even graffitied on the odd wall in town. It seems New Plymouth is not a great example of quiet resistance. Meanwhile, on the other side of the planet, the strategists in their expensive suits are quietly working away in the background to make sure it all goes to plan.

But for now, Daisy is just happy to continue putting her energy into spreading as much surf stoke into the Taranaki community as possible. As I'm leaving, she shows me her office, a concentrated form of more surfing paraphernalia, and the latest photos she took down the coast. She begins energetically clicking away on the mouse, standing back with smile after smile to let me see what I'm missing while I'm back on the East Coast. Sure, they were sweet waves, but I couldn't help imagining the looks on the faces of her peers at the college reunion when she turned up. The words 'chronologically frozen' would've been rife. It got me thinking, is the act of surfing itself the mythical fountain of youth? 'The surf has got this influence over us. It's just so calming. We're out there floating on this fibreglass and we've got no control over it. And it's just so different, I think it must be all those negative ions being generated off the ocean. I often tell people to try it, especially in summer. Get up early and get out in the surf by half past five and see how different your day will be. When they do, they all tell me it's the best thing ever.'

Craig Levers

Aaron Topp

PHOTOGRAPHER
PIHA

Sunset Beach, Hawaii, and trigger-happy photographer Craig Levers is loitering around the neighbourhood taking snaps of the raging surfing scene being played out in front of him. He's got his orders from the editor at home to bring rolls of classic Hawaii back, or else. And he's making a good job of it too; there are more blue waves and tanned skin in those films than one mag can handle. He's feeling good about himself, and is not only anticipating the editor's whip to be left stashed in its cupboard for another month, but perhaps this time maybe a little bonus cheque left on his wooden chair back in his cubicle. Yes, life was good in Craig's world.

That was until he bumped into expat surfing legend, Allan Byrne. After listening to Craig spout on like a chipmunk on speed about all the great images of famous surfers tucked away in the bag slung over his shoulder, Allan's more than obliging to help a fellow Kiwi out any way he can, and has an idea. He offers to take Craig to Darrick's house.

For the first time since he stepped off the plane, Craig's smile disappears. He's suddenly the whitest guy on the continent. 'What, you mean Darrick Doerner? Big-wave legend, hellman, Darrick Doerner?'

'Yeah, he's a good mate of mine,' Allan says, but senses this journo's about to lose it. 'Hey, look, man, you gotta be cool about it though, OK? Just try and relax.'

They pull up outside the house, Craig grabs his gear, takes a breath, and they head in. Allan introduces him to Darrick as 'the photographer from *New Zealand Surfing* magazine', and asks very politely, on Craig's behalf, if it's OK to shoot a couple of photos. Craig notices the hint of a wink from Allan to his Hawaiian comrade. Being the butt of these two legends' little joke was a tiny price to pay for the shots Craig was getting. He was pulling out every trick in his photographic repertoire, doing the craziest effects, constantly repositioning the two staunch grown men like they were a couple of storefront mannequins. Finally, happy with his efforts, he sticks a stiff thumb in the air, 'that's a wrap, thanks guys'. Feeling pretty smug with himself, he heads out the door to put his gear away.

Craig remembers the moment vividly, 'That's when I looked down at the back of the camera as I was sticking it in the car, and just went, oh, crap. I couldn't believe what I was seeing — where was the film? I was thinking, no, no, no, what the hell am I gonna do?' In the end he thought, stuff it, loaded the camera, and hoped like hell they wouldn't realise it was same one. He waltzed back inside and said, 'Hey, I just shot with that other camera, so I just wanna get a couple more with this one, that cool?' He got them to recompose their positions, and began shooting again, paranoid they were going to notice. Out of that whole session he ended up with one shot that worked. He was stoked.

Craig started off his youth immersed in the '80s skate scene in central Auckland, growing up with the Tony Hawk generation. As far as he was concerned, back then the coolest people on earth were the likes of Jay Adams, Tony Alva, and the rest of the Z-Boys who were setting any empty swimming pool in the state of California alight with their radical moves and don't-give-a-shit attitudes. He wasn't alone; it was a time when the youth of the whole world were absorbing themselves in the scene; having the chance to watch Stacy Peralta work his magic at Auckland's Skatopia was every kid's dream come true.

To keep themselves up to date with the latest happenings in the Northern Hemisphere, Craig and his mates would collect the original *Skateboarder* mags, doing their best to emulate what they saw. It was in this publication that Craig became exposed to the amazing images of photographer Glen E. Friedman. 'I'm pretty sure it was those early shots of the Dogtown crew he took, but there were those crazy ones of Duane Peters too, at the Upland skate park. Then there were the Black Flag and Henry Rollins images, and of course the original Suicidal Tendencies album cover. He could capture the culture like no one else.' Craig may have been young at the time, but the revolutionary images left a resounding effect on his grommet vulnerability. It wouldn't be until years later, when at a mate's flat he was shown a copy of Friedman's famous anthology book, *Fuck You Heroes*, that the penny would drop. It was at that moment he realised just what sort of influence the legendary L.A. photographer had played in guiding him on his journey behind the lens.

'Some were out of focus, some were dark, just all sorts of weird things were happening, but I was controlling the effects . . . It was the perfect creative outlet.'

But trying to define the exact moment Craig and the camera became the one entity is impossible. 'I didn't make a conscious effort to take up photography. It's what my passion was; it just took me a while to work it out. Looking back in old family albums there are quite a few that I took as a kid; then in sixth form I messed around with it a bit more seriously. But it wasn't until the early nineties when I started surf travelling that I knew I had to start documenting the cool stuff.' He tried writing a diary, but that only lasted two days. He was working in a surf shop at the time, when his boss offered him a sweet camera with a big lens for a hundred bucks. It was all completely manual, but Craig thought it was the cool. The first film he developed had generic shots of parked cars and stuff, but when he saw the images, he thought they were awesome. 'Some were out of focus, some were dark, just all sorts of weird things were happening, but I was controlling the effects. That fascinated me. It was the perfect creative outlet. From that moment on, each day literally became like Christmas Eve, or like when you're a grommet and you know you're going for a surf the next day. Seriously, taking photos rated right up there with those. I couldn't sleep.'

As a kid, and like many Kiwis during their passage of adolescence, he would spend all hours on his polystyrene surfboard catching the walls of whitewater. At night he would lie on his back with his arms outstretched, his front, fire-engine red from the rash, his back, hot-rod red from sunburn. Then he'd do it all again the next day, then the next. Finally, when he was 11, his parents got him an old Bob Davies single fin to use. Skating started to take a backseat as he found he was progressing and having more fun out in the surf than he was with the modern wave of skateboarding. Skating's fate was sealed when his father, someone who Craig says was the coolest dad ever, started to take him out to Piha most Saturday afternoons so he could read the paper in peace while Craig went for a surf; the bonus was the driving lesson — that included fishtails on the gravel — on the way home. 'Then, on the Sundays I used to get up almost at dawn to catch the bus back out there again. We had to stick our boards in the storage underneath, and on the way up to Piha we'd be sitting there listening to them sliding back and forth, crashing against each other. Sometimes we'd get off the bus, find a fin or two smashed, and you just knew it was gonna be a long day watching everyone else surf your waves.'

'We very much lived Fear and Loathing. We took surf-gonzo journalism and embraced it, because that's what we thought we were supposed to do . . .'

By 18, Craig was immersed in the nightclub scene, partying, girls, staying up late, sleeping in late. One morning he woke and realised the city life was spiralling him down, and worse, he hadn't touched his board in months. He walked into a travel company and bought himself a one-way ticket to the Gold

Coast. For the next two winters he surfed non-stop with every other hotshot surfer in the suburb, while keeping close with other pockets of Kiwis on their surfing pilgrimages. 'We were in the "North Shore flat", so we'd hook up with the guys in the "Gizzy", or the "Naki flat", or the "Mount flat", and hang out, get pissed, go for a surf, whatever. It was an awesome time. With the surf so accessible, and the quality of it so good, by the time I came back to Piha, I definitely felt I'd gone up the pecking order.'

And it's where he's been based for the last 16 years, living in a place that overlooks Piha out one side, and Karekare out the other. He takes me to his back yard and shows me the old log flume that the millers used back in the day to push the mighty timber down to the waiting ships below; it's a bizarre sight, like a giant earthworm has pushed its way through the Waitakere Ranges. Then he turns back to the house, points to an empty space, and I swear I hear him sigh. 'And that's where I had my half pipe. I pulled it down a few months back after I busted my knee.' He shakes his head. 'Mate, we had some great times riding that thing.' Sure, he's reached 40, but that's about where the normality ends. Even the silver streaks in his hair, a standard sign of age for most, gives him a dynamic appearance that suits the boardies and T-shirt that have been his work uniform since he can remember.

Back inside, I sit at Craig's breakfast bar while he brews one of his coffees — his speciality. For a guy who's spent the last 15 years photographing some of the best waves and surfers around, his walls are strangely barren; just the odd piece of art here and there, the well-positioned surfboard or two sitting in a corner, a noticeboard bearing a wide-angled photo of someone pulling an air on his back yard half pipe, while a group of beer-drinking mates watch on from the veranda. Very Friedman. He pours the brew and my cup begins throbbing. 'My photos are all in these files.' He points to a cluster of plastic boxes. 'I'm currently going through them for a new project I'm doing and getting the good stuff out.' Being a smartass, I try to call his bluff and request to see a photo of . . . oh, I dunno . . . how about somewhere random, like the Fijian surf break, Frigates?

Within seconds he's handed me a clear file with the trannies of the left-hander. 'It's such a hard place to photograph,' he says, like he has his own clear file of knowledge from each place inside that head of his. I take a sip of coffee, swallow my impertinence and remind myself of the company I'm keeping. 'I never intended to become a surf photographer,' he continues. 'I learnt from an early period that if I was holding a camera, then I wasn't surfing. And I wanted to be surfing. Thing was, even though I was very interested in the technical aspect and commercial side of photography, the surfing kept dragging me back in. I think it's my nature that my hobbies become my work.'

After having a few images published in its pages, when Craig was 26 he was asked to apply for the editor's job of *New Zealand Surfing* magazine. At that stage it was a three-horse race. Craig felt like he could do the imagery as well as concentrate on the advertising revenue, but admitted to finding the writing side of it intimidating. In the end, one of the horses pulled out, and Craig and Chris Berge, a guy he knew from the 'Gizzy flat' from the Goldie days, got dual roles — Craig did the photography, while Chris, an accomplished journalist, did the writing.

'We were as thick as thieves, me and him. We very much lived *Fear and Loathing*. We took surf-gonzo journalism and embraced it, because that's what we thought we were supposed to do — we were in our late twenties and living the rock'n'roll surf journo lifestyle. The shit we did to get a story.' He shakes his head. 'Mate, we were loose. If we weren't goin' surfing, like at a competition or something, then we'd get on the piss and create stories. We'd shout first round, then shout last round. If anything was going, we were in. Some mornings were hazy, but we never let the truth get in the way of a story. They were the glory days, for sure, and produced some of the best issues in that time.' But after three years of chaos, Chris reckoned his liver couldn't take any more. Suddenly, Craig was flying solo.

But things were about to get much harder for him. Craig committed himself to moving back in with his parents to help his mother care for his dad as he battled the final stages of cancer. It meant taking shifts with his mum; she watched over his dad during the day, while he handled the night. Between the two of them they worked like clockwork to nurse and monitor his father until the day he died. 'It was awesome that I was able to do that for him, to be there for those last six months and put all my own issues to the side. But at the same time, it took a toll on our lives. Particularly me, because I didn't know how to grieve properly. Dad had been this super-fit guy, full of vitality. He played tennis until the cancer became too much. In those final few months he ended up skin and bone. I guess I had a certain amount of bottled anger because the symptoms were there for a long time and he did what every Kiwi guy would do and swept it under the carpet. Then after his death the doctors kept saying he should've come and seen them sooner, which is a shithouse thing to tell us afterwards. The day Dad died I went out and got absolutely roasted. I'd always been immersed in the drinking culture, and the irony was that when he was sick, I didn't drink at all because I had a job to do. But that suddenly all changed. Alcohol seemed to dampen all the remorse and sadness I had. Dampen the memories. I suddenly began using drinking for something else other than a good time; now it was a way for me to escape.'

Craig spent the next year or so going hard binge drinking. He became increasingly unfit, increasingly unhappy. He'd heard people call alcohol a depressant, but had never really understood it, especially the long-term effects on depression. It got to the stage where, when he was surfing at Piha, all of the guys who he knew he could surf just as well as, were surfing rings around him. At over 100 kilograms he wasn't catching anything, and when he did, he spent the whole time stomping cockroaches on the wave to get speed because of the extra mass around his midriff. 'I remember saying to myself, I'm an editor of a surfing mag and I can't even surf — I'm so unfit. While I'm not saying I had an epiphany or anything, at that particular moment I decided I was going to get my act together.'

> He became increasingly unfit, increasingly unhappy. He'd heard people call alcohol a depressant, but had never really understood it . . .

It's kind of fitting that Craig can also recite the date of 20 March 2003 as the last time he touched alcohol. His father's death three years prior had become the catalyst for him allowing alcohol to take control, so that date in March marked the day he took it back. It rolls out of his mouth like he's reciting someone's birthday date, and in a way it is. It was the day he looked to climb his way out of the darkness and emerge a different person. He wasn't foolish enough to say 'no more forever' to drinking, he didn't actually ever think that he'd stop it for good; instead, he thought he'd just take a break from it for a month. But that month came and went so quickly, that he decided to extend it for another one, then another and so on. In that time he was having experiences he hadn't felt in a long time. 'Every night I was having a better and better sleep. Physically I was feeling good, I was getting a high off the way I was feeling. The body gets used to familiarity, like the whole four-o'clock-beer-time thing and so on, but once I'd finally broken that cycle, I was sweet. Now I relate alcohol drinking to all the bad times and being unhealthy. That works for me. Not saying it's a struggle not to drink, but I've taken responsibility for what happened, and I'm definitely OK with guys doing it around me. I was in that scene long enough to know the fun factor they're getting off on. It's just not right for me any more. I've realised the further away I've got from drinking that any guy over the age of about twenty-eight who gets overly drunk tends to look really ugly, not cool at all, and my acceptance and tolerance of those guys suddenly drops. I'd much rather be in control.'

His reinvention of himself didn't just stop with alcohol. With the combination of what he was achieving and starting to eat properly, including an initial cleansing diet, within three months he'd dropped the excess weight and was back to a healthier 78 kilograms. Surfing was there the whole way, too. And it played a massive role in his transformation. 'I wanted to focus on regaining what I'd lost in the surf. As I got amped again about surfing, it suddenly became this self-fulfilling experience. The more I surfed, the more weight I lost. The more weight I lost, the better I surfed. My mates were noticing it out in the waves, and I had great genuine support from some of them, which was so effective for me. I was super-lucky that surfing was there as the mechanism to do it. Surfing has this centring effect. I find if I haven't done it for a while I start getting away from what's important. Surfing refocuses you. There were moments where I'd be in the moment on a wave and it'd instantly stop the mind chatter and the "what ifs". It was absolutely the saviour for that, that's why I carried on doing it. Physiologically my body had found that energy source and I was getting an endorphin release, and combined with a couple of satisfying rides, getting a physical high off it the same way a gymhead does after an hour session on the weights.'

He decided if he could do his own extreme make-over, then the mag could do the same. In 2004, they changed the size and format, relaunched it, and watched it go from strength to strength. 'Looking back, the body of work around that year was the best I've ever done. It's like when you wind up, everything else winds up around you. I don't want to sound like the cheesy motivational guy, but if you think positive thoughts, then positive things happen. I was suddenly this smiley, happy Craig again, because I was happy with what I'd achieved with Dad and being able to successfully revamp the mag. I decided that year I wanted to head overseas for over two months surfing and shooting, because it felt right to do it and because the mag could afford it. We ended up getting pumping G Land, Teahupoo, Australia, and amazing waves back here at home, everything just worked out crazy.'

Eventually Craig became editor and remained in that role for seven years — the longest of any before him and arguably the best. He used Chris's former writing as an inspiration to improve his new responsibility of photographer and journalist, something he found easier to grasp once he accepted the fact that it was up to him to keep the issues flowing off the printer. In the end, he found he actually enjoyed developing the story just as much as pushing the shutter button.

To be honest, the letters 'CPL' have been an oddity for me ever since I was a grom looking at those early shots of his. Other photographers would use their normal name in the acknowledgements, and I could never get my head around the whole three-letter thing he insisted on using. I longed for a vowel or two to go somewhere. It screwed with my head for years. In fact, if you're a non-surfer reading this, it's likely doing the same.

'Cock-Pulling Leper was my favourite one,' he says with a laugh, referring to the day he walked into the Piha carpark the day after his first photo was published, and was accosted by his mates wanting to know what 'CPL' stood for. 'Someone just blurted it out. It was classic. I've probably perpetuated it myself the most.' The thing with Craig, apart from the fact he doesn't take himself too seriously, is that he's lived and breathed the punk ethos most of his life (it'd been playing on shuffle since I'd arrived), and where he can, he'll pull two very big fingers to over-commercialism. So back in the day, when no one really knew whether the whole surf mag thing was going to last, and photographers were doing all they could to set themselves up by getting carried away with full names, company names and even website addresses in their credits, Craig took a stand. 'I just thought, stuff the lot of you; I'm just going three initials — C-P-L. I mean, as an editor, I was having to type all these guys' different names everytime they had a photo published . . . it's just so much easier to push three keys and get it done with, without all the bullshit baggage.'

Ah, yes, that punk ethos. It's what made Friedman's photos so gritty, so raw, so alive. So alluring. His images — his subjects — have withstood the tides of fashion and to this day they still look like they're dictating what's cool, and maintaining that kick-your-ass-if-I-want-to attitude. 'It's the eyes, you gotta have the eyes,' Craig says, 'that's the key. And being involved in the scene, whatever scene it is, is critical. Friedman did that, he immersed himself in whatever scene he was into and it shows in the images. He's intimate with his subjects and they're allowing him to be there because of his integrity.' Craig shows me the highly acclaimed anthology of his first 15 years of surf photography, aptly named, *PHOTOCPL*. There are definite echoes of Californian style on each page, yet at the same time there's something very unique and Kiwi about the images. Maybe it's because Craig's mostly used well-known local surfers, some photographed over a space of many years to emphasise the journey from upstart wonderkid to pin-up surf idol. One thing's for sure, each image has that special surf wairua that he's looking for. 'In the past, I've seen some coffee-table books about surfing, but they've missed the mark because the photographer wasn't really that into the scene. All they've done is seen a hole in the surf-book market and decided they can fill it. I mean, Friedman had it right, if you want to differentiate between good and great, you've got to immerse yourself in the scene, there's no other way. I'm constantly amazed at the amount of photographers being published who're just spectators and not actual participants in the surf lifestyle. I couldn't do it any other way.'

But he's quick to admit that he's not the first to capture the essence of the

'I'm constantly amazed at the amount of photographers being published who're just spectators and not actual participants in the surf lifestyle. I couldn't do it any other way.'

Kiwi surf culture on film, and says he was also inspired by someone much closer to home. His predecessor at *New Zealand Surfing* magazine, Mike Spence, set the standard early on in the piece. 'It wasn't so much his images, which you almost took for granted as being great. The real gold in Spencey's work was his ability to involve the viewer in the lifestyle shots. Back when New Zealand surfers despised having their picture taken, they'd fully freeze and do the whole "school class picture" pose. Spencey won them over and got the shots that shared the surfers' personalities. These were the ones I wanted to emulate, and that's what I hope to perpetuate.'

Early on in his time as editor, Craig realised he had the extra benefit of being able to tell a story through the images he took. So each trip he went on he'd think about the sequence he was shooting and how it was going to eventuate in the mag. His senses were acutely aware of what was going on around him, making sure that he was prepared for that one image that was going to induce maximum stoke from the reader. 'Sometimes there are just these shots that come, and I think "dude, that's the one". It all comes down to the timing and lighting, and other factors that aren't necessarily in your control. There's a lot more calculation with certain shots, removing the variables so you're in the right place at the right time to produce an image that is unique from anything that's been done before.' To help demonstrate what he's talking about, he pulls out a photo of Luke Cederman taken from behind the wave. 'I identified that angle four years ago and decided I had to get a shot of it. It actually took me three years of trying at Indicators [Raglan] to get it. I knew it had to be in the evening, the general wave size, the surf manoeuvre, and there's only a few surfers out there who could do it, so there was always going to be heaps of failed attempts. Finally, this one time I had all the conditions right, went to take the photos, but the wind was too offshore. So I had to then add another variable — the wind had to be slightly sea breezy, otherwise there was too much spray between the lens and the surfer.' It paid off. The shot made the cover of the following issue.

I ask him if there was ever any pressure to constantly show images of the big names in the local scene? 'Put it this way, I was always stoked to get photos of Maz [Quinn]; his surfing is incredible, because put simply, the photos you get of the guy compared to most of the other surfers were just so much better. If

I hadn't shot him for a long time, then after a while I got the opportunity to, then when it came to seeing the photos I'd be stoked, because every turn of his was a fin-bust, or something else that gave the image the X factor. Jay [Quinn] and Bobby [Hansen] were the same. As a photographer, you want to shoot the best surfer you can, 'cause it's going to eventuate in the best shots you can get, and at the end of the day, that's what makes a mag. I guess that's why there's the criticism of the surf mags that they just show the same surfers all the time. But you know what? They're the best surfers in the country, so that's why they're there.' But just as I'm about to go on with another topic, he's quick to make one last point:

'When I'm on a photoshoot with surfers, what I really like doing is getting the best shot of them individually. And at times, maybe that was to my detriment as an editor, because I often sacrificed the quality of the magazine by having the best photo I could get of that surfer to help tell the story, as opposed to using the best surfing photos of the trip in general. So I think sometimes people would look through the mag and ask, why's he there, he's not even that great a surfer? But it's the best photo I got of him, so it stays; it's one of those intangibles.'

And his most memorable photoshoot? He sits back in his chair and smiles as though it's an easy question, but hesitates answering it, like he's trying to find a second-best instead. In the end, he just lets it go. 'I was in Hawaii a few years back to shoot the Kiwi guys, Maz, Chris [Malone], Blair [Stewart], and Daniel [Kereopa], who were involved in a WQS comp over there. One of the days, Backdoor [the right-hand break off Pipeline], was pumping and there were only a couple of guys out, and one of them was Kelly [Slater]. I'd set up on the beach and was getting sick sequence after sequence of him; he was surfing these perfect ten foot waves — amazing. He would be putting his hands in the waves, holding himself up, and moving around, you could see it all happening behind the curtain . . . to shoot that level of surfing was mind-blowing.' He laughs coyly. 'To say "Kelly Slater" is such a cliché. But it's such a prime example of what I mean by photographing the best surfers — they're such a pleasure to shoot.'

Craig's life as a photographing journalist, who just happened to sit in the chair with 'editor' etched on the back, meant that surf trips overseas like the one just mentioned were a common occurrence. Four to five times a year he'd head to Auckland airport with his trusty camera bag slung over one shoulder, and surfboard over the other. And he wouldn't come back through that airport for at least another 10 days. That's right, for 50 days a year he was not only paid to travel overseas and sample the best surf, but he got to do it within the company of the country's best surfers. All in the name of a good read, of course. 'Yeah, I could tell you the down-side of it, but I'd sound like a spoilt brat if I didn't say it was an absolute dream job. I never once took it for granted. I was so privileged to be in that position.'

For the first decade he felt he had to take on the role of manager. After a while, though, he got sick of playing camp mother, and found, especially with the younger crew, if he made them accountable for their responsibilities, then things went more smoothly. That allowed him to focus on the job at hand, and there was a very serious one to do; although it all sounds like a utopian lifestyle, like everything in life, for every reaction, there's an opposite and equal one — the pressure on Craig to deliver the goods on these trips was immense. 'When you go away you're held accountable for absolutely everything that happens. There's a dynamic involved in being a photographer on those top-level trips. If the weather is bad, or the surfers aren't performing, or you can't access the breaks you thought you were going to access, or if the surf travel company doesn't live up to expectations, then the photographer's seen as a kook. That's the way it is, the photographer is always the scapegoat. But you go away knowing that fact, and it's a small price to pay when you come back with sick shots from exotic surf.'

'. . . this was a real New Zealand surf mag. And all of a sudden, it added not only the surfer's perspective, but added a whole country along with it.'

Having all that experience of overseas surf has given Craig an appreciation of home most surfers couldn't comprehend. As New Zealanders, we can be too quick to pick up any one of the surf mags in the local bookstore, see tropical waves peeling off in translucent perfection, and assume that, yeah, the waves are always better over there. Perhaps some of us are put off by having to rubber-up from head to toe to avoid the cold winters, or the murky water in areas of our coast. The fact there aren't any coconut trees when we look back at the beach, or a dedicated surf-camp around every new bay. Or maybe it's just our good ol' culture of not believing we're any good. Whatever, like I said, Craig's travels have taught him one very big lesson; there's so much New Zealand has to offer.

'When I started at the mag, it was my perception that everyone thought our waves were substandard because the New Zealand photos were not as good as the overseas ones. So everyone thought they were better. I can tell you, after fifteen years of travelling around the world documenting its best surf locations, then going around our country and doing the same, that the waves in New Zealand are absolutely world-class. Kiwis just somehow think that things are better overseas. That's bullshit. The waves I was surfing last week at Bethells were as good as anything you'll find overseas, absolute world-class. I mean, you want to surf Indo perfection, go to Indo. You want Pacific perfection, go to one of the islands. Don't think that the waves are any better than here, though. Every single trip I did, I'd come back thinking how good we've got it here, wave-wise, lifestyle-wise. I don't think most people realise just how good it is. It frustrates the hell out of me that our culture has that conditioning of "we're a pack of miserable bastards who can't appreciate what's in our own back yard". I'm definitely a flag waver, because I've been to these other cultures and been fascinated by them, while fully appreciating them, and witnessed how other human beings interact with each other in their own unique ways. What I've learnt out of this is that we've got it so sweet here. That's why, when I started at the mag, I really wanted to change the perception of what our waves are like, to get guys stoked in their own back yard, and at the same time strengthen the pride in our own surf culture.'

One way he approached the challenge was to emphasise the fact that *New Zealand Surfing* magazine was all about 'our coast'. Too often, Craig found the pages would be full of some surfer riding a wave, but for all the reader knew, it could've been anywhere. To do the job properly, Craig swapped the surfboard for a pair of flippers and homemade waterproof housing for his camera and, like any good Kiwi bloke, put his body on the line and got out there amongst it. Before long, he found he was achieving what he set out to do. 'By getting a water-shot I could get the background at the same time and show the unique land mass in the shot. That way I could start to hammer home that this was a real New Zealand surf mag. And all of a sudden, it added not only the surfer's perspective, but added a whole country along with it.'

Craig, who surfs everyday it's good ('North Piha is my favourite wave in the world'), says the unique thing we have as a country is our isolation from the rest of the world. We've grown up with influences, instead of an influx of visitors, and that has resulted in a cool surfing culture that you won't find anywhere else. A stand-out feature of the culture, for him, is our bicultural identity in the waves. 'We definitely embrace a lot of iwi and Maori identities in the surf, and that's eventuated in some of our best surfers. We went through a huge trend a few years back where the Maori motifs and brands came along, and it was so cool. Most surfers should realise that their sport is a Polynesian sport. Americans would love to say it's a Hawaiian sport, but it's not. All the Polynesian nations surfed. Maori were surfing way before European colonisation. This country of ours has got a real deep history of surfing, and I'd like to see that recognised more.

'The thing I like about surfing is that it doesn't matter who or what you are, whether you drive a BMW or live out the back of a shitty van, the ocean is still going to push you down. It's the ultimate level playing field. It's non-racial, non-bigoted, it treats everyone equally, the way we should regard everyone. To me, it's a living thing. I tend to humanise each wave, like they're different people. Every one has its own character.' I asked whether he thinks they're male or female. 'Depends. I would say the vast majority of the time, though, they're women,' he says with a laugh, 'especially the more gnarly ones.' He takes a moment to think about it. 'I'd take it even further and say the more you surf, the more you even tend to humanise different swells. Every fresh swell is different, depending on how it's been generated. They have different patterns and after a while you can learn to acknowledge those patterns. Like, you can have two south-west swells hitting the same Piha bank over a two-week period, but they can be completely different-behaving waves. The more you understand and appreciate those nuances, the more you appreciate surfing.'

Most of us are weekend warriors when it comes to surfing, lucky to get a wave in on a Saturday or a Sunday between work and family commitments. At night we like to lie in the darkness and relive that one special moment from the last surf, or the month previously, keeping that memory's flame alight, for fear that if we don't, it will be placed in the recycle bin with all the others past their use-by date. But I wanted to know whether Craig still holds room in that surf-ravaged brain of his for a particular surf moment to shine. To my surprise, he doesn't muck around — he sits up in his chair and things start to get a little animated. Suddenly, we're a couple of surfies recalling particular rides that left us with a lifetime of stoke. One of his stories was based in Piha and how he successfully scammed his mate Paul to go for the first wave of a set while he paddled for the bigger one behind it. Craig bottom-turned, stalled, and found himself in the barrel of a lifetime. 'The opening was a tiny hole in front of me, so I pinned it to reach it. As I came out into daylight the next section threw out over me and I was in the barrel again. The whole time I'm thinking, I've gotta get out of here, but as soon as I'm out, I want to get back in there again. When you're getting tubed it's like you're surrendering to the wave, it's the one thing you

'It's the ultimate level playing field. It's non-racial, non-bigoted, it treats everyone equally, the way we should regard everyone.'

can't control. It's up to the wave to let you out or not. You hear these clichés about time standing still in the tube, but it never does for me. When people talk about time slowing down, I think all they're really talking about is their adrenalin levels are so high, and their senses are firing so much, that time seems to go slowly. Barrel riding is still the absolute best thing about surfing. Reos, floaters, airs, they've all been included in the surfing repertoire, but the barrel is still king. The best thing about that wave I scored was everyone saw the whole thing. A few of the boys paddled up to me and told me it was the best barrel at Piha they'd seen.' But like I said, we were just a couple of surfers talking shit, so I nodded energetically and sounded stoked for him. An hour later we were down at the Piha RSA getting one of its legendary meals, when Paul, the guy he apparently scammed, just happened to be there. Did he remember Craig's wave? Like it was yesterday. Craig claimed it and we headed to the pool table.

Modern technology has also strengthened our surf culture and emphasised our uniqueness. Yep, today's travelling surfer now relies on their computer way more than the old power of anticipation. IT geeks have become admired by surfers everywhere. They've transformed the way we surf by giving us our own crystal ball each, one that predicts where and in what condition the surf is going to be, not just tomorrow, or the next day, but seven days out, with freakish accuracy. Who would've thought? Back in the day we used to get a newspaper and turn straight to the isobar map to get a 24-hour picture of what the surf conditions were going to be like. A trip through town became a search for a flag waving to see what direction the wind was blowing. Just ask the next mature-looking surfer in the line-up how they used to predict swell, they'll tell ya (just before snaking the next wave on their longboard). 'What's happened in New Zealand is we can look on the Internet and target a swell approaching, right down to a tide. That's why, out of all the countries in the world, due to our proximity to the coast, the Internet has meant that us Kiwis have better quality waves more often. We can now work out when our workload needs to be done by, or accommodation sorted, or whatever, so in three days' time, when that swell arrives, you're there. In the past it wasn't that we didn't have world-class quality waves, it was just that getting to them at exactly the right time meant that the window of opportunity was infinitely smaller.'

Our environment is something with which every surfer has an emphatic bond, whether they realise it or not. Those of us who do understand that our wave playground is only as clean as the water coming into it, can be quick to stand on top of our cars' roof racks and speak our mind. But while we are seen as the keepers of the ocean, we also have a dark secret that could easily turn our groundswell of positive debate into a grovelling shorebreak. Earlier it was mentioned that Craig's success has been a result of total immersion in the lifestyle. That means he's acquired complete understanding of the good, but also an acknowledgement of the bad. And thankfully, surfing hasn't many negatives. But if surfers really want to achieve that squeaky clean image that the public have credited them with, the one that detergent companies would kill for, then there's just one thing we need to change.

Our surfboards.

'To be a hard-core surfer you live your life around the weather, so we're acutely related to the environment from that perspective. But look what we ride. We're riding this hideous petrochemical cocktail of pollutants. They're gnarly not only to the environment, but also the people dealing with them. That's why Clarke Foam [formerly the world's biggest supplier of foam blanks to the surf industry], got out of them before the shit hit the fan. All these former workers who had latent asthma, and shapers contracting cancer from the contaminants from the fine dust particles; that's why so many shapers have jumped on the computer-shaping machines, because they can stay behind glass and watch it happen. Some may argue that a surfboard is just a tool of the trade and technology will provide us with better alternatives, but we as surfers, we're the ones who create demand for that product. As a surfing consumer, it's up to us to say we don't want to use those boards any more. And there are already shapers out there who are passionate about meeting that sustainable demand, who've experimented with biodegradable products and such. Unfortunately, other mainstream manufacturers out there pay a bit of lip service to the environment, and simply appease the consumer's conscience, so the progress gets stalled. But if you put that one glitch to the side, then in general, sure, surfers have a valid voice because we're at the coal-face. As surfers, we are unconsciously in tune with the weather and it's not until you're talking to a non-surfer that you realise how aware of it we are, and that's a great gift surfing has given us. It's this grounding that has led to a lot of surfers becoming proactive in matters that affect the environment. I think we could stand up way more than we do on certain topics, because after all, we're the guys in the water, we're the ones physically experiencing these changes. We are the "Johnnies on the spot".'

Above where Craig's sitting there is a large framed photo of a long-haired surfer doing a big cuttie, and I find myself staring back at it through the course of our conversation. As it's the only one on his wall, I wonder about its significance. It also makes me think what the last 15 years of his life were like; after all, he was the kid looking through the front window of the candy shop but never actually stepping inside. He says in his last five years he's had a shift in a way of thinking, in that it is now more important for him to surf than to take photos. He laughs when I ask if he finds it easy to leave the camera back at the house when he heads for his daily surf (he calls it a dichotomy, by the way). What I found out is that today's Craig is in many ways still the same as 15 years ago; he's still a surfer like the rest of us. And that image above his head? That's him. Taken by Mike Spence during a session at Karekare in 1992. And just to accentuate it, on cue his little email chime rings out on his computer. Suddenly he's this grommet as he begins clicking away on the mouse, showing me photos on his screen that his mate's girlfriend took of them from last week's surf at Bethells. He's like a kid at Christmas again, stoking out on the images of himself, just like we all do. To see the country's premier surf photographer so excited over simple images taken on a cheap digital camera was compelling.

'Dude, I'm just like anyone who surfs. I'm first and foremost a surfer, everything else falls in line to perpetuate that. All I've ever done is scam ways to surf more.' He laughs, 'And I guess I've been successful in my scams.'

Aaron Kereopa

Aaron Topp

CARVER
RAGLAN

When a professional American couple wanted a memento of their holiday in New Zealand, they didn't rely on a digital camera stuffed with images. Nor did they decide to video every activity in the anticipation of getting home, shoving the tape into a player and watching it once or twice. No, this trip was special, it deserved something unique, contemporary, something more than their favourite moments captured in a four-picture combo frame hanging on the wall.

On the plane over, the husband, an IT specialist, had picked up the American in-flight magazine, *Outside Traveller*, and seen an article about a surfer guy at a sleepy seaside village at their destination, a guy who did magical things with surfboard blanks. He had an idea. He showed it to his wife, a heart surgeon, and she agreed. When they touched down they proceeded to look him up, and before they left for home again they visited him at his place in Raglan.

It probably sounds easier than it really is — tracking down Aaron Kereopa, I mean. I had to call on all of my journalistic skills, begging and pleading with complete strangers to throw me a bone, before I finally got him on the end of a telephone line. But that's the way he likes it; living slightly below the radar suits his quiet existence. 'If anyone wants me hard enough, they'll find me,' he tells me, shrugging his shoulders unashamedly. 'You did.'

At the moment, Aaron's working in his garage so he can stay closer to his pregnant partner, Jasmine, and their two-year-old son, Kai. At the back of the garage, beyond the hanging outrigger canoe that you have to watch your head on, the lawn mower, bicycle, numerous paint containers and plastic sheets, is the 10-foot-long surfboard blank slowly being turned into an exquisite piece of art destined for the San Franciscan couple. Already it's obvious it's going to become a conversation piece — like any good bit of art should do but at which so few succeed. It's covered in pencil marks, aesthetically depicting a tiki-esque character performing various activities over the four bodies of Maori-influenced hammerhead sharks. 'This is their trip,' he tells me, running a finger over the image. 'Here's them caving, at the beach, running. I used the hammerhead because it symbolises strength.'

Aaron's relationship with surfboards started when he was a kid growing up in a farm environment across the Raglan harbour, in Te Akau, a district where his parents sheared sheep for a living. While playing down at the beach one day, he and his brothers found an old Bob Davies surfboard. They took it home and paddled it around the creek until the fibreglass started peeling. In search of a new lifestyle a couple of years later, Aaron's parents picked the family up and moved out onto a small spot of whanau land above Manu Bay. 'After school we used to watch everyone below surfing in the water,' recalls Aaron. 'They'd be hooting and there'd be cars zooming and in the weekends we'd be watching contests, listening to them blowing the air horn. Dad used to tell us another shark's been spotted. Every half hour or so he'd say, yep, there's another one. We believed him until our older bro went down and said, nah, man, they're having a contest and there's a party on tonight. The parents tried to keep us out, but it was only a matter of time.'

His younger brother, Daniel, joined the nippers club and would come back raving about the little boards they got to ride, so Aaron went down to check it out and was instantly attracted to what he saw. 'I was the first one to question the olds about what was going on. We're living here, I told them, and while we're stuck jumping off the jetty for fun, those guys below our house are hooting way louder. My parents tried to tell us surfing was for bums, a bunch of useless, lazy louts. No good for nothing. That was entrenched in us. But I used to look at my aunties, smoking durries, unfit, fat, and then over at the surfers, skinny, fit, ripped, and that's what I wanted to be a part of. So I kept hounding Mum to give in and finally she did; she saved up and got Daniel a surfboard from a local doctor. The rest of us got our first boards left behind from some cousins who stayed once. A little later I managed to get one out of Mum, a twin fin. I had no wax, no wetsuit, no leg rope, no idea. But I was straight out there with my cousins. They were wondering why I was slipping off all the time. The next day, Dad got me some wax.'

A week later Aaron was trimming along the waves confidently, and a love affair with the ocean began. 'From that moment everything changed. I was there from dawn to dusk. I'd go down in the rain and cold just in a pair of shorts. I wasn't gonna be a labourer [although he did, briefly], I knew I was in store for better things. I thought, if I can do this and feel like this, imagine what I'll be like when I'm with those guys sitting out the back.'

On our way down to his studio, Aaron shows me where he and his family lived during this period. These days it's nothing more than a derelict aluminium shed with a key rusted permanently in the sliding door. They never locked anything, he tells me. The family have long since moved on, except his younger brothers have adopted it as a hangout to use for parties and after-surf sessions. It's a world away from the time when it slept 10 of his family marae-style, tarpaulins covering the dirt floor. His studio is not far from here; keeping with the privacy theme, it's just a short walk down a secret path off the beaten track. He built the circular building himself and lived in it for a while. Through the last of the trees out the front you can smell the salt air and hear the pounding of the waves breaking on the Manu Bay reef below. Some days he'll sit on the logs and watch, listening to the ocean speak to him. But most times he'll make the trip down, paddle out and talk back.

Inside the studio are sketches on the wall, names and addresses of people he has to contact, a few surfboard blanks and some of his early pieces. Across one wall in large lettering is a Maori prayer; it's there to keep him centred and focused. Hanging at the back is a series of signs painted for a local exhibition based on the over-hyped property boom. There's Mugstown, Why Fite, and Catchy 22, all directed at the exploitation of the local real estate market and the wealthy out-of-towners who've forced up rates, affecting people who have been here for generations. In the centre of the studio, below a hanging light bulb, is a new blank, untouched and at waist height. Aaron grabs a pencil from a jar and with his left hand behind his back for composure, starts sketching curves across the foam surface. As we quietly talk I sense he's already starting to drift into another world.

Aaron was inspired by the artist, Kevin Baker. Aaron was in his early twenties when he saw 'this Maori boy from the East Coast' on TV with a piece of art made from a carved-out surfboard with 'No Nukes Pacific' inscribed on it. Man, I can do that, he thought. Up until then his only foray into art had been scratching his school desks with compasses, following the lines on his hand with a biro, doodling on the top of text books, a bit of tagging. 'I always thought art was something I could do, it was easy for me, like a walk in a park. These days, three days' work is like three minutes, that's how dazed I get. When I was at school I'd look at my hand and it'd be covered in ink and the teacher would be telling me off again.'

That's not to say he was a slacker at school; quite the opposite. From his own admission, he was a good student, excelling at maths and geography. He earned a scholarship to Wesley College as a prospective Maori leader. He boarded there while the rest of his family's life changed without him; his mum started commuting to Hamilton to look after street kids and gang members and the homeless as a chef at the church. His dad threw in shearing permanently and took up painting houses. His brothers threw themselves into surfing their front yard, and Aaron played catch-up during the holidays. He went to polytech for four years and doodled on the top of his text books during the lectures. The following five years he avoided job requirements, collected the dole, and became a full-time unemployed surfer. The irony wouldn't have been lost on his parents.

But the day he saw the future staring back at him on the television his life took a turn in a second. 'I looked out the shed's window at all the broken boards dumped on the grass, and thought about how I could get into them. I started stripping off the fibreglass with my hands. There were airborne shards everywhere and the sound of resin snapping. My hands were bleeding and all my bum mates were laughing at me, but as I carved with a butter knife and spoon I was getting stuff off my shoulders, and it felt wicked.'

It evolved from there. At first he didn't want to give any of his art away. Each piece was a new part of his healing report card, he says. This was a way he could have a say in the world, leave something behind in life, not just a docking-in ticket at some factory. 'You hear people say, that guy could dig a hole, he was a hard worker, or that guy sure could grow the best onions. But if I can make people think about things and be better people, help them cross a bridge someway, then that's worth working hard for. I'm just a Maori boy down the road, but I can do something in my artwork, because they'll reach places I'll never reach, they'll live on far longer than I ever will. My messages will change over time, they'll evolve as the owners hand them on and others see their own part of the story in it, add their own bit of ownership to it. I'll be stoked if it comes to that point, then I would've started to make some sort of difference.'

> Some days he'll sit on the logs and watch, listening to the ocean speak to him. But most times he'll make the trip down, paddle out and talk back.

Aaron says there's nothing more humbling than sitting in an income support office with a new baby and no money. He and Jasmine were in their early thirties and had just spent their last $20 on petrol to get into town. When they got home there was a text message. 'I've got a buyer,' it said. 'That's how it was, one extreme to another. In the end we just had to let it go and let things happen. We accepted long ago that if we want to live a life like this, then this is how it's gotta be. It's not up to me any more, or about risk taking. Sooner or later things will fall into place for a reason. More money doesn't mean go out and buy a house, it's about more freedom to do what we want, do more art, enjoy life, whatever. Just not piddling it up against the urinal at the pub.'

While things started to happen for him in the local art gallery, Kanuka Design, a shop owned by Jasmine's mum, it still wasn't enough and at times it'd be another month of riding the rent if they didn't make a sale. Aaron's big break finally came much further south. A couple of pieces of his had been used to help sell a new house in Queenstown; if it sold, the owners got to keep the art as well. It was effectively expensive window dressing. Not only did the house sell, but when the owner of a new gallery in town, Toi o Tahuna, paid a visit to the house, he was blown away by the originality and quality of what he saw hanging on the wall. A call was made to Raglan and suddenly Aaron was preparing for his first exhibition in the big time. 'I've always been surrounded by art in life, but I'm not qualified, I've no formal training, so I had no degree to say you're an artist, buddy. Toi o Tahuna was taking a huge risk with me in that sense.'

Aaron did 16 pieces of work for the exhibition, working on it for six months solidly. Through his research, he'd found every artist with a successful exhibition had used a theme in their show. Aaron thought hard about that and after days of scouring the corners of his imagination, he got his pencil out and started sketching a pot of fish heads. 'They say it's a Maori delicacy, but nah, man, it's not, it's just a pot of fish heads,' he says. 'I chose the fish head 'cause I could carve it, pull apart the gills, the scales, teeth, bone structure. You can tell a lot from a fish head — you know where they came from and what their lives were like. So I was going to do a lot of fish heads as the main theme. I did the first one fine, then went back to doing something about surfing. I think too much, and the first thing I dream about is going surfing, paddling, anything to do with the ocean. I just piss off the subject and revert back to waves, sunsets, barrels, giant swells. I just think about what patterns the wind makes, like the onshore winds, if you look inside the tube when the winds going one way but the wave's coming this way, you get a criss-cross effect. I try to put that sort of stuff into real life.' In the end his theme was all about him. 'If I'd sold three pieces from it I would've been happy, but I ended up selling ten.' Jasmine corrects him — it was actually 12, she says, you lost count at 10.

The next big step is an international art fair in Miami, but there's a financial risk and no guarantee they'll get the money back, even if they make the cut. Having the backing of a well-respected art gallery helps, but Toi o Tahuna is still young in the industry. There's also the small issue of the size of the reputation of the artist. But that's happening fast. 'I need to get up to the stage of Ralph Hotere, Simon Kaan, Rangi Kipa, Tony Ogle, all those guys. If I get to their status in the art world, what I say will be more recognised, my art could be used as a platform to make political statements. I'm still a small fish really, but I'm moving towards that.' In the meantime, he has been asked to do a few small things, like baptise newborn babies. He can't help smiling at that. 'I'm normally the guy drinking the refreshments.'

Aaron's work is carving its own niche in an already busy art community. He's come a long way from the days where he'd give his pieces away; now, one of his larger pieces of work will sell for up to $17,000. That's a lot of money, there are a few cars in that, he tells me, like he's torn between his charitable nature and the reality of providing food on the table. So for now he's happy for it to sit on the shelf. Not that it'll stay there for long. Doing commission work, like the piece in the garage, is what he'd like to focus on, where he can talk with the client and get to understand their thoughts and feelings, thus allowing him to say more with his tools. 'I could mass produce fish heads and make a nice comfortable living and pay the rent, but I'm not into duplicates. When I'm fifty I'll still be making art. Whether it's worse or not, I dunno. The fun is there. It's just like surfing, you can have a shit day and go for a surf and feel much better. Same with my art. You go do art and do something new, you walk out of the shed eight hours later but it feels like five minutes, that kind of buzz.'

Aaron fidgets as he talks. I watch him twist his cap yet again; this time the peak settles sideways. When he grins his whole body lights up and he looks like a cheeky schoolkid. For all his reserved nature and perceived shyness, I start to find he's got an aura of calmness around him that acts like a field, holding it in while drawing others to it. If he's not happy, he says, then the client will get shit quality, so he makes sure a balance is maintained in his life. Jasmine helps keep him focused, although she finds it hard to agree with him when he says he's going to work, then proceeds to grab his surfboard. 'But that's how all the work comes about,' he justifies. 'In the ocean is where I get inspired. You're experiencing it, all the emotions. Am I gonna make it? Is that shark gonna get me? Will I see killer whales today? You don't get that sitting in a studio somewhere.' Jasmine says he is always dreaming, thinking about his work. Aaron is trying to change the perception of work, to something that should be fun, if only for himself to embrace. Leading into an exhibition the stress from the demands results in him scrambling to produce the goods and that means his health suffers. He'll break out in coldsores, get dandruff, and he'll worry some more and find himself scrambling even further into the early hours to get the work completed. He can't think straight. He hates feeling like that. But that's when he's most productive, when he disappears into another zone, and it's no surprise the pieces made during these intense moments are normally the first to go. Why is that? I ask. He pauses, then chuckles. 'Maybe they like buying my dandruff,' he finally replies.

'My hands were bleeding and all my bum mates were laughing at me, but as I carved with a butter knife and spoon I was getting stuff off my shoulders, and it felt wicked.'

'I was brought up working hard. If you didn't have blisters on your hands then you weren't putting enough effort in. But that ain't nothing on this, this work is emotionally and mentally exhausting. The best thing is I have people around me. No matter how ugly I am, they're still here for me. They bring me back to reality. A good support mechanism who love me for who I am. That's why none of my family has any of my artwork, I don't make anything for them. Everyone knows me as Aaron, not Aaron the Artist.'

If you're wondering just how good a carved surfboard can actually look, then Google him. I have to admit, I originally questioned just how far you could take a chunk of discarded fibreglass. A bloody long way, I find out. Like me, you'll be blown away by the talent of the guy. The pieces are even more impressive in real life. Sure, it started off with a couple of kitchen utensils, but his work is now bona fide world-class material. Each piece is painstakingly detailed, every tiny groove hand painted, often twice and in a special order. 'I let emotion guide my colours. Sometimes the carving will look better with certain colours, even though I didn't plan it that way. Some foam will be more absorbent than others. Some pieces come to life by themselves and I let that guide me.' Each one is as unique as a wave. And there are plenty of those portrayed, sometimes blatantly, other times much more subtly, but nearly always masked as a flax-woven material, as found in a kete. Look a bit closer and you'll often see things that weren't apparent at first, like that surfer emerging from within the barrel. Tiny, painstaking detail. 'Every piece that goes out has got my wairua, my DNA. It's my child, my skin and blood are on it, I've lived my life around it. It's a part of the family by the time it leaves here.' Like a modern-day Geppetto, when somebody buys a piece, Aaron has a problem with freighting it — it's like a kid going to school, out into the big world. That's why he gives every piece a lifetime guarantee to be fixed if something happens. As of yet, he's never had to act on that promise.

Aaron doesn't see his art as staunchly Maori. In fact, he resents being called a Maori artist. The original Kereopa was of Ngati Porou descent, but Aaron acknowledges he now has stronger links to Tainui in the west and Ngati Hine in the north. Aaron's parents were both whangai-ed, brought up by their grandparents, so he and his siblings' aunties and uncles became their grandparents instead. Full Maoritanga was never passed on. It is a dirty stain on our country's heritage that te reo was almost lost completely as a result of his parents' generation being punished at school if they spoke it. Te reo was reserved for dinner time in the privacy of the home or used during formal settings such as hui. Aaron was never encouraged to speak, although he knows bits and pieces, but that's another journey he says he'll go on in the future. Lots of people still expect him to step up and take a leadership role in the hapu. Without the natural teachings being passed down from generation to generation, he has had to rely on the understanding of Maori protocol he picked up during his time at Wesley. There, the Maori world was unveiled through his involvement in cultural activities. He and four others from Wesley were hand-picked to paddle for the Maori Queen as warriors. They went down to Ngaruawahia to learn traditional paddling and haka.

In 1988, at the age of 15, Aaron went to Canada for four weeks as part of a cultural exchange with the indigenous Indians. Then he went to Hawaii on another exchange. All this time, the group was training, reciting prayers, enacting customs in an attempt to jump start the culture that was in their blood. But it was too late for Aaron, he was a rebel without a cause, and most of it went straight out of his head. He was stuck looking after the old folks, being the bum boy, taking care of the paddles and so on, although he admits he found watching the older guys draw facial tattoos on the performers fascinating. But that wasn't enough, and when he left college he left it all behind. 'I thought people were putting too much pressure on me. It was too full on. I ended up turning my back on it and going surfing instead. I started doing my own interpretation of what I was seeing. I was aware of what others thought about Maori at the time, the stereotypes — you know, snotty noses and lazy — and I knew I wanted to change that perception, but didn't know how. I was looking at the stuff non-Maori were making to make it look like Maori stuff, and I was thinking, come on, man, as a Maori that doesn't explain anything about me. So I thought the best thing was for me to explain it myself, rather than someone hang a plastic tiki in front of people and say this is what Maori people are about, a plastic tiki.' He shakes his head slowly, adjusts his cap. 'That always offended me.'

'I don't want to be racist, I don't want to be trapped in a box where Maori are talking about one thing, and Pakeha are talking about us in another. Surfing opened up all these doors to other ethnicities. I can sit at Manu Bay and meet Hawaiian, Spanish, English or listen to some Portuguese having a conversation beside me, and yet here we are as a country bickering between just two of us. Soon it's gonna be none of that, just Kiwis. New Zealanders. Surfing opened up a huge door to express all that. The carving became an avenue to express my frustrations and at the same time it was a way I could attempt to build a bridge between the two cultures. I think I'm still going through it, but I've used surfing and Maori culture to express myself, I've taken what good Maori think of Pakeha, and what good Pakeha think of Maori and blended them together in a hybrid of contemporary and traditional.'

Like his siblings, Aaron was taught a ritual very early on in his life and he still uses it every time he enters the sea. He bends down and splashes water in a certain way, towards the east to where the sun rises, the last stroke of this action being to his head. It's a way of blessing himself, a time to let Tangaroa know to watch over him as he enters his domain. When every new piece is completed, Aaron signs the back of it with his hapu, favourite surf break and the date, then takes it down to the shore and blesses it the same way, to protect and empower it on its journey. 'The day of Kai's birth I blessed him in the ocean. He's already been surfing with me in the tiny days. I want him to appreciate the naturalness of the beach and the ocean. Every time I touch water, it's my life. Surfing is all about me. It's freedom, you can go into yourself if you want, to a place where you don't have to worry about anyone else's rules, but just when you think you're in control a wave can slap you in a second and remind you you're not. It's been the best thing to ever happen to me'. He takes the moment to look across at Jasmine playing with Kai. 'Or us,' he says, still staring.

What are his best moments? Watching his brother get barrelled, mates getting barrelled, getting barrelled himself. According to Aaron, the tube is king. 'Just standing up inside it and breathing, it feels like the board's not there. To come out of something like that you feel so lucky, you're full

> '1've taken what good Maori think of Pakeha, and what good Pakeha think of Maori and blended them together in a hybrid of contemporary and traditional.'

of energy. It's also about those times when dolphins share the same wave as you, or you're simply watching somebody else experience the same emotions. Surfing has taught me to live life to the fullest with what time you've got. Treat every moment with preciousness. The biggest decision you ever have is what kind of life you want to lead and how you want your body or soul to evolve. I've got a few friends I've watched go wayward, join the mob and so on, but you choose the life you want. Believe in it, let it out into the universe and watch it come around. I've always tried to listen to the older people tell me how to live my life, but some of them had ended up being shockers. This is my life, I don't want them to mess it up, I can do that myself if I choose to.

'Life is bigger than just an office job. Tomorrow's not promised to anybody, even if you're tucked away comfy in a nice cosy little nest egg somewhere. If you're there, you're dead already. Surfers are at the peak of experiencing life to the fullest, they're at the brink. I reckon I've died at least five times already. You get a sense of calmness in the world when you're drowning; you're down deep, nowhere to go, you just have to wait until you can get up. It's not nice to be that deep, when really you should be on top. Surfers will always be there discovering themselves, they're the pioneers of it. Some older surfers will sink off into their comfort zones, but there are still old salty dogs out there soldiering on.

'It's changed the way I think things should be. I know there are people who feel I should be at the marae, speaking fluent Maori, eating all the food, smoking the durries, beers in the weekend at the pub. But life's healthier doing what I'm doing, there are more choices, better opportunities. Twenty-plus years on I'm still seeing different things in the surf. All my boards are getting longer. I'm now getting into stand-up paddle boards. Last week I was outside Indicators paddling on my outrigger miles from the closest surfer, riding this giant groundswell as it journeyed to shore, and here I was, evolving again. What I do in the surf is what I make on the land, and because I'm doing that it sells. It's a huge compliment in itself. And people say, so you're an artist? But I was surfing yesterday, so does that make me a surfer? A paddler? I am what I am. I'm all the one thing.'

Ian King

Brian Herlihy

MUSICIAN
AUCKLAND/TORONTO

Ian King could be the quintessential throwback to a 1970s surf movie. Over the last 15 years he's ridden any surfboard as long as it had a single, double, or quad fin set-up. For 10 of those years he's spared the slaughter of beast, bird and fish as a staunch vegan. He hasn't supported the local barber trade for a good long while, and his whiskery growth says the same for the razor industry. His views on the desecration of the environment are well articulated and laced with passion. I expect him to say he lives in a hut made out of driftwood at some secret surf spot north of Orewa, playing his acoustic guitar to an audience of stars and the moon and the sound of a small fire crackling.

Heck, if the guy was any more laid back he'd disappear down the back of the couch he's sitting on.

Then again, he could've easily come out of the period when bands like the Ramones, the Sex Pistols, The Clash, and The Damned were single-handedly creating an anti-establishment movement in Britain's urban dwellings through anger-induced rock. Despite first impressions, Ian's actual occupation involves living the typical rock'n'roll lifestyle we all once wished we could, as lead guitarist for New Zealand's premier punk band, The Bleeders. Acoustics be damned. Sending power chords at 100 decibels to tens of thousands of amped fans is nothing new to him. He's bloody good at it.

Ian hangs and surfs with his childhood surfing hero, well-known Californian, Thomas Campbell. He's toured and played on stage with his childhood music heroes, AFI. He's cameoed in the same surf flick as legends Dane Reynolds and Rob Machado. He's recorded music in New York. He's co-hosted a rock show on Sky's Juice TV. He seems to be living two parallel, almost fantasy lives, with rich experiences suggestive of someone who's looking at life after retirement. Yet all this has been achieved by a guy who was born two years after the 1970s ended. While most of us struggle with just one life — we often fill it up like a house collects junk — Ian flits from world to world at will, like an open archway has been built between them.

It started at an early age when he was introduced to the worlds of music and surfing by a dad who rode longboards during the day and played the Hammond organ in bands at night. He tried to get his eight-year-old son into the keyboard, but Ian wasn't interested in being stuck static behind some immovable object. His parents offered him the guitar and the two of them became inseparable. Soon he was belting out Jimi Hendrix riffs, and playing Stevie Ray Vaughan covers at family friends' fortieths, while the adults cheered on the cute, chubby kid with the oversized Samick Stratocaster copy. Music took hold of his imagination. He dreamt of one day ditching the living room full of half-drunk family and friends, and playing in front of a real crowd, with a real stage and real sound system, some cool lighting and hot chicks.

He became heavily influenced by his parents' Rolling Stones albums. He began listening to his brother's skate music, bands like Fugazi, The Ramones, and Suicidal Tendencies; it was angry and incoherent at times, but according to

Ian, it was also pretty good pop. He began watching Taylor Steele surf movies and would get entranced by the punk-inspired soundtrack of bands like Minor Threat, Bad Religion, and Pennywise, and particularly the Californian band, AFI, whose entire back catalogue became a favourite in his music collection. While others in his age bracket preferred musical mainstream, he was drawn to the loud, alternative, much more mature sound. When he got to college, his dad and a few of his friends came in to save a decrepit musical department by offering to start a blues band for third to sixth formers. They played songs from the Blues Brothers and other old soul music, while back at home Ian emulated bands like WASP and ACDC and Slayer, the left-of-centre sort of stuff. When Ian hit 14, he found a couple of other guys who knew a bit about the punk sound he'd come to love. They started doing a few covers and attempted their own stuff. They got a couple of gigs, which led to other offers. The audiences began getting bigger. The group played during the Devonport riot days.

But it wasn't all loud chords and black T-shirts. The ocean was Ian's solace away from the noise and commotion, a place to be inspired, even from an early age. Every summer the Kings would escape the city climate and travel to Whangamata, where Ian's dad would push him into the whitewash on his old Roger Hall twin-fin. Ian had a paper run and saved up enough for his first surfboard — a standard thruster — when he was nine. He started surfing with his dad and learnt to appreciate, and prefer, the hollow waves of the East Coast. By the age of 10 he was doing run-of-the-mill manoeuvres like cutbacks and floaters, getting off on how much fun something so pure could produce. 'It's about that moment when you take off, bottom-turn and feel that rush and flow of water beneath your feet,' he says, recalling those early memories. 'There's nothing quite like it. It's just you and nature.'

Ian was working at Backdoor Surf in Takapuna when I caught up with him. Not exactly rock'n'roll, but during the day the need for rocket-fuelled guitarists in town is pretty thin. Something surf-orientated seemed the natural alternative. We chill out in the staffroom out the back and talk over the noise of the fax machine. In the beginning, Ian sits forward slightly so he can drum his fingers quietly against his leg between questions, like he's keeping himself on edge, sharp, pumped, perhaps as an antidote to watching people scroll through racks of branded clothing all day, stuff he'd never wear himself. Or maybe he's just not used to doing the solo interview thing without the rest of the band present. Eventually he sits back, but his fingers, purely out of habit I realise, don't stop.

He points a thumb at the wall over his shoulder and tells me none of the dozens of shiny new surfboards in the next room appeal to him. Instead, his current arsenal of sticks resembles the sort of styles you might find lying dormant under an old family bach, or in the rafters of your uncle's shed. He gets his kicks from riding thick, heavy creations like his 1960s-inspired longboard, the single-finned egg, his classic 1970s Bob Davies, or any of the numerous twin-finned retro boards he's collected. To the non-initiated, you can be excused for glazing over that section; they're foreign descriptions even to many longstanding surfers. That's why you won't find them in most of the surf stores around the land; they're deemed too crusty for the majority of grommets, who make up the biggest slice of the monthly sales pie graph. Although, as an example of his stance, Ian was only a grommet himself when he found himself asking his dad more and more if he could borrow the longboard for the days when the surf was no more than a lazy swell crumbling its way to shore. Each time he took it out he realised the fun factor and purity of riding waves remained, while around him he watched frustrated shortboarders compromising style and speed to maintain momentum.

> Soon he was belting out Jimi Hendrix riffs, and playing Stevie Ray Vaughan covers at family friends' fortieths, while the adults cheered . . .

He ditched the thruster and got his own longboard, taught himself the traditional techniques, and embraced the grass-roots ethos associated with riding such a board. He tells me the last time he rode a conventional shortboard was somewhere in the early '90s. He didn't give a toss that others would ridicule him. He listened to punk music and with that came the dissident attitude of not wanting to be just another waxhead, or another whipping boy for a pretentious surf industry. In a sport emblazoned with coolness, in Ian's eyes, riding 20- and 30-year-old designs was the epitome of 'it'. While the others wanted to emulate guys like Kelly Slater and Taylor Knox, Ian had no desire to follow their campaign aimed at progressing the sport with their revolutionary moves. Learning to ride a diverse array of surf craft as smoothly as possible was much more inspiring than joining the rest of the surfing wannabes popping another reverse ollie or backside air. Even when he began competing on the national longboarding circuit, frustration set in when he saw what the surfing mainstream was trying to do to the art of soul surfing. 'Longboarding is for when it's small, or if you're really good, like Hawaiian legend, Bonga Perkins, who can ride a longboard at Pipeline. The average New Zealander who watches a longboard contest will see a bunch of surfers replicating shortboard manoeuvres in slow motion, which just looks ridiculous in my opinion. It's like shortboarding with training wheels.'

But there can be a compromise between a traditional style of the trim and glide of a longboard, and the snappy speed of a standard thruster, and this is what's making Ian excited about being in the water lately. His four-finned 'fish' design — another name for a short, wide, thick board, with a rounded nose and large swallow-tail bottom, much like the bird — has been getting the most use lately, as those early feelings of speed on a wave make a return, while all the purity and freedom of riding a longboard is retained. After 10 years of longboarding manoeuvres, and acquiring a reputation among his competition peers as a master of executing them, he's being refreshed by putting the shorter version into places on the wave he hasn't ventured into for years. Maintaining a smooth flow and drawing deep arcs require a more disciplined set of skills than the traditional hack-and-slash of modern surfing. And it's this combination of perceived simplicity and an aging surfing demographic that's seeing retro-inspired boards start to make a comeback. While Ian gets his boards made for him by master shaper, Dain Thomas, someone who specialises in old-school surfboards in Australia's Byron Bay, many Kiwi shapers are now churning out their own versions, shapes they haven't had to make in a long time. Ian is watching the movement with a hint of trepidation. 'If people want to ride boards like that and experiment they should, but at the same time, I think it's kinda funny that the current trend is that everyone wants to get all retro. To me, it's never been like that. I've always seen it as a different way to treat the wave.'

When he was 20, Ian was plucked from another band with the promise of starting a group dedicated to punk rock. They began practising and by the end of the year were playing a few shows. They recorded a couple of songs and were picked up by the student station, BFM, regularly making the top 10. They released an EP and people started happily squeezing into Auckland's King's Arms Hotel, despite the shows being sold out. Girls would feed off the tall, mysterious-looking lead guitarist with the chocolate eyes, while guys would go into fits of apeshit fuelled by the energy coming off his six-stringed inferno. Later, Ian would look back on those early concerts as some of the biggest highlights the band experienced. Like some clichéd music story, it was only a matter of time before a representative from a record company came to a concert to see what all the fuss was about. Afterwards, he knocked on their band's door with an offer of bigger things. But the boys weren't easily bought. They took their time discussing the implications, while the record company courted them with fancy dinners and lots of drinks. They eventually signed the deal with Universal Records, with the intention of using the extra money to get a bigger recording budget and make a better-sounding album that they could confidently release to an international market. The Bleeders had just had their first taste of the big time.

Their manager would organise three-week tour dates, then leave them to their own devices. On the way to the concert venues around the country, Ian would sit in the back and party up with another band member while the other two, a couple of non-alcoholics, navigated the countryside. It didn't take them long to work out that in a world of rock, alcohol created the roll. Suddenly, they were drawing straws to work out who was on driving duty. 'They were definitely good times; it could get pretty wild,' he says, smiling as if it was anything but. 'It was an eye-opening experience as to how good that lifestyle can be, as opposed to playing in a band, going home afterwards, and thinking, well, that was nice.' They perfected their stage presence and made a name for themselves as one of the most full-throttle, hardcore acts in the music scene. They put everything into a show; their music is punk, it's aggressive, it has a defiant attitude and they epitomise it all. Members of the crowd run from the stage and step on people's heads to see how far they can get. There are fights, both on and off the stage; it's not uncommon for the singer to lash out and punch someone in the head if they get too close. All the while, Ian and the other four musicians don't miss a note or a beat or a lyric, but later they'll laugh about it all during a break. It's how a Bleeders concert goes down. Afterwards, they'll hang out at the bar and drink and party with the punters. If the night looks like closing down, they'll head back to the hotel for more shits and giggles. There's been a bit of damage here and there, but so far no bills for a fixed window or replacement TV — they don't make enough money to be in that league, Ian says.

At the big concerts, Ian says looking out at tens of thousands of moving people, like when he's standing on the main stage at The Big Day Out, has a sense of the ocean about it. 'It can be mind-blowing to see that many people, it reminds you of gazing out to an empty ocean.' What's more daunting, I ask, playing to a massive crowd full of expectation, or surfing a solid swell? He doesn't need to think about it. 'Knowing you're three feet inside a breaking eight-foot set is way more daunting. The crowd's easy.'

In a sport emblazoned with coolness, in Ian's eyes, riding 20- and 30-year-old designs was the epitomy of 'it'.

The band got their wish for better quality recording and were paid to travel to New York to make their last album, Sweet as Sin. No five-star accommodation here, though; they stayed in Jersey City, five lads from down under amongst non-English-speaking Hispanics. Universal gave them an allowance, which went straight into the party machine. Two months later, when production wrapped up, they boarded a plane for London, where their manager got them a gig opening for The Misfits. In 2006 they opened for Motorhead at the St James. The same year, The Bleeders won Best Breakthrough Artist and Best Rock Album — an enviable collection of awards for anyone in the music industry, although Ian plays it down and says it's not that big a deal. But when was the last time a punk band, traditionally ignored for music accolades, won those awards? Never, before or since. The Bleeders are it. So, yeah, it kinda is a big deal.

The biggest highlight for Ian was touring the whole of Australia with his heroes, AFI. Since their early music of the 1990s, they had marked the soundtrack of his longboarding life between the ages of 15 and 25. It was surreal, he recalls, sharing the same stage as them, tapping into their massive loyal following and getting to hang with them after each show. The tour also meant the band got their first real taste of Australian exposure. But timing is everything, and circumstances meant they never got the opportunity to hammer home the point with a follow-up tour themselves.

So what's Ian doing working in a surf shop? It's all part of the big plan. By the time you're reading this, he and the rest of the group will already be playing out their American invasion from their new home in Toronto. Why so far away? Despite their success locally, in hindsight, it seems they were the right band for the right time. Suddenly, punk ain't cool any more, in New Zealand's tiny music industry at least. In America and Canada it's never lost its army of devoted fans. Living there makes good sense. They'll get set, organise some tours over their summer and record a new album afterwards. Then they'll keep penetrating for a month at a time, returning to Canada after each trip to plan the next step. The connections they've made in the Northern Hemisphere means if they're asked to tour, they're already Johnny-on-the-spot. That's the big plan. Still, nothing's promised to them. 'You don't make any money being in a punk band in New Zealand, unfortunately. You definitely suffer for your art. Everything we make goes back into covering bills, maybe a bit in the bank so we can carry on making music comfortably. We want to get to that level permanently, where we're self-funded, anything else will be a bonus. It's going to be a long shot. If it doesn't work out, it's gonna be a good party for a year or so.'

'There are fights, both on and off the stage; it's not uncommon for the singer to lash out and punch someone in the head if they get too close.'

Canada may claim the titles for the best skiing and mountain biking destinations in the world; however, as a surf spot, it barely makes a blip on the radar. Ian's taking his board anyway, he's got it sorted. But if it wasn't for a freak event a few years earlier, things could've been a lot different. When longboarding legends Thomas Campbell, Tyler Hatzikian, Devon Howard and C.J. Nelson were touring New Zealand looking for locations to shoot Campbell's latest surf movie, *The Sprout*, things were going fine until their van broke down at Whangamata. To 99 per cent of the population, they were just a bunch of cruising Californians with an even bigger bunch of surfboards on their roof. When Ian's dad happened to come across them down at the beach, he knew exactly who they were. He and his two sons had watched endless hours of footage and seen plenty of glossy images over the years of these same guys as they kept the classic ethos of longboarding alive and well. That night, Ian arrived from Auckland to find his biggest surfing inspirations sitting around the family dinner table. They stayed and enjoyed the Kings' hospitality and Whangamata's waves while the van was fixed, and thanks to a shared surfing idealism, the Kings and the legends have become lifelong friends.

Ian's toured around both countries surfing and filming with Thomas Campbell, and made the final cut in the New Zealand section of *The Present*, a movie with a cast that boasts some of the superstars of style, guys like Dave Rastovich, Joel Tudor, Rob Machado and Dane Reynolds. Ian's stayed at their homes in Malibu and Santa Cruz with them on numerous occasions, and Campbell has been back to New Zealand to stay with him. When Campbell picked Ian up from Devon's house in San Diego late one night, on their way to Santa Cruz, he suggested they should surf Malibu. Ian looked at the dashboard clock as it flicked to 1 a.m. 'He's a pretty eccentric dude. I'd never surfed it before, but he wasn't taking no for an answer. I could only just make out the waves coming on the full moon, but couldn't see the rocks. I remember turning around and paddling into one, standing up on the waist-high peeler, not knowing what's coming, but seeing the moonlight sparkling on the wall of the wave.' Ian was stoked. They went back again at the end of the trip and surfed it again from five in the morning to five at night. It was the best wave he's ever experienced. Being able to hang with them, he says, definitely does wonders for his surfing. So while he's researched potentially good surf in Canada, he still thinks it's going to be easier to fly to California, use a board stashed there to surf for a couple of weeks, then fly back.

But treading water has taken a toll on his musical creativity. The closest he's got to performing has been a television role he scored as a co-host for a dedicated rock programme on Juice television on a Tuesday night. As far as picking up a guitar, nothing new has come out of him for a while. That'll change quickly, he promises, when he heads north, starts being stimulated by a wider outlook on the world, and takes the time to look at New Zealand from an outside-in perspective. I find it hard to imagine the guy sitting opposite me ever gets pissed off about things, he seems way too mellow and level-headed to let anything bother him. Then again, maybe I'm just staring at Ian King in his soul surfing persona. 'People always used to ask why I rode longboards when I listen and play punk rock and heavy metal. Longboarding is a lot more like my personality, yet I vent what anger I have through my music. It's like a release. You can create really intense life in music, then you can create what life is really like when you surf. They're both extreme opposites, but they fulfil one's life pretty well. If I didn't have surfing, the music side would suffer without those mellow times. Normally, the best stuff you write is when you're passionate about something or it affects you directly. It's hard to write something when you come home from work and just pick up the guitar, because I think music, like most art, is an emotional thing.'

As his surfing has matured with him, it has taken more of a role of maintaining that point of balance in his life. While he enjoyed surfing previously, it was just something he did in his spare time. These days, Ian's finding he understands the holistic side of surfing even more so; appreciating the ocean, its environment, the landscapes and the sea life. For him, living in the city for so long has turned the coastline into a place of sanctuary, even escapism from a society in hyper-drive. 'I fear people's ignorance for always striving to get ahead in life at the expense of other people, the environment, animals, whatever.' Ian studied geography and sociology at Auckland University, which raised his awareness of environmental practices and people's quests to benefit themselves; understanding cause and effect, and the right and wrong, of a commercial world.

His family, who Ian says are not environmentalists outright, gave him the grounding that helps him to think about the world in a lateral sense, trying to appreciate how everything is connected in some way. It was this upbringing that instigated a life-changing decision for him when he was 16. He was stuck behind a cattle truck on his way to a competition at the Mount, when he made the connection — the stock on the truck weren't going to a happy place and would eventually end up on someone's dinner plate. That night he went to a vegan restaurant, had a veggie burger, and it all just clicked; why eat meat when all these other alternatives are out there, options that are friendly for everyone?

He turned vegetarian for a year, weaned himself off fish and chicken, did a bit more research, then took the final step to 100 per cent vegan. 'It can be hard and testing on tour, a huge pain in the arse when you're stuck in some redneck town and you find yourself eating hot chips and bread or chippies. But you make sure you eat good when you're in the cities. There are ridiculously good vegetarian places in New York dedicated to vegans and vegetarians, you name it, they've got an alternative to it.'

Ian's arm bears a picture of a Moby Dick-inspired scene of a giant sperm whale destroying a Japanese whaling boat. It's still a work in progress. He's thinking about adding a giant squid eating some dude as well. The image is a mixture of things: his passion for the environment, his disgust at whaling. He laughs and says it's way more subtle than getting 'I'm a vegan' tattooed across his neck. 'I think surfers immerse themselves in the environment way more than other people. They see first-hand what pollution can do and how fast it can do it — [more so] than the average Joe living in the 'burbs. Regular people don't quite get that experience like surfers do. Even subconsciously, the most staunch non-environmental surfer is slightly more environmentally conscious than the next person down the ladder who isn't a surfer. Surfing at Takapuna Beach in a storm isn't pleasant; all the sewage and overflow end up on the beach and make it go a crappy brown. I think there's been some bad decisions made by the government on environmental issues, and there's going to be a fair few more with the new government that are going to see us heading down the same destructive route as California. That's definitely something I could write a good punk rock song on.'

Even subconsciously, the most staunch non-environmental surfer is slightly more environmentally conscious than the next person down the ladder who isn't a surfer.

Like digging up a certain Whangamata estuary to make a marina? It's a joke as far as Ian's concerned, just another example of how New Zealand's short-sightedness is going to destroy an important feature of the local natural environment. There has been hot debate over the decision, and Ian has been frustrated at how the media have had a field day portraying the opposition as a small group of simple-minded surfers and a few local Maori standing in the way of local businesspeople, pushing for their self interests. 'It's a super-beautiful estuary, especially at high tide, and it doesn't need to be another Pauanui. They're gonna turn it into another shithole just so a handful of wealthy dudes can park their boats at another place on the Coromandel, twenty kilometres from a place they can already park at. They're going to destroy a habitat and an environment for thousands of people for years to come.' We talk more about what's happening; black sand mining, family campgrounds now exclusive to a fortunate few, the proposal of a natural spit being subdivided on unstable land north of Whangarei Heads, and the ruin of the well-known beach breaks at Pakari Beach due to the mining of its sand. All are issues he's confident talking about.

But there are some things we're doing right, and Ian points out that the marine reserves being put in place around our shorelines are at the forefront on a global scale. 'There needs to be more around the place, like in National Parks. The coast is so easily affected by pollution. We're still a long way away from where we should be, but we're getting good at establishing them. As much as fishermen might despise them, if they look at how the fish are being depleted on our shores, and the amount of fish bred in these areas, then they would have to realise it's a good thing in the long run.' Education is the big thing, he says; the public need to be made more aware of the environment and get in behind it. 'I would hate to come back from Toronto and find the relaxing of environmental law in New Zealand. Otherwise, I can see overseas investment trying to get the most out of the land, not paying the prices they should be, or bothering to offset the pollution to the environment. It would eventually destroy our image portrayed overseas.'

The simplicity of what the ocean provides has become reflected in his philosophy on life. Living in two worlds, it seems, is a good thing, if you can get it right. Exercising both sides of his brain keeps him grounded, despite the successes he's had and the opportunity to name-drop a storm of people. For all anyone knows, today he was just some dude making coin in a retail store, an everyday occurrence, and that's the way Ian likes it. 'I just wanna enjoy life for what it is and not try and ruin it by chasing the carrot of money. There are better things in life than trying to get the dream house and the next designer shoes that many people get hung up on. You forget to stop and take stock of how good your life already is. Lately I've been thinking about how much better my life could be, but when you stop to smell the roses, I definitely couldn't have asked for better than what I've experienced so far through both music and surfing. There hasn't been a time where I've felt the needle come close to bursting the bubble. I guess I've never aimed that high, though. I've just enjoyed it for what it is. If my life turns a shitty direction, I can prop it up with the other side. If the music doesn't work out, I've got surfing experiences to fall back on.'

So how does surfing make him feel? 'Pretty damned good. There's nothing I'd rather be doing than going to a beach with a box of beers and some food and surfing with mates for the day. It's pure enjoyment, pure relaxation, pure adrenalin, it's every good human emotion wrapped into one. The music is good, it's great partying and so on, but it's a short experience. I'm happiest when I'm at the beach.'

And this is where I leave Ian, about to get into a car with his mates to catch a fresh swell somewhere north of Orewa for a couple of nights. Away from the city lights and blocked motorways. Somewhere where he can express his love of surfing with another soul arch across a luminous green wall of water as the setting sun closes the day. Later on he'll probably take one of those beers he mentioned, and with a crackling fire beneath an audience of stars, perhaps he'll reach for that acoustic guitar.

Andrew Forrester

Aaron Topp

FILM DIRECTOR
PAPAMOA

As a boy, Andrew Forrester found the placid waterscape around his home of Lake Rotoiti boring. He pined for something that moved by itself, without the need for a skimmed stone or the ripple from a trout's tail. Something with a pulse, like it was alive, something that suffered mood swings of violence and tranquillity and everything in between. Something that would satisfy his birthright as an Aquarius, providing him with an arena to challenge himself through bodysurfing or in various watercrafts. To lie with his eyes closed under its surface, listening to the pulsating hiss of the earth's greatest mass accepting him as its own.

He was happy, then, when his parents decided to head north to the coast, to a small rural settlement called Papamoa, a community that embraced alternative lifestyles. Andrew was 13 and it was the late 1970s. Here he would remain for the next 30 years, enjoying an open love affair with its waves.

These days, Andrew lives with his partner Michelle, a homeopath, and their toddler son Jordan, in one of the many quiet cul-de-sacs of a very different Papamoa. The street has been custom-designed, with paved roundabouts, quaint street lights and a series of towering palm trees guiding my way. It looks nice, it's designed to be, but it is nothing out of the ordinary for this place. It's typical of the look and feel our coastal expansions have become — sterile, Californian-inspired habitats of culture from a can. Perfect real estate fodder for the thousands of (mainly) Aucklanders jumping provincial ship to start a new life of seaside bliss. I park outside Andrew's house and walk past the 'For Sale' sign hanging on the gateway. His Rottweiler, Coco, announces my arrival long before I knock on the door.

Any surfer over the age of 25 will remember the *Coastal Disturbance* movies of the mid-1990s. The four quintessential videos represented a time when the surfing market's appetite couldn't be satisfied. A time when big egos, long hair and any colour but fluoro ruled the waves. Andrew was the right man at the right time. He brought local waves and local boardriders to the living rooms of the surfing community. Films we Kiwis could call our own to be found in any video rack, beside the power names of the surf movie industry like McCoy, Brown, and Steele.

So much has changed since then; televisions are a fraction of the thickness, and the disc has relegated the videotape to a box in the shed where we also left our ability to grow hair past our ears with dignity, and our ability to look cool while screaming lyrics at the front of a Muse concert. I didn't know Andrew back then, but I doubt he's changed at the same pace in that time. I can picture him with the same moustache above the magnetic smile he flashes as he opens the front door.

Andrew's progression into surfing was as natural as pulling the curtains back in the morning and checking the conditions from his bedroom window. His first fibreglass board came not long after he arrived in Papamoa, an old single fin. There weren't too many surfers in the area to learn from, so he taught himself. The memories of those first sensations are still vivid, he tells me, while we sit at his breakfast bar with a brew, Coco resting at our feet. 'You always remember that first amount of speed you get. You go from wallowing around in the ocean to suddenly moving at pace. That was the factor that did it for me. From then on I was going to the beach and thinking to myself, how do I control that? How do I harness it? I think I managed to get to my knees for the first few rides, wobble around, bang my shins, keep falling off, but I thought, hey, I can do this. I had a desire to be a waterman, someone who could ride anything that was lying around, so I experimented with various boards to learn the different sensations.'

It was a time when television, eager to tap into the exploding market, was showing coverage of the Australian competition, 'Surf About'. Same time every week, he'd gawp at the top surfers dancing on the waves as they broke across his screen, studying elements like their foot placement or body position. There was no question about it, he had to ride a surfboard like those guys. Back then, Simon Anderson hadn't even made the thrusters, and everything was still twin fin. Andrew was being inspired by Queensland guys like Rabbit Bartholomew. They surfed fast on what always seemed to be everlasting top-to-bottom waves. Andrew begins recalling these scenes from 1980s surf movies to me, like they're mini epiphanies — I suspect even more so for the footage itself than just the surfing prowess on show. ' . . . Rabbit would be gliding along, then stall, put his hands behind his back, and get barrelled for a few seconds. Watching that I was like, wow, and he's just standing there, no pressure, that's so cool. I liked looking at those waves and the idea of being a natural footer, riding those endless right-handers . . .'

In the 1980s, Papamoa's surfing population was just a handful of guys. Andrew and his mates would travel up the road to the Mount, looking to progress their surfing. Up there, the whole surf thing was starting to boom; it was the place to be seen on a board, while Papamoa was quickly getting the reputation as a poor cousin. That title didn't bother the boys, who soon discovered the Papamoa Domain had as good a surf as anywhere else they found on their road trips. They left the hype to the Mounties and relished the fact they were riding perfect waves that barrelled in waist-deep water (these days, he says, the waves break about a hundred yards offshore when it's good;

'Times change, sand banks change, storms come and go and shift the dynamics of what you ride.'). With a few of the older crew they eventually set up the Papamoa Board Riders Club. It didn't have an official building, but they'd use the local surf club as a base for meetings and social events. One of the key people involved was Wayne Lowen, a top rider at the time. Wayne was not only known for his shaping of surfboards, but was also a champion who came second in the Pan Pacific Cup in 1987 to a young Kelly Slater; it was a claim they held as proud as any cup in their cabinet. They began holding local competitions, and enjoyed a new era of memberships and seeing different faces in the water. Soon, a weekend would see a van-load of guys going on a surf trip when the Domain was flat.

The club became a catalyst for the surf community to get together to check out the latest surf films, an event Andrew always enjoyed. '*Wizards of the Water* had one of the coolest things I'd ever seen. Derek Hynd riding a twin fin on these really crappy waves in Sydney. He was doing all these different types of three-sixties, real revolutionary stuff. Thing was, he had a front foot strap, and sometimes he'd disappear into a barrel and come out facing backwards, leaning back. I had a little five-foot board at the time, so I ripped a strap off my windsurfer in the garage and bolted it on to my board, and headed out into the surf to try to do what I'd seen. Even to this day, the three-sixty is a favourite manoeuvre of mine.

> It's typical of the look and feel our coastal expansions have become — sterile, Californian-inspired habitats of culture from a can.

It's that fun factor, something that helps mix the surfing experience up.'

For all his love of watching them, though, to my surprise, Andrew can't remember ever wanting to make his own surf films. Like surfing, his progression was a natural one; he saved some money, then, at the age of 21, headed to Australia and bought a VHS camera, one of those big, black, boxy things that clanked like a train shunting when you pressed the eject button. He was stoked. Back home, he sweet-talked his mum into filming him surfing, but she didn't really get it, so he did the same with his aunty, with much the same result. One day, out of desperation, he set the camera up on a wide angle in the front garden and went surfing, but nearly all the shots had him out of frame. He went to the Mount Pro Am in 1985 to do a bit of filming, then captured the Raglan Pro Am in 1987, just small stuff, editing a few snippets here and there to show some mates. They'd head to Gisborne or Mahia or Raglan with the camera in the boot with the rest of the luggage. If it was really good when they arrived, Andrew would offer to film the boys. 'When we got back and started watching it, they'd be like, hey, that's really good; if you put some music to that it'll be awesome. Somewhere around then a friend turned to me and told me I could make a living out of this. I didn't think much of it until about seven years later, when I had an opportunity to start filming the pros. When you start doing good guys and good waves, things go up a whole other level.'

With a notebook starved of any professional contacts, Andrew made do with following the 1988–89 competition circuit to get them all in the one spot. There were six events in a year, but he focused on a few of the local events: Labour Weekend would always be Taranaki, Queens Birthday was the Gisborne Cold Water Classic, March and April were the Raglan Pro. By the 1990s, Andrew's hard work had paid off. He got the attention of the owner of Seasons Surfboards in New Plymouth. He offered Andrew an opportunity to work with their sponsored riders to make a promotional video. 'They were some of the best surfers in the country at the time, guys like Glen Campbell, Pipi Ngaia, and Jason Mathews, who's the best power surfer the country's ever seen. He's the guy who'll paddle into the biggest waves without a jetski. Kelly Lovelock, Motu and Dwayne Mataa were the others, all big Taranaki surfers at the time when the place was the hotbed of talent. They made filming so easy. Before I knew it, my connections were building at every competition.'

With filming experience and confidence building, Andrew followed the circuit again in 1991–92 and ended up with hours of footage, but he didn't know what to do with it. So he turned it into a video called *Back to the Beach*, which, he admits in hindsight, was very average by today's standards ('Most kids would rather trash it than watch it,' he says). Despite this, at that time *Back to the Beach* was the only Kiwi film in a starved market, and over two years it went on to sell 400 copies. It turned out to be a big stepping stone in his career; suddenly he had the attention of the surf industry, and it was eager to give him feedback, mainly in the form of 'give us better waves, surfing and music'. The market had spoken. Andrew set about delivering.

Although his notebook was filling fast with the phone numbers of surfing drawcards, Andrew found his bank account was in no state to match the benchmark films of the time like *Storm Riders*, which enjoyed a A$110,000 budget. The reality was, his last bank statement showed he might be able to squeeze $10,000 and still leave a bit for some groceries. 'I was ringing up Dick Hoole in Australia, who was working with the film legend Jack McCoy, trying to get information out of him to find out how I do this. No one in New Zealand was doing anything. Andrew McAlpine did it once back in the sixties, then it all stopped. There was a big gap there and I wanted to make it happen.' He started working part-time at the TAB, filming races in the weekends, holding a cumbersome camera for hours on end at horse- and car-racing events, as well as developing a small corporate client base, to help him financially and to give him more experience in the technical side of filming. He also decided to base the structure of the movie on the popular *Hawaii '90* movies, where ads were placed in between each surfing chapter. It could have been easier for him to pitch the project to one big name in the surf industry and get a lump sum for their name, but the money wasn't there. Andrew just wanted to shoot great waves and great surfers and keep creative control of the movie. If someone with the best barrel wasn't sponsored by the name on the movie, Andrew felt they should still be included. There was no way he was going to risk the integrity of the film.

Andrew travelled a lot with Logan Murray, a veteran surf photographer from Gisborne. While the surfers were doing their best to put a show on in the waves at any of the numerous beaches in the North Island, the two lensmen would often end up standing side by side on the sand, eyes watching the world pass through a small window in their devices. During their first shooting session together, Logan told Andrew a good movie has good waves, good surfers and good lighting, which, given that he can still recite it to me after a decade, must've been good advice. Although he learnt quickly, there were subtle differences between the two mediums. 'A still photographer is always going to be looking at the one shot, but with video you're looking at the whole thing, thinking about the editing process, whether to keep that wave because a surfer falls halfway through.'

Then there were the angles, the ones that made Jack McCoy so famous. Sometimes Andrew would paddle over a wave as it rolled beneath him and he'd look back towards the chaos and be hypnotised by the circling oval of energy. It was at these moments he wished he had a camera to get that special angle, to make the dream reality. In 1994 he got a water-housing system made up to fit his camera and suddenly he found a new dynamic to filming. He could now get up close and personal with surfers, feeling the spray of water on his face as they passed, or capture the roar of a breaking wave as it drew near. Despite the big names and the high level of surfing on display, there was still an element he couldn't control. Mother Nature, consistent with the rest of the female species, when not making him guess, would keep him waiting. 'Capturing how perfect surfing can be was the key. I lost count how many days I'd be sitting at a place like Raglan waiting for the offshore or swell to come. The best days are always going to be the good swell, no wind, great light, nothing's affecting the wave, it's breaking perfectly. But even when you have everything just right, the wind can change direction and the opportunity's gone.'

'From then on I was going to the beach and thinking to myself, how do I control that? How do I harness it?'

With 50 hours of footage shot over 1993–94 and whittled down to a 60-minute feature, a title borrowed from the name of a surf shop in the Mount, and generous assistance from Craig Levers at *New Zealand Surfing* magazine, the first *Coastal Disturbance* movie sold 1000 units at about $40 each; impressive when you consider a good rugby vid back then was doing 2000. But Andrew is quick to state he was lucky to get a fraction of those profits for each video once all the costs were included. After calculating a whole year's worth of work, he decided he would've got more on the dole.

An objective of the CD series was to make it totally New Zealand. Apart from the odd travelling surfer coming through the country, the rest of the surfers were to be Kiwi, the waves Kiwi, with music to reflect it. Andrew hounded record companies, pitching down the phone line an image of their band and the hottest surfers in the country in sync with each other on every surfer's television. It resulted in his mailbox being crammed with a heap of free demo

CDs. Looking at the list of bands used, you are automatically transported back to a who's who of 1990s New Zealand music. Andrew's biggest break came when he developed a relationship with Wildside Records. They'd recently signed an upcoming group by the name of Shihad, a fresh, raw sound with intros that fitted his movie perfectly. Then there were The Dead Flowers, Pumpkinhead, Hallelujah Picassos. The relationship with Wildside went right through to the fourth CD (although Shihad's move to Australia meant Andrew had to pay a bit more for their music). Later, in CD2, he'd use music from The Exponents and Headless Chickens, two bands that were being played on mainstream radio everywhere. Regardless of a band's popularity, Andrew promoted all the music he used the best he could, aware the surf community were also typically big music fans, like himself. 'A guy from Wellington band, Monkey Puzzle, was so talented. His music was punk with a modern edge, a really great sound and he didn't even charge me, he just wanted to see the music immortalised. It was great having that mix of underground music mixed with the better known ones.'

Andrew stuck to the same production blueprint for the series (which has since been digitally remastered and made available on DVD). Each movie would start off with a brief showcase of what to expect for the remaining feature, and always to a Shihad track to help raise the blood pressure. It would feature a new break, based on either common knowledge or rumoured local folklore. One particular place he wanted to capture was the East Cape district during the cyclone season. By CD3 he had his chance. With a giant low sitting north of the Bay of Plenty, he packed a car with camera gear and surfers and headed to a secluded break east of Whakatane. When they arrived, there was already a bunch of guys out enjoying the giant groundswell peeling along the river bar. Unfazed, Andrew started setting up the camera on the stony shore; they were perfect waves and their shape and surroundings made them unlike anything else he'd filmed for the movie. But he was soon confronted by some agitated locals, who didn't like the idea of

. . . he was soon confronted by some agitated locals, who didn't like the idea of their break being exposed to the masses.

their break being exposed to the masses. Andrew managed to reason with them — probably when they saw how laidback he was — and they let him continue shooting as long as he promised never to reveal the name of the magical spot. I try to get its name out of him years later, but even now his lips are sealed. He shakes his head at me when I start rattling off places. Nope, nup, nah. I don't push it and we drop the topic with his integrity still intact. In the final cut it was simply referred to as the 'East Cape'. It was to be the only negative time he had in all the CD filming.

'Out of four movies there's about two hundred hours of footage. Finding a favourite section is really hard. Pipi Ngaia was always really a pleasure to shoot, because you always knew he was going to get as close as possible to you to get that perfect shot. There were others who did that too, but I have some really vivid memories of surfing Rocky Lefts in CD2 with him that stick in my head. I watch that section today and it still gives me a tingle, the whole session came together that day. I've had great times at Matakana and Shipwrecks too, which the surfers involved are still raving about.' Andrew's biggest break came when the WQS arrived in Raglan in 1995. It was his chance to make his own televised surf show/video, a tribute, in a way, to the hours of grommethood he spent in front of the TV. To do so, though, he had to get the best footage out of the pros in the short time they were in town. Timing was everything. With help from Paul Hogan, Andrew grabbed some TAB mates, borrowed the work cameras and talked future weatherman Brendon Horan into being a presenter. Andrew then negotiated with TVNZ that he wouldn't charge for the time; he just needed the footage to be used for his own CD series, to which they agreed. They shot a TV show with three cameras on the beach and Andrew in the water. Andrew's moustache bristles as he smiles and recalls how they pulled it off. 'You've got Occy [Mark Occhilupo] and Luke Egan warming up for their heats on the beach, and I'm sitting there filming, thinking, wow, these are the guys that Jack McCoy films, and I've got them.'

The *Coastal Disturbance* series, and his more recent longboarding feature, *NoseZone*, have even gone on to sell in America. Andrew's been told by some of the older Californian crew that the footage reminds them of how the waves used to look in their own back yard prior to the '70s. 'I guess it's because we've got quality waves that aren't polluted and great landscapes. We're really lucky here. We worry about sewage, and some of it can be stopped, but at least we don't have the nuclear power plants near our ocean like in some places in the world, where they use the water to cool the turbines. And there's no oil and sludge or tar on the beach, like in California, that sticks to your feet and wetsuit, and makes you feel like you're walking through a dirty gas station.'

Andrew gets pretty emotive when our conversation turns to the current state of the environment, both climatic and political. Does he think there are changes to be made? Damned right. For a guy who enjoys a good discussion, I start to feel I've just found a pet topic of his. For the next half hour we head down different roads of thought, taking us as far inland from surfing as we can go, only to come back to the coast again. Andrew is pretty adept at bringing a conversation full circle to make his point. 'I think we need to get back to basics, back to growing some of our food. The oil reserves aren't there and in our lifetime we're going to see massive changes. Even as surfers we use those resources; the foam, fibreglass, neoprene, they're all non-renewable. We need to, as a global surfing community, change the attitudes of the manufacturers to supply us with more sustainable products. Part of it's starting to come in already with some surfboard manufacturers, who are thinking of change and have started using different methods.'

We discuss the rising cost of fuel, how it's affecting surfers and their ability to maintain a large portfolio of surf breaks, and its imminent effect on compounding localism as they decide to surf the one area. Andrew is all too aware of the surge in population in his own back yard. He's been observing it every year as the first spray of spring sunshine entices people back to the waves. There are more kids paddling out, and the surf life saving club is enjoying increased membership. Andrew says the waves are getting more crowded at the Domain, but mainly on the peak. 'Here at Papamoa, it's a tourist town, we're always gonna get crowds. But I don't get mad, I just accept it and find another break somewhere else down the beach.'

It's more the effect the increase in population is having on the environment he's been a part of for the last 30 years that's the centre of his concern. While he acknowledges there's always been some sort of development here at Papamoa, he's now watching the resources become more used, especially in the summertime. 'We're lucky to have a section here, but new homes being built in the neighbourhood have no space between each house. I've noticed the newer homes are better quality, but the developers are squeezing more of them in that area. You just have enough room to put the barbecue out, have three people around, and it's overcrowded. Then the neighbours are looking straight at you.' With their choices of lifestyle being consumed like the land around them, and with old-school coastal communities with a similar climate as rare as a claustrophobic developer, Andrew and Michelle are seriously considering packing up and starting again. To get back to basics. Even if that means looking offshore. The sign on the gate is just the first step in a journey they hope will end in a fully self-sufficient house somewhere in the Pacific Islands. 'As surfers we are free. It's that free spirit that's making us move. Growing our own food, going fishing, buying our own organically grown beef. The waves are great over there.' He pauses, and I can see him momentarily picturing the perfection as he nods his head lightly. 'But I'll have to hone my reef-riding skills, though.

'My partner, Michelle, is keen to learn how to surf. She loves nature and she understands my love of surfing. Getting onto a surfboard will be easy for her. I can't wait for her to share that stoke with me. Same with my son, it's only a matter of time. I'm looking forward to teaching him the appreciation of the water, watching him adopt that inner peace surfers have.' Andrew's seen his share of guys in the water who have lost that ability to see what surfing is and what it can gift. They instead choose to taint the water with aggro, spreading their negative vibes like a waterborne virus. 'They're not going to be happy in any situation, those guys, they're missing the point. They're not letting surfing heal themselves. It's a sad fact in this society that we've become conditioned to violence. Look at the TV news, what do you see? Why don't we see the good news happening? Some of it's found its way into surf movies these days, showing guys getting cut up or fighting. One of the key things Laird Hamilton says is his favourite board is a 'tanker', a longboard. Here's a guy riding the biggest waves in the world, riding a massive array of watercraft, and he's saying

> 'That stays in your body and your partner and friends can always tell afterwards that you've had that change, you're relaxed. It changes you for the better.'

121

his one board to have is a standard longboard because it's fun. I think guys out there get stuck in a rut and think they have to only ride certain waves on their six-foot boards. That's crap. Get back to the fun factor. If it's two-foot, ride a Mal, ride a twin fin in sloppy conditions, ride an eight-foot wave on a gun, whatever, just ride what's there and have fun. Stop being so aggro.'

It was a cyclone stalled in the Pacific during 1998 that left a profound effect on Andrew. As lines of giant groundswell were marching upon the BOP coast, he was busy capturing a couple of guys surfing off the main beach at the Mount. Through his lens they looked like tiny stickmen against the massive faces of liquid glass breaking 300 metres out to sea. The size of the waves and the light southerly conditions grooming each set were making it the swell of the decade. It was a moment surfers wait for their whole life. The reason they go out in grovelly, wind-affected chop, or spend hours talking over beers and barbecues — the one swell. The one to be forever at the front of the queue in their memory. The one where they proudly let their mates know 'Yesterday, bro. Epic.' Andrew knew all this, and despite the footage he was collecting, he couldn't resist it any longer. He went back to the car and returned with his board. As he made his way across the sand towards the surges of whitewater racing up the land, it occurred to him how still and eerie everything was. Like the rest of the world had ceased, the distant growl of the giant groundswell breaking the only reminder that he wasn't the only thing still alive. He waded into the water. 'For some reason it was an easy paddle out, and instead of the rumble I heard from the beach, it was quiet. It was so clean and glassy. I remember taking off on the first couple of double-overhead waves and I could hear the board slicing through the water, when normally I'd have the wind howling in my ears. It was a surreal sensation. I was sitting there afterwards in the water thinking, wow, Mother Nature has really given us something special today. I think it's the bigger swells that have that effect on surfers, where you feel you love your surfing. You're paddling to catch the wave, that first drop, when you realise you've got all that power behind you, the sensation of what I'm gonna do after that first bottom turn on a wall of water as it looms over you. The excitement of those first sensations is there, it always will be, but as you get more experienced, the adrenalin is a controlled adrenalin, thinking about how I'm going to get more out of it. Afterwards, you always come in from the water feeling pleasantly exhausted, but it's a feeling that's hard to explain to someone who doesn't surf. It's about being at one with the ocean, with nature. When you've been out there on a good day, at your home break, you come in thinking, yeah, the ocean didn't get me, so there's always that sense of elation, that sense of achievement, definitely the adrenalin. That stays in your body and your partner and friends can always tell afterwards that you've had that change, you're relaxed. It changes you for the better. It makes you feel good.'

Ken Thomas

Aaron Topp

ARTIST
RAGLAN

*I should've known better than to ask Ken Thomas
what he was afraid of. The guy had been out all
night, first at the pub watching the league, then
at a local's thirtieth, then at another's fiftieth.
Today was the start of daylight savings too, so
when I rocked up at the arranged nine in the
morning, it was only really eight and he'd had
four hours' sleep. He told me to come back in
another hour at least and closed the door, leaving
me standing beside a broken surfboard wrapped
around a tree in the garden like it had been left
to grow there, or perhaps to issue a warning. I
took my pen and wrote in my notebook: straight-
up guy.*

A few hours and several coffees later, after listening to the 51-year-old talk of broken bones, shotgun-wielding locals and being held down by giant Hawaiian waves, it was just too tempting to probe him with a question that, if he answered, would mean opening up to a complete stranger. But when he stood from his deck chair and leant against the railing in silence, rubbing a palm over silver stubble that could etch metal, my cocky journo grin left, and I suddenly felt like I'd overstayed my welcome. 'Shit, mate,' he says in the deep, raspy voice left behind from the previous night, 'that's a bit heavy.' He takes his sunglasses off and hangs them above his cap. For the first time I see his eyes, and they're giving me my answer already. He leaves me sitting on his veranda and I start packing up. I'll show myself to the door, thanks.

For the record, Ken didn't leave me for long. I hear his voice call out from inside: 'Wanna smoke? Iced coffee? Glass of water?' I decline all three politely and he sits back down in the chair beside me and lights a roll-your-own. I unpack my gear again and suddenly start to appreciate how the sun feels after a long winter, kinda like how the second part of the interview unfolds.

Ken has been living in Raglan for a quarter of a century now, coming and going a few times in that period. He lives here with his wife, Jenny, and their two sons, Jimmy and Hugo. He was born in Mangakino in the King Country and grew up in Hamilton. He first surfed at Whitianga, where it didn't take long for him to stand up. He'd head straight for the beach while his mates yelled at him to go sideways. He got into it more when he scored his driver's licence at age 15. By 18, the lure of the surf had drawn him to the sleepy seaside village of Raglan. Back then there were only six full-time surf locals and he became part of the second generation of surfers to call the place home; the first lot had settled in the 1960s, establishing the Point Boardriders Club at Manu Bay.

Ken took a year away from Raglan and headed to Taranaki, where he lived in a farm house, worked in a dairy factory in Kapuni, and surfed Stent Road by himself. He headed to Sydney and discovered he had a a talent for art. A friend of his was into Greenpeace, so with nothing more than a pen, Ken drew a humpback whale with a calf for him and suddenly it was being featured as a print and sold. His friend asked for more, so Ken evolved it into animation. He sent some samples in to a surfing magazine and secured himself a regular feature — a full-page cartoon. Hyped up at the time with the explosion of surfing in Oz, he returned to Raglan three years later, reignited the original surf club, and began facilitating contests and movie nights.

Raglan was recently voted the nicest place in the country. Like many one-saloon towns around New Zealand, Raglan has been swallowed up by the frenzy for all things quaint. Observing the place on a typical Friday night, I saw cafés fully booked for dinner functions, pockets of young professional women walking the street with excited springs in their steps, a cluster of groms hanging out at the local takeaway, two new BMWs, one Bentley, and a bustling Four Square. When Ken first arrived, Raglan was hardcore and staunch in its ways, with a large Mongrel Mob presence. The pub could be a heavy place, he says, but that was part of the fun, there was always something going on. Surfers hardly registered, they were the scum of the place. 'It's still a nice place physically,' he says, taking a moment to think about how much it's changed. 'If you'd been away for twenty years all the buildings are the same, except now they're cafés. The reserves are in the same areas. It's shaken that Wild West image, it's not considered like that any more, no more than Rotorua or West Auckland.' He has a laugh at that last one. 'It's a popular place here now, a real melting pot, very international. A good party town.'

It's a standard answer, something from the local textbook of pleasantries, I'd imagine. But I can't help feel change is something a guy like Ken doesn't accept that easily. There's no disputing surfing has climbed the rung of respectability and now it's fair to say this place owes a lot of its appeal to the image surfing has in the modern era and the town's recognition of the quality waves in its back yard. There are, though, some mixed feelings in the surfing community about just how far the appeal has to be pushed before people start destroying it. A classic case is the new development at Manu Bay, the most popular of the three breaks at Raglan. And it's here, at the heart of his surfing, where I find Ken's reservations.

For years Manu Bay was natural, just a big green paddock with an old access track running through it, but things are changing quickly and guys like Ken aren't that impressed. 'It's turning into an asphalt jungle; they put the road close to the beach, like it's part of a cityscape now, like Dee Why Point in Sydney. It's not country any more, that's the big difference, you're not getting away from it coming to Raglan. It's all being bought up by a bunch of speculators, people wanting to change the place. People that'll blow in, blow out, and leave no community spirit behind. Oh, this is a nice town so let's #%@! it up the arse and make a buck.' I can see that he's gonna continue, but something below us catches his eye. His 15-year-old son, Jimmy, walks below the deck with car keys in his hand. Ken calls out: 'Where you heading? You taking a board? Great.' It's enough to break the moment, but he's made his point. Ken relights his smoke and sits back. 'It's just typical of what's happening around New Zealand now,' he says with a slight shrug of his shoulders. 'This place is no different.'

While still at college Ken started shaping his own surfboards. When he moved to Raglan no one else was making any, so he did a few more. He opened up the surf shop in Raglan and sold them as the brand, Rockit Surfboards. So it was only natural when Ken first travelled to Hawaii back in the late 1980s that he survived by using this early form of art. Back then, Hawaii was the undisputed surfing mecca, the only recognised big-wave spot in the world. Its reputation of turning boys into men in just one wave attracted gung ho surfers from every country, every day. Ken was different, though. At 30, he didn't need to prove himself to others. He was there searching for purity, the sensation of riding something that was so beautiful, so perfect, so deadly. It was his surfing rite of passage. The first day he arrived he headed out to Oahu's North Shore, sat on the beach and watched mountains of white water being generated by the massive swell hitting the reef, and felt the sand vibrate beneath him. He'd never experienced anything like it. He reached into his bag and pulled out a bottle of duty-free Scotch and began sculling. He watched some more. Eventually he grabbed his board and paddled out.

He and an Hawaiian made a home on the North Shore in a run-down shack surrounded by coconut trees and began making surfboards out of necessity. They called them Poi Dog Surfboards after the locals' little fighting dogs, which were fed on the staple Hawaiian diet of poi and taro. Back then, the Shore was run by a big Hawaiian guy, Robert Napalipali, otherwise known as the Prince of Haleiwa. He had sent many a tourist surfer packing prematurely, but was impressed with Ken's ability to charge out in the water and give respect when back on land. He took Ken under his wing and introduced him to the neighbouring Hawaiian families. Six months later, Robert paid Ken a visit at the shack to let him know he was now considered a local. 'Since then I've realised there's certain kinds of people in the world. There's the guy who can go anywhere in the world and be a local, living for the day, that kind of person. Then you get the other kind who come in, do their thing, piss everyone off, then leave.'

But living on the Shore wasn't all about warm water and laid-back living. When the waves are pumping for six months of the year everything's fine, it's a 13-kilometre stretch of coastline full of guys throwing themselves into big waves, loading themselves full of adrenalin, walking around bristling with confidence that blurs into a non-stop party atmosphere. But for the other six months there's nothing to do but wait, and according to Ken, it's like living a constant rugby game all day, all night. This is the sinister side of the Shore, where guys resort to proving themselves on land instead. Things got pretty wild, Ken reckons — a lot of drugs and disputes. Heavy moments where he was faced with guns and baseball bats, where being an honorary local meant he couldn't exactly hold up the 'I'm a tourist' card whenever he wanted to distance himself from it all. So with no other choice, he charged that stuff too.

Ken was surfing the more obscure spots back then, places that have in the last 20 years become crowd favourites, like Backyards and Velzyland. 'I was getting off on the adrenalin. What I thought was a huge ten-foot wave was just normal for the locals. The waves are intense, too. I saw a guy get killed on a six-foot wave. It's intimidating at first, but after a couple of weeks you get used to it. The biggest stuff I rode was at Sunset, Backyards, Outside Velzyland, Laniakea, and Outside Puena Point. When you're out there in that situation, when building-sized water is moving towards you, there's nothing going through your mind; that's the thrill, it's like dynamic meditation. You're reacting, you have to charge, you have to attack to catch waves. Should I paddle over it? Should I paddle into it? It's just decision processes all the time. It's scary, but it's good. I've gone back years later and seen the guys I used to surf with on the smaller

> Things got pretty wild, Ken reckons — a lot of drugs and disputes. Heavy moments where he was faced with guns and baseball bats . . .

129

days at Rocky Point and Log Cabins, guys who were a few years younger than me, and they're now charging the giant swells on jetskis, and I'm like, yeah, that's so wicked.'

The last time Ken went to Hawaii he found a place changed by the hand of developers. He realised his earlier arrival had coincided with the beginning of the end, when Hawaiians still lived in the traditional spots, before they were pushed into Pearl Harbor City because they couldn't afford to live in paradise any more. During his visit he only recognised one local Hawaiian at Sunset Beach. He returned to Raglan saddened by what he saw. He rekindled his shaping days and started producing KinaBoys Surfboards. That name, though, would change again when he teamed up with hotshot surfer, Glen Campbell, and together they started Fever Surfboards, a shape on which Glen went on to win the national champs. In his career as a shaper, Ken has produced over 1000 surfboards. While he's retired from supplying the mass market, he'll still shape the odd one every now and then. I suspect it's his way of keeping the embers glowing. Just another avenue for his creativity.

Hawaii was responsible for art entering his life in a way he'd never anticipated. Using a bit of brown paper and some pastels, he did a drawing of the shack they were staying in. He redid it, this time as a painting, using fluorescent surfboard paint. Everyone seemed pretty impressed, so he did few more. When he got back home, Ken approached a mate who had a handcraft store in Hamilton with an old butchery out the back. Ken cleaned up the room, put on an exhibition of his paintings and sold every piece. He had another exhibition, again using surfboard paint, in the Waikato Society of Arts. He was reviewed well, but the writer suggested Ken would be better off using quality paint. At the time, Ken was brimming with creative drive, but he had reservations about whether being an artist could pay full time. 'A good artist friend of mine, Hadley Hodgkinson, helped me out. Back yourself, he always told me, do what you feel like doing, otherwise it'll never come out.'

On the wall of Ken's house are some of his original pieces, still glowing with streaks of fluorescent blues and greens and yellows against black-and-white latex roof paint. These are sentimental to him, stuff he'll never sell. They were painted back in 1988 when he was single and working out of his own graphic design studio in Hamilton. He looks at them now and as an artist he still thinks they're hot. One in particular, the attractive woman at the bar, looking relaxed as she draws longingly on a cigarette buried in her hand, is a poignant representation of Ken's first impressions. It's of Jenny, and it was painted not long after they were introduced to each other by a mutual friend. Ken clicks his fingers — that's how quick they connected. She bought the painting from him; he married her 10 years later. She's got a good eye, he says.

His studio is on the way to the surf. It was a big old barn at one stage. He purchased it and the land it's on before all the area was handed back to the local hapu. He's got a great relationship with them and makes sure the area is looked after. When we turn up, one of Ken's mates is selling plants out of the back of his truck. Ken gives him a vertical handshake and they talk about last night. His mate was in the band playing at the thirtieth and hasn't slept yet, but he'll see Ken in the surf later.

The studio is in various stages of production. At the eastern end is a freshly hung canvas protruding from a background that reflects just how much energy Ken puts into his work. There are slashes of colours, notes to himself, blends and things that filter to the floor then spread around the room, over the rows of paint tins, paintbrushes and beer crates. The place looks like a rainbow has exploded. The walls are covered in a collection of Ken's large paintings, ones done over time. He points to a multi-coloured fish fighting a rod's line that's taken him 10 years so far, that one over there, six hours, that one, 20 minutes, the next one was six years. And all done at night while the rest of Raglan sleeps, so he doesn't get interrupted. There are a lot of curves in each one. It's a pleasure thing, he says, it's nurturing, curves of waves, curves of a woman. And there are plenty of those depicted, mostly naked. Every picture, abstract or not, is derived from real moments, experiences he's had. I look up at the lady sensually bound in black leather strapping standing in the corner of a boxing ring. Yeah, even her.

There are racks of canvases ready to be transformed into a work of art. He hand-makes them all with the highest quality timber and material he can find. They're so tightly bound they have a five-millimetre concave you can't see. Above them is a horizontal bar hanging from some rope, it's a place to hang or do chin-ups. Above that, amongst the rafters, are rows of his old surfboards. Against a wall is a large amp and an electric guitar that he uses to belt out riffs whenever the urge arises. He's got a lot of friends who are good musicians and he enjoys jamming with them, as long as they play in E. Loud, thumping music helps drive his art; he'll crank it up, grab a beer, light a smoke, get pumped and in the mood. Then he'll reach for a brush, mix some paints, and start moving around, making noises, getting sweaty, grinding his brushes into the thick canvas, putting it on, scraping it off, spreading paint residue across the wall behind; for the next six to eight hours it'll be one part art, one part forbidden dance.

After being a full-time artist for an easy 10 years, Ken reckons he hasn't settled on a style yet. Even still, walk into the art gallery in town and it's pretty easy to recognise whose work is for sale on the walls. His art is like a loud rock group playing unplugged; you know there are a lot of gritted teeth behind those grungy blends of colours. It results in images that are quite stirring. 'I still love underground comics, Crumb and all those guys. I like how it's black and white with them, there are no grey areas with some bullshit plot. They don't pull punches. That's what my art's like, it's physical. I use heaps of paint, it's a workout when I do it; the more exhausted I am at the end, the better; they're the ones that come out wicked.'

> Then he'll reach for a brush, mix some paints, and start moving around . . . for the next six to eight hours it'll be one part art, one part forbidden dance.

But it's not the exhaustion that'll stop him. Ken has more bound energy than many fit teenagers. More often than not, it's when he gets interrupted by a phone call, or a friend calling in after hearing the bass and seeing the barn's yellow light in the night, that he'll look back at the work and suddenly the painting's finished. If the visitor is there he'll ask them if they think it's completed. Yeah? Sweet then. 'All my friends are creative people, so they give me a lot of inspiration. I get off on their energy, whether they're builders, drainlayers, sculptors, they're all the same kind of person. They inspire me, how they get on with life, without the egos. I don't like to call myself an artist. I tell people I'm just a painter. Most artists I've met tend to be flaky, have a sense of self-importance, with some sort of problem. I'm definitely not the tortured artist type, my art celebrates life; it has a dark side, but it still celebrates it.'

Ken moves between an existence of solitude and being surrounded by family and friends. This is how he rolls. His surfing is no different. Often he'll wait until everyone else has gone in, and as the first stars start to show in a sunless sky above Manu Bay, he'll paddle into the final wave of the day and soul arch it to the beach, old school style. But surfing stimulates social interaction as well, he says. You learn manners real quick, although he admits now that he's the old man out there he's conveniently forgotten this and takes most waves he wants. That's the right he's earned. 'I hated the old guys that did that to me, but that's the natural law of surfing. If you're cheeky or say something stupid you're gonna get a smack in the head. So you soon learn how to deal with other people, how to get what you want without upsetting others, and those are good life skills to learn.

'Surfing demands great physical dexterity, it can be an intense and competitive situation. It keeps you fit like nothing else. It's so natural, you're immersed in something that's not man-made for a change. You're not on some rugby field, you don't have to look at a bloody ugly house or hear cars going past. As soon as you hit the water, even on a city beach, half of the world is natural,' he says, extending his arms out sideways, 'you can't see any other human when you're out the back, you're isolated, you're in the wilderness. You're straight away involved with the planet. You're in contact with the infinite. Most people can't justify doing that, they're so busy doing what they think they should be doing, they don't know how to make time to become one with the world. Sitting around between sets would seem unproductive to most, but they don't get the implications or the essence of doing that. For me, it's that connection I make. I guess that's the way creativity works, letting that power flow through you 'cause you're connected.'

She's a woman, Ken says of the ocean, a grin and a nod of his head accompanying the statement, like he knows I know what he's talking about. Everything a woman does, he continues, the ocean does; she can be just as sensual, but if you're not using all your wits, she'll do ya over. The grin turns to laughter and I find myself joining in. So how bad did she do him? He'd been held under by many a wave in the past, but none of them could compare to the big day he had at Hawaii's Sunset Beach. He was fit, experienced, island savvy and his confidence tank was bulging. Yet when he paddled into a giant wave that was finally hitting land after days of unhindered travel, he found himself being pitched over the falls. He watched the reef 20 feet below start approaching as man and surfboard were thrown into a freefall like they were merely floating debris. Suddenly, what he thought he had on land didn't count for shit. 'I didn't expect it to be so black down there,' he says, describing what it was like being driven so deep underwater by such a powerful force. 'I'd never been held down like that before, it was so unfamiliar. I just kept getting drilled further below and I couldn't work out what was up and down. I started thinking this could be it, so I relaxed, sorta let go, and accepted now was my time.'

But while his body twisted and somersaulted through the darkness, he hung in there, and as the hurricane conditions outside his body mellowed, his survival instincts suddenly kicked in. He started swimming in a direction he hoped was the surface. His head broke through and he took in one supersized portion of air while another wave, just as big, began falling directly above him. Again he was driven down. 'I didn't get much time to get a breath because I was puffing so much. When you're out in the big surf it's such a workout that when you eat shit you're already out of breath. Go for a run for a hundred metres or so and see how long you can hold your breath for, it's damn near impossible, maybe a second or two. That's what happens when you're surfing and you're working hard at it. It's actually exciting when faced with that challenge.'

Moments like that have helped build Ken's foundations of appreciation for life. But it seems throwing himself into physical challenges is the way he's always been. He was in the local pub when he was talked into playing rugby — he was 31 at the time. Someone else talked him into playing league, so he did that a few times. His coach would tell him he was soft, so he got harder. For the next 11 years he became a regular starter, until one Saturday his leg snapped the wrong way. The coach reckons he almost threw up when he witnessed it from the sideline.

Then there's the small X-ray image of an elbow joint held together by seven large screws, which is pinned to the wall of his studio. Ken's still recovering from smashing his elbow into pieces while keeping up with Jimmy as they snowboarded down Treble Cone last winter. He admits the steep section was way over his ability, but he managed to stick it anyway and was riding out when a gust of wind knocked him off course and he lost control. He made it to Dunedin hospital with a couple of codeines from the ski field's first aid kit. That's a hell of a lot of pain, he thought, looking down and expecting to see bone through skin; something had better be broken 'cause I shouldn't be grovelling like this. He found out afterwards that he'd snapped his radial head into four different pieces and the surgeons had done their best to screw it all back together again. A few months later, though, and his movement was still restricted, so he found the best specialist in the business and asked him what could be done. 'He wanted to chop it off and stick a titanium one in, but I'd have to put up with replacing it every few years when the cartilage wore out. So I went to another specialist — his business card had a skeleton on it — he said, nah, we'll have a little tutu first, if you can't live with it we'll have another operation before the titanium. His reputation could take a dive with that decision, but I was impressed because he was keen to see if we could get it back working as naturally as possible. He had that waxhead attitude, there was no ego; if it works, we won't go any further. It's good now.' He moves his arm to demonstrate. 'I should be back snowboarding next year.'

'Surfing demands great physical dexterity, it can be an intense and competitive situation. It keeps you fit like nothing else.'

With his arm out of action for 12 months he had to find some way of providing for the family, as well as quenching his creative surges. Years earlier, Ken had started Backdoor Surf in Hamilton before selling it for two grand. He takes me to the side of his studio and into a large room that he's converted into a very tidy and well-presented surf store, packed full of product. He's drawn upon his experience and is selling his own brand, Mountain Surfers clothing, using his own print designs done locally in Raglan. He's had quite a bit of interest from other stores, both in New Zealand and abroad. The shop has turned into a range of possibilities for him and his family; it's a place for Jimmy to work in his holidays, it's an avenue to start selling his KinaBoys Surfboards again, and most importantly, it helps sponsor his art. Most artists in the country rely on another source of revenue — the dole, a grant, a rich partner — but Ken's confident the shop will do well enough to make getting food on the table that much more of a reality. There's also Rockit Records, a music label he's started on the side. He has local indie band, The Clap, signed on. He co-produced the video for them, did some animation, and filmed it entirely inside the art studio, complete with cameos by himself. He's tapped into YouTube and MySpace and it's now watched by thousands of people worldwide.

But now that his arm's back in action, he's busy chewing through a thick file of ideas and inspirations. Already he's produced 16 pieces, with more in the pipeline, each one as diverse as the next. While he hasn't settled on a style, painting to a market is definitely not what he's into, and he's staunch when he tells me he'll paint what he likes. He has to out of necessity, it keeps both him and his art fresh. 'You've gotta do what you like doing, not what you think other people like, otherwise it backfires on you every time. That's a lifelong battle with anything creative based.'

So what is he afraid of? Not much these days, he finally answers. It seems everything he does, every situation he finds himself in, Ken is driven by his confidence to succeed, or break himself trying. 'Beauty has its own integrity, it's inspiring. If you recognise beauty, you can back yourself and do

'Do I go for that wave or wait for the next, it doesn't matter. Take that approach to life and nothing's gonna disappoint you.'

anything you like 'cause you know you can tackle anything. Likewise, surfing sets you up for life because you have to make these snap decisions. There's no right one or wrong one, it's just a decision. Do I go for that wave or wait for the next, it doesn't matter. Take that approach to life and nothing's gonna disappoint you. You'll be at peace. That connection, everyone has it, it's whether you make the time to be aware of it or not. Most people have those days where everything happens, a lucky day, but for some people it happens all the time. It's not a coincidence, it's your personal power, you're letting it happen, you're not controlling it, it's just happening for you. Someone walking in when that painting needs to finish, ringing someone up and they've already arrived at the front door. You can get your life to a stage where that's happening twenty-four hours a day, but if you're worried all weekend about getting to work on Monday morning, then you're not going to notice those things. That's where surfing clears the head. It doesn't matter what sort of day it is, raining, sunny, onshore, perfect, you always come in feeling really good, you're stoked, it's so uplifting. You've washed your sins away.'

Nick Toa

Aaron Topp

SCULPTOR
WAITARA

'The energy of Nick Toa.' Sounds like something out of Hollywood, huh? The next summer blockbuster, full of special effects, overpaid actors, and a seat-pulling promo campaign leading into some exorbitant premiere where the leading actor does something the weekly magazines can't get enough of, embedding the movie once and for all in the part of your brain that controls Friday nights.

Its sequel well underway before it makes its first million.

Spin-off toys. Video game.

Happy Meal tie-in.

It could be all this, but it isn't.

Instead, it's a story about Nick Toa, resident of the seaside town of Waitara, North Taranaki. A place steeped in a history spanning hundreds of years, complete with scenic river of the same name, golf course, police station, and two car dealerships. An east side and a west side. A town flanked by two orphans left over from the Muldoon 'Think Big' movement of the 1980s: the nearby decommissioned Motunui gas plant and the Methanex gas plant further up the fertile valley. A close-knit community of just over 6000, bonded together through its love of sport and the proud Te Ikaroa-a-maui meeting house, found on the historical Manukorihi Pa.

The day I rolled into town, Waitara didn't feel too vibrant. This being my first visit, I'd taken a wrong turn off the main trunk line and found myself navigating its residential streets. For a mid-Sunday morning there wasn't much activity, no kids on bikes, no dads mowing lawns. Just a cat perched on a fence post following me with its eyes. The overcast sky was keeping everything in a state of greyscale. The wind was blowing in gusts. The Waitara bar was flat.

When I pulled up at the Toa residence, things started to change.

I stood outside the gateway gazing up at the giant figure inside the property, his rust-coloured head clashing against the blue starting to show in the broken cloud. It looked like a shrine left by some lost culture that'd discovered metal, a god of some description maybe, or perhaps a keeper. Its massive hands were at rest in prayer position at its chest, while socketless eyes watched for something to the east. Later I'd find that it's purposely facing this direction to greet the rising sun, to capture the energy and transmit it to the viewer. And strangely, that's how I felt, invigorated in its presence. It would be my first foray into the energy of Nick Toa.

Nick has spent his whole life in Waitara. He was brought up on the west side of town immersed in the staunch codes of rugby and league and boxing. He excelled at all three, with some of his family expecting him to follow in the steps of Waitara's many sporting heroes who've claimed national honours. As far as surfing went, that wasn't something he discovered until he got to intermediate school and began hanging out with the east side boys who had a monopoly on the surf club and the river bar. All their hyped-up talk of surfing appealed to Nick. That winter he found himself down on the beach with his new mates, surfing in his rugby jersey, and afterwards laughing around the bonfire they used to thaw themselves out. He was hooked. 'I got a milk run and saved money to buy a board, but I wasn't game enough to take it home,' recalls Nick. 'I had to hide it at my friend's house, and sneak down to the beach to use it. I eventually stopped playing rugby, I stopped playing league and I became a full-on surfer. When my father found out I'd quit those sports to focus on surfing he went ballistic; he thought surfers were drug addicts and losers.' Heading inside I pass a quiver of boards lying on the lawn by his front door. They're stacked on top of each other like they're used so much it's no use storing them properly. Nick tells me his teenage sons Jaemyn and Logan have turned into mad surfers; he's nodding his head, stoked, proud that he introduced them, and daughter Haylee, to the sea early in their lives.

'I eventually stopped playing rugby, I stopped playing league and I became a full-on surfer.'

At an age where many men are starting to let themselves go, at 44 Nick reminds me of those well-proportioned gymnasts in the Olympics. He looks like the sort of guy who could bound into a back flip at any moment, or lay you flat with a lightening right hook. He's got a firm handshake and a big smile behind that thin goatee of his. And he's got a habit of laughing after each sentence — a release of nervous energy, perhaps — which just emphasises that smile again. He's like a compressed spring with stored impetus.

We sit around the family dinner table and talk while his children make cameo appearances. Nick's first memories of surfing are still vivid. 'I can remember paddling out and catching my first white wash, just bellying it in. All of a sudden I was aware of this energy in the ocean where I didn't need a motor to drive, or wind to push you. I've tried kite surfing and windsurfing, but they don't compare. Doing radical manoeuvres and tube riding to me is secondary to that energy source. I've pinned it down to that source you're tapping into, that's what attracts me. Now I've transferred that awareness of energy into my artwork.'

As a kid, art was just something in which Nick had an interest. He'd always be drawing in his textbooks or scribbling something for his own enjoyment. As for sculpting, he was raised by a father who encouraged Nick and his four brothers to use his tools and understand their purpose. Nick used to create models out of objects or Plasticine. As he got older, he started to take more notice of his famous uncle, Darcy Nicholas, and the paintings he was producing, fascinated by the way the images could spark emotion. He bottled that observation and decided he'd come back to it one day to try to understand it. But for now there was no use wasting his youth on an old man's activity like art. While he had physical and athletic abilities he was going to savour the moment. He put that plan in his head and carried on going hard.

'He reached into his pocket, pulled out a wad of cash, and gave it to me. He said he'd take another hundred when I had the time.'

As Nick matured through grommethood, he got to hang out with some of the older crew. They were a hardcore group of surfers who lived and breathed the surfing ethos. They'd let Nick ride in the back as they journeyed down to the reef breaks south of New Plymouth. It was here the boys from Waitara created a reputation as the heaviest crew on the coast. 'We'd turn up at Stent Road and everyone would get out of the water. They'd never argue with us, they treated us like we were a gang. You'd regularly see guys getting punched up. I was just a grommet thinking, oh, God. But thankfully you don't see that any more, it was a totally different world to today. I'm not into localism, never have been, and I'd never indulge in that violence. A couple of gang members here who surf, they leave all that culture on the beach and we treat them like everyone else. These days it doesn't matter where you're from, if you're out there surfing, it's all sweet.' Nick was brought up on a marae from birth to 16, when his grandparents died. He was raised to appreciate Te Whiti and his preaching of the philosophies of Raukura (the three feathers), meaning: glory to God, peace on earth, and goodwill to all mankind. 'The elders sat us down, pointed a finger and told us we had to live by that. If they ever caught you fighting then they'd pull you over by the ear and give you a good growling, just to keep reminding you.'

Back in the 1990s, Waitara was a breeding ground for national surfing champions. Nick was hanging out with a couple of them, Jason Mathews and Pipi Ngaia, who used to take the piss out of Nick's strange, yet powerful, surfing style. As time went on, however, he was talked into entering a few comps and ended up beating them in a couple, something he holds as his surfing milestone to this day. 'From there I ended up doing the contest circuit thing and the old Pro Ams around the country. After a while I worked out that's where you can achieve glory for yourself, but it's not the real thing that was attracting me to surfing. I still do the odd contest here and try to win, but I'm really going into them now just to be a part of the social side of it.'

Nick became a qualified fitter and welder, a job in high demand around the oil and gas fields in the area, and continued throwing himself into sports that satisfied his desire to be challenged. It was here that Nick claimed Taranaki and Auckland welterweight titles in boxing, even building his own ring behind the house out of scrap pieces of metal welded together. It's got a movie set feel to it, like you're walking into some gladiator scene. It has a couple of boxing bags and there are weights lying on the floor. Thick rope, like the kind you'd find attached to a giant barge in a wharf, is wrapped around four poles, forming a miniature ring, perfect for teaching his boys the sport. Nick says they're showing a lot of promise; they only know one direction, forward. It's the sort of thing every male wants on their back lawn, but that most haven't got the balls, or energy, to build. Nick laughs coyly when I ask what his wife Janeen thinks. She 'accepts' it. These days, Nick focuses more on coaching boxing in the gym at Bell Block up the road, only getting back in the ring to spar with the older guys. It's all a part of the aging process and the passing of wisdom. And it's here the next chapter of his life began, when at the age of 38 Nick felt his knees creaking and aches and pains started to appear in new places.

It was time.

Nick quit his job and enrolled in a Bachelor of Visual Arts Degree at the Western Institute of Technology in Taranaki (WITT). His thinking was simple; if he was going to give this art thing a decent go, then it was worth doing it properly. The course would save him 20 years of trial and error.

Nick naturally thought that painting was where his calling was and forced himself to give two-dimensional work a go. But he admits, no matter what mediums he used, he never felt satisfied with what he was doing. He soon found something else that rang true. 'I liked the three-dimensional work, where I could walk around it. From one creation I can feed another ten works off it. To me it seems more real, if I paint it's merely an illusion on a flat space, and you're just tricking people. A sculptor is more honest, what you see is what you get.'

With a family to support, taking himself away from his financial security blanket was a gutsy move. Especially when Janeen was training to be a teacher as well. There were times when Nick would sit on the couch, feeling the emotional weight of the bills pinned together by a magnet on the fridge, and wonder what the hell he was going to do. Surfers have a reputation for being cruisy, go-with-the-flow types of people. That's fine if you're having a couple of beers with one on a Sunday arvo, but even Nick knew the businesses in his bill pile weren't likely to be run by a bunch of laidback surfers. Still, Nick has always lived his life around one golden rule: when life is getting difficult, he'll just tell himself that it'll be all right, and somehow it always is. The next day he was flicking through the paper looking for part-time work when he came across an ad: rock carvings wanted, cash up front. He got on the phone and the voice on the other end told Nick to come around with what he had. Nick took his only two pieces in. The buyer was interested, but laughed when he found he was looking at the only two in existence; he needed a hundred, and he needed them by tomorrow. 'I was so hard up that I told him I'd be back, same place, same time tomorrow. I worked all night and all the next morning. I turned back up with the hundred, and said, there ya go mate, a hundred of them. He didn't believe I could do it. I said, now you know I don't talk crap, mate, maybe we could do some more business? He reached into his pocket, pulled out a wad of cash, and gave it to me. He said he'd take another hundred when I had the time. I went straight back home and started again.'

Now that that period of his life is behind him, Nick has gone back to his trade, working on the gas plants in the area, including on the rig offshore, where he stays for two weeks at a time. 'I think it's good to do art without money becoming a driving force. Using art to support a family, I learnt that it can take you to a really sad place if that's all you're doing it for. I feel like I'm selling myself and my art out if I make money my main agenda. My art fire will

Justin Summerton surfing Aramoana. *Gisiele Alves*

Murdering Bay, Otago
by Justin Summerton.

Justin Summerton. *Aaron Topp*

Hobbit Island by Justin Summerton.

Ben Galbraith at home in Wainui. *CPL*

Ben Galbraith in the 'dungeon'. *Brennan Thomas*

'New Wave' billboard.

From *Every Second Friday*, illustrated by Ben Galbraith. *Brennan Thomas*

Daisy Day.

Craig Levers.

Craig Levers surfing Samoa.
Digga

Aaron Kereopa. *Aaron Topp*

Surf blanks into art:
(above) *UFO Fish* and (left)
Time Machine Surfboard
by Aaron Kereopa.
Toi o Tahuna Gallery

Ian King. *Brian Herlihy*

Ian King 'firing up' on stage.

Andrew Forrester and his son,
Jordan. *Aaron Topp*

Ken Thomas. *Aaron Topp*

The Outsides by Ken Thomas.

The Wardrobe
by Ken Thomas.

The Quiet Winter by Ken Thomas.

Nick Toa and 'Steel Man'.
Aaron Topp

Pauanui Point by Tony Ogle.

Surf Pals by Tony Ogle.

Tony Ogle surfing Ahipara. *Brian Herlihy*

Tony and Elena Ogle with their
sons, Luke and Jamie.
Tony Ogle

Rob Baker. *Aaron Topp*

Limestone creations by Rob Baker. *Rob Baker/Aaron Topp*

Jess Santorik. *Aaron Topp*

Jess Santorik in her 'backyard'. *CPL*

Daryn McBride and his triplets, Lennox, Harper and Willow. *CPL*

The Domain by Daryn McBride.

Beneath the Mist
by Daryn McBride.

Daryn McBride competing on the national longboarding circuit. *CPL*

Damon Meade on assignment filming.

Surf art by Damon Meade.

Peter Lambert at Rocky Lefts. *Aaron Topp*

Graveyards
by Peter Lambert.

Arawhata
by Peter Lambert.

Andrew McAlpine with
the original waterproof
housing for his camera.
Aaron Topp

Matt Hishon surfing Tairua. *Cory Scott/New Zealand Surfing* magazine

Raglan through Matt Hishon's eyes.

Fran Kora. *Aaron Topp*

Fran Kora surfing in Indonesia. *Miles Ratima*

Dr Dave Jenkins receives the inaugural SIMA Humanitarian of the Year award from Liquid Nation Ball co-founder and SurfAid USA board member Santiago Aguerre. *Courtesy SurfAid*

Dr Dave Jenkins with a mother and her malnourished, anaemic baby and SurfAid staff.
Bob Barker/RovingEye.com

Dr Dave Jenkins with villagers of Betumonga, Mentawai Islands.
Bob Barker/RovingEye.com

die out if I do that, and I'd probably end up just redoing what I know sells. I'd go stale.' Now that his natural ability as an artist has official recognition, Nick can let his art foster without the extra pressure. Already the community has recognised his abilities as a hands-on artist, while his soulful nature and holistic approach has brought commission work, in particular for the highly sensitive act of creating headstones for past loved ones. 'I sit the people down, find out what the deceased was about, then go and digest that through my creative process, then sculpt something out. After it's done I show the family members the result and they often start crying because it's so close to what they think the deceased would've liked. It comes down to the energy you feel when you look at the object, not what you see. The mauri is what I've been deeply investigating. That looks like a tree, but what's the feeling you get from it? Visually is not important, it's what you're feeling when you look at it. What's its energy?'

. . . the energy he talks of is the undiscovered energy, the impossible yet alluring mystical realm of faith, the energies of the unknown . . .

Nick explored this concept deeply while he worked on his degree. Relying on concepts like mauri, or wairua — roughly defined as a vessel holding a particular kind of energy — he could perceive the art from a variety of angles and create a more holistic image of the work. This is most apparent in his carvings, where he uses extensive use of the spiral as a symbol of energy — it represents 'that which is intangible into a comprehensible dimension'. Nick says the energy he talks of is the undiscovered energy, the impossible yet alluring mystical realm of faith, the energies of the unknown that can only be tapped into by believing (or assuming) in them, then having faith in that belief.

If you're confused, you're not alone. In day-to-day life we're moving fast, we're working to deadlines, we're driving at 100 kilometres an hour, we're surfing our 80 channels at 10 seconds a push. In many respects we've lost our ability to look at something and marvel. The Eiffel Tower, the pyramids, the Sky Tower (to an extent) were all designed to radiate energy to the viewer, to emulate the feelings we get from a majestic vista, a mountain stream or a kauri tree. You know that feeling when you see something that makes you pause in your tracks? You're not able to define why, but something powerful radiating from it is stimulating emotion. Nick's training in that phenomenon climaxed with the building of the giant at his gateway — the 4-metre-high 'Steel Man', as he calls it. Its body is made up of hundreds of pieces of scrap metal, welded together and giving an effect like bark on a tree. 'I think about where the products have come from before I use them. Each one of those pieces on the Steel Man has special significance. It was an off-cut left from the engineers at WITT, all handled by young men making their start in the world. I used those because I knew they've already put all their creative energy into doing what the instructor wanted, so the pieces still have that energy in it. Their mauri has carried through.'

Nick's eyes are always searching for inspiration. Looking for that next thing that makes him pause and think of the possibilities.

To demonstrate this more, we drive to Nick's gallery in town. He tells me it's a work in progress as he unlocks a door in the main street, bending down to pick up the pile of mail that's accumulated on the floor. He did six months' work in the space of three in here, often sleeping the night in the shop. He's now transformed the derelict store into a cave of industrial metal; rectangular and oval pieces meshed together aesthetically to form walls and archways that curve towards you like you're in the intestine of a giant machine. That's one way of describing it. Nick designed this place to evoke analogies like this, to make the viewer a participant in the process. In the future, people will come here to look at the art inside the art. 'I rolled some feathers in class once because someone said they didn't care whether anyone saw their art or not. I said that they were effectively masturbating, doing it on their own for their own pleasure. That was a big debate. After that the viewer became a big topic in class, and how they can be included in your art. How you can manipulate their emotions. That's why I try and get how they feel about my art, not just how they view it.'

He shows me a mask he once carved. It looks Maori or Polynesian, from one angle it could be Celtic; it's actually a hybrid of many cultures, he tells me. Out of all his work, he'll never part with that one. Across the wall and positioned as a feature amongst the strands of metal is a similar-styled face peering down at me. It's carved from pounamu. It lights up fluorescent green with the flash of the camera. There are limestone carvings and more of those small pieces of work he used to decrease the strain on the bill-laden magnet on the fridge. All have distinctive South Pacific styles to them. Nick is of Te Atiawa and Maniapoto descent, but resents the label of Maori artist just because of what he looks like. Maori art was drilled into him from a young age. He spent a lot of his time on his marae, which has always been respected throughout the country for its immaculate and detailed carvings. 'As a kid I'd look at those and feel power from them. I guess that's when it was instilled into me. No one told me what each one meant, so the fascination has remained. Once someone explains their relevance, then my appreciation will be placed in a box with everyone else's. They put a spell on you, you're stuck there. I'm not a Maori artist, that's someone who has been shown every notch and curve and how that translates in Maori terms. Some Maori play on it because Maori art is selling really well overseas, but that's not my approach. My art is a hybrid of traditional Maori and contemporary art. It's a result of how I've lived my life. To come up with something else would mean forcefully removing myself from it all, but I couldn't do that. You don't just say, I want to scoop the whitewash from that wave because it doesn't suit. I just want to go with the flow like a surfer, and it's the same with my perception. I'm an artist, that's it.'

We make our way over to the Waitara Board Riders Club, one of the oldest surf clubs in the country. A two-foot wave has arrived and is peeling along the submerged sandbank — a couple of groms are already paddling out the river in anticipation of something bigger building. Nick points to one of the large rocks lining the river outside the WBRC building. He tells me about the time he was pulled over and charged for not having his Warrant of Fitness renewed. Being a poor student he couldn't afford the fine, so he found himself facing community service. What did he do? He offered his time to the clubrooms in the form of a carving. It has the face of a tiki, with a mouth partially buried in the earth. He says it represents how the Queen's laws are consuming tangata whenua. He laughs at the irony he's created. Not that he's bitter about it; quite the opposite actually. 'My grandmother was in charge of our iwi. I remember her saying to me as a youngster, look, forget our old ways, they're gone, there's no use for them in a Pakeha world. Being a Maori to her was all about remembering who you are, your whakapapa, and where you're from. You recognise those, she'd tell me, then you don't need to know anything else. This country has just been a progression of people arriving, Pakeha are just as much part of the time continuum as Maori, that's what she was saying. I get scorned often for suggesting Pakeha are just another iwi that came to New Zealand. But if we can accept that, then it would help with racial relationships.'

You can tell Nick's eyes are always searching for inspiration. Looking for that next thing that makes him pause and think of the possibilities. I ask if he ever finds the creative reservoir empty, but he shakes his head firmly. 'I'm always creating things. It doesn't have to be art-related, either. I see boxing as a creative thing. I'll try throwing a punch in a weird way just to try and be creative. Out in the surf I'll try doing a manoeuvre in a strange way just to try and be creative. I'll give things a go to see how it feels. I do it all the time. Everything I do is about being creative. It's a way of life. I don't like to fall into routines. Even at work I get into trouble because I'm constructing modules for sites, and my peers tell me they've been doing it for thirty years one way, but I come up with a new, more efficient way, and the boss goes, what are you doing? That's not the way! I find that fascinating how people get stuck in their ways like that. Then they become blind with their blinkers on and refuse to change anyway, when to me change is a way of improving yourself. Without change you just become stagnant and die.'

Nick once created a series of waves carved in limestone. Naturally everyone figured he was exploring the connection between wave riding and sculpting, cliché surf art. But Nick would fold his arms, shake his head, and urge them to 'look a little deeper, mate'. They still didn't get it. They probably won't. But on explanation it becomes quite obvious. During his study, Nick was thinking about the waves of energy from the sun, and how some pass through the earth. Then one day a mate told him about the day he was on the main street of Opunake when an earthquake hit, and he watched a wave roll up it, moving cars and rubbish bins, just like a wave in the sea would. That image stuck with Nick. That's what the sculptures were about, how the land itself can form a wave. Nick pauses, then sits forward suddenly with a look of inspiration — what if you could ride an earthquake on a skateboard? We explore the possibilities for the next five minutes, Nick driving the conversation the whole way, eventually concluding that, yeah, you probably could.

On the really big swells that pound the Taranaki coast, Nick would tie his gun to the roof of his car and venture down Opunake way, the stereo the only thing keeping him company. He'd drive past the popular reef breaks with the knowledge they'd be reduced to massive lines of whitewater, to the only place on the coast that could handle a 10-foot wave, Mangahume. While people would arrive to sit safely on its shore and amaze at the raw power of the waves cracking like thunder, Nick would sit on the end of his car bonnet and observe its personality, to calculate the groundswell's pulse; watching how each set would have a wave that broke rank and made its own rules. Then he'd silently get into his wetsuit and wade into the water until the power of the white foam around him made it too difficult to walk any further. The spectators would watch the man on a toothpick begin paddling towards the rolling mountains of ocean. 'You take the risks during those times, but you take on a sense of empowerment as well, throwing your life to the luck of the gods. Surfing is a form of escape. I've toned my attitude down a bit with my age,

'I've been taught some big lessons by the ocean, mainly when I'm pinned on the floor and wondering if I'm going to get back up to the surface.'

but back in the day I'd always aim for the biggest spot on the coast at the time. You can chuck your board in the car and find a break where you're completely alone. I've been taught some big lessons by the ocean, mainly when I'm pinned on the floor and wondering if I'm going to get back up to the surface. The sky always seems brighter and the birds louder when you do. Nothing like a near-death experience to appreciate life. No one can call surfers chickens, because you won't get anywhere surfing if you're not confident. Surfing is just as scary, just as thrilling, just as hard as rugby, but you don't get injuries, concussion, or limp around for a few weeks like on the field.'

Although the big-wave charging days are behind him, when he can he'll still take on a solid Stent Road to keep the thrill alive. Something that hasn't died is the feeling he has for surfing, the one that was sown as an 11-year-old. As an adult, there have been times where his job has meant weeks away from his board. 'When I'm away on work projects I get grumpy. Every second thought is about the ocean, and when you finally get into it that energy absorbs me. Other surfer mates have talked to me about how they feel when they come out of the surf, like a battery that's been recharged. It's an addiction and the addiction gets satisfied.'

Back at his house we walk past a metal mosquito the size of large dog. Nick's work always has some sort of environmental element to it that relates back to the land. This one, he says, represents the local oil industry; like a giant bloodsucker it burrows into the land, takes the earth's black blood, then flies somewhere else to do it again. 'Surfers are environmentally aware. We're always looking at those sorts of things, whereas Joe Blow in the office in some high-rise, they're oblivious to it — out of sight, out of mind. A surfer's voice is valid, it has to be. Surfers should be one of the first groups approached when looking for it because we're there, we're often wallowing around in it. When you're seeing all sorts of things coming out the river here you hate the fact that it's happening. Sometimes the smell is overpowering.

'That's where local groups like the Black Sand crew take a stand. Around here they're prolific. All the key surfers and us older crew are backing it. As a consumer, we need to make them accountable to come up with alternatives or more restrictions. Same with the oil companies — they want to come in, suck it up and leave. They have to adhere to the restriction the public put in place. I'm a practical environmentalist. I admit we all do things that aren't necessarily good for the environment, but I'm into keeping pollution to a minimum.' Nick sculpted a huge carving out of a bank down on the red sandstone at the beach one day. The block had sat there for years and years and he'd always wanted to carve it. Finally, he took some tools down and made a massive carving on it to celebrate the foreshore and seabed debate. 'Within a week afterwards, the hikoi went to Wellington, the legislation came through, and the ocean came in and took the carving away. How fitting.'

As I leave Waitara to begin the five-hour journey back to the east, I think about how Mark Twain once said: 'And what is a man without energy? Nothing, nothing at all.' I think of the last few hours with Nick, a surfer living in the middle of one of the country's energy sources, creating pieces of art that convey their own energy, someone who has a personal energy that's somehow attached itself to me, and I think, yeah, that old Yankee bastard's right: the energy of Nick Toa. I turn the stereo up and settle into my seat. A bright orange light reflected from the rearview mirror sends a band across my eyes. I look up to see the sun dropping towards the Tasman, leaving Waitara to rest, for now. Early tomorrow it will be back, casting new energy across the land.

And Nick and the Steel Man will be there when it does.

Tony Ogle

Aaron Topp

ARTIST
AUCKLAND

I'm sitting opposite Tony Ogle in a stylish café somewhere near the industrial area of Onehunga. The place has been converted from an old library and has retained the shelves of books lining the walls so that people can browse while they wait for their coffee. It's a perfect backdrop to talk about literary matters, and inevitably we do; he's just finished Tim Winton's latest surf novel, Breath, *and was impressed by how well the Australian author encapsulated the spirit of surfing.*

'It's an activity that leaves you with an indelible impression, because it's special,' Tony says. 'We're not particularly special people, but we do a special thing. That's what I like to think of surfing as, something that's uniquely common between us.'

As the waiter places our orders on the table I move one of the books I'd brought with me to make room, and notice his eyes scanning its cover. His face glows. 'Big waves, huh?' he says, pointing to the cover image. 'What's the biggest surf you guys ever been in?' he asks. Tony and I barely have time to shrug our shoulders and start making hand gestures before he's cutting in again. 'I was on the great Astrolabe reef of Kendavi, a hundred miles south off Suva's biggest island, on a twenty-one foot boat, flying six hundred feet straight down in fourteen-metre surf. I was inside the barrel at dead low tide. Ended up spending twenty days on water, had to swim ashore, first one to survive in five hundred years.' He turns and begins walking away. 'It was phenomenal stuff,' he lets us know over his shoulder.

'I could feel the surge, feel the energy, I was tapping into it. There was excitement and fear in trying to control that.'

Tony uses the moment to make his point. 'Isn't it funny how the waiter saw the picture of the wave and felt he had to express? Surfing becomes an important component of our lives like that.' He looks back in the direction the waiter went, smiles, and shakes his head. On this occasion, however, we agree there's probably a connection between the waiter and recreational drugs.

Tony Ogle spent his adolescence in or close to the sea. He describes his preliminary training as being the son of a keen boatie who'd take him and his brother out water-skiing or exploring the Hauraki Gulf. Living on Auckland's North Shore, he'd swim at Campbells Bay where his grandmother lived, or Milford. At other times he'd take to any one of the pristine beaches in the Bay of Islands where his family often holidayed. In the winter he'd spend his time as a skilled soccer player while he waited for the warm seasons to draw him back to the ocean. He recalls being 13 and sitting on the sand one summer watching a small group of surfers riding the waves. He still remembers how much fun they were having. It looked so cool. A few days later he got his hands on a surfboard and began the long journey towards learning how to keep the soles of his feet pressed against the thin layer of wax. The foreign sensations, his lack of co-ordination, and the unrelenting power of the sea made for a cocktail of ugliness — he was a million miles from the skilled watermen floating around him. Yet Tony processed all those sensations and savoured each tiny moment of progress. Then finally one day, his life changed forever.

'It was just a rush, standing up. I could feel the surge, feel the energy, I was tapping into it. There was excitement and fear in trying to control that. Suddenly I stopped playing soccer. Summer or winter, I was out surfing.' Tony's telling me all this like it just happened yesterday, but his stoke of surfing has long matured since those early impressions. Now, at the age of 49, Tony finds that surfing has its own niche in his life; it's as normal as seeing his artwork hanging in Helen Clark's office, as comfortable as the skate shoes he's wearing. 'I told someone once that surfing is the epitome of outdoor sports, and they laughed at me. They said, well, you've never tried mountain climbing before. But I've climbed a few cliffs, so I can get an idea. It's difficult to find an activity that matches the purity and simplicity of surfing. Maybe gliding could come close, riding energy waves in the sky? But even then surfing is different, you're so close to the action when surfing, close to the energy. That's what's kept me there all these years.'

Tony left a lasting first impression on me. I'd been told by someone that their art-dealing family member would often talk of the 'charming Tony Ogle'. And I think there's a lot of weight in that description; his tall figure matches his casual suaveness. He speaks in a warm, articulate tone that complements the smile and demeanour that defy his age by decades. Even the well-worn denim-jacket-and-black-sweater combo adds to the whole clean-cut, guy-next-door package. I'm not surprised that one of the females at the table next to us is taking random glances across at him, although that could've been because he's one of the country's most well-known artists. But I doubt it. The thing that left the biggest impression on me, though, was how relaxed he was. Initially, I put it down to two things: one, being an artist, and two, being a surfer. Something that went with the territory. But I soon found Tony's outlook on life these days reflects a philosophy he's had to work hard on in recent years.

Back in 2003, Tony paid a visit to his doctor. He hadn't been feeling well for a while, and some lumps on his neck were beginning to trouble him. After a preliminary biopsy it was confirmed he had a non-aggressive form of lymphatic cancer. Naturally, he was blown away. He started thinking of all the worst things possible when he was presented with the diagnosis. How could it happen to me, he thought, after years of keeping myself so healthy? He was in shock. Over the following few weeks he tried to piece together the puzzle, looking for an answer, or combination of reasons, as to why. He found lymphatic cancer had a high incidence among farmers who use a lot of chemicals, such as pesticides and other sprays. In the past he'd dealt with a lot of cadmium-based colours and hadn't always followed the best practices, often getting paint on his hands or breathing in the fumes. But while that seemed a plausible explanation for this illness, it was just a hunch, and was going to be near impossible to prove.

There was also a deteriorating long-term relationship Tony was dealing with at the time. He and his partner had just built a home together at the beach, amongst nature and overlooking Bethells. Tony was living his dream — a creative life by the sea — but in reality all it did was bring underlying issues between them to a head. She was a city girl at heart. When Tony acknowledged things had to end, he soon realised how hard it was to let everything go and how messy these things can get. The stress set in like a storm.

The cancer is in Tony's lymph glands. It's one of around 15 sub-groups of the type. While Tony hasn't had to take any medication for it, every six months he has to have a CAT scan. 'I've accepted it now,' he says, 'I've tried not to let it get away on my mind too much, and the more I can do that, the better I am, because if it does get away it can work against you. I try and feed as much positiveness into my life as I can subconsciously, because the more I acknowledge it, then the more I give in to it, and the more it's going to be there.' As the initial shock turned to acceptance, he decided to make a few life-changing decisions on where he was going and what he was doing. He started to think about what he was eating, what he drank. He began managing how much stress he was putting himself under. 'I looked at my life, looked within myself and re-evaluated a few things, like how I was relating to people. I think I'm a lot more relaxed person from how I was back then.' At the same time he was invited to a friend's place for a dinner party. There he met an Italian girl, Elena, and found they had plenty of common interests. She was a breath of fresh air, he says, and best of all, she loved Bethells. They were married soon after, and these days they find the location is a fantastic place to raise their two boys, Luke and Jamie. 'I thought I was going to be sick a lot, so for better or worse I threw myself into becoming a parent.' He laughs. 'It just seemed so right with Elena. Underneath all the extra effort and energy you put towards your family, there's a strong sense of positiveness that runs through it. I think in many ways it has made me stronger too, given me something more to live for.' Important too, was his decision not to give up surfing. 'Surfing helped in that period the same way it's always helped me. When I surf I tend to leave any troubles and worries back on land, so for me it was a positive escape from the anxiety of what I'd just been through. When I surf, I appreciate every moment now for how special it is.'

Tony has a far deeper understanding of his body these days, and if something changes he can normally feel it straight away. He's felt lumps come and go, and he knows what symptoms to look out for, like the night sweats that can be a sign of things progressing. The scans don't worry him as much any more, despite them changing from an annual schedule to six-monthly again. He may need chemo in the future, but the important thing is he's mentally prepared for it. It's a slow progression, and the longer he can keep the cancer in a non-aggressive state, the longer he knows there's a chance there will be a new technique or better cure discovered. The changes in his life have all helped, he believes, and that warm tone turns staunch when he tells me it hasn't worsened. In the meantime, all he can do is remain positive. 'I've always been a very positive person anyway, but it's helped me cherish life even more, because none of us know what's going to happen tomorrow. As I said to someone recently, I've just become part of a club nobody wants to belong to, and it's a big club. When you're in it, you begin to realise how many people are affected by it. It makes you appreciate what living's about, that's the one benefit you can say about it. Life is certainly designed to be cherished.'

'It makes you appreciate what living's about, that's the one benefit you can say about it. Life is certainly designed to be cherished.'

Previously Tony would produce six prints a year, but since the diagnosis, he's dialled that back. Working from home, however, has meant the biggest challenge has been managing his work ethic better. It's too easy, he says, to work an eight-hour day, then at night do the book work, or go down the workshop and make wooden canvases. In the weekends, if there isn't surf, he might work through because he can see on the swell report the seas are going to be good later in the week. He acknowledges he has to find a balance, especially now with a family, because there's a table that needs food on it. He realises that ultimately his health is the health of the family. His mental wellbeing is the wellbeing of the family. These days, he doesn't commit to an exhibition every year. He believes he's fortunate that he can supply new print works to various galleries around New Zealand that deal exclusively with him, which helps maintain a regular income and keeps the pressure off. The days of having an art gallery dictate whether or not he can take a winter break with the family are long gone. 'I'm not working to crazy deadlines any more. Back then I'd turn into a madman trying to get things finished. People wouldn't understand why I was so committed, but I have to be, no one else is going to do it for me. I'm not employed by a company, I am the company. I feel very blessed that I can do what I love, especially combining my two passions, surfing and art, together.'

Art was always there for Tony. He describes himself as a kid who just happened to be 'visually aware'. At school he'd have a pencil in his hand in readiness for capturing his surroundings on paper. He became attuned to whatever environment he found himself in, and when he wasn't drawing what was around him, he'd do random stuff, like tracing maps out of atlases because he liked how the shapes of the lines flowed. He became very aware, too, of illustrations in picture books, and how some styles appealed to him more than others. The old Commando comic books were a classic example — certain issues would capture his attention more than others. Looking back as an adult he can see this inherent ability influences the way he sees the world, the way he sees surfing. 'I guess I see things aesthetically. I appreciate things on that level, and surfing to me is highly on that level. I never tire of the beauty of the perfect wave. That's why I like to depict them in my work.' For all the pieces of art he's done with swell in them, Tony admits it's difficult to paint a wave convincingly.

He's had to work hard at it over a long time; there are still plenty of examples in galleries where other artists have tried to do the same, but the result is a wave that looks like a weak ripple. The experience Tony has had of scouring the New Zealand coastline for the last 35 years has meant he's become acutely aware of the change and mood of the weather, a reflection of how his own awareness has evolved over the years. His searches for inspiration over that time, and the reinforcement of his impressions, have dovetailed well for him.

It was only natural Tony would take art classes at high school, despite the school system insisting any student who chose a path that was activity-based would be downgraded academically. In his final year at college he applied for a fine arts course, missed out, but was picked to do a graphic design course instead. He would frequently walk to the fine arts campus over the hill to look in the galleries to keep a foot in the door, whilst he continued with his design studies. Like most young, highly creative people, it didn't take him long to be sucked into the advertising industry. In 1981 he walked through an agency's doors at the same time that the business began losing its biggest clients. Over the next few weeks he watched employees and customers come and go through those same doors, and he sensed the bitter taste of what he'd let himself into. His creative reservoir transformed from a freshly picked plum to a withered prune, as creative control was sucked from him by account managers and ambivalent clients. His proudest achievement was to paint the creative director's beer fridge. A few months later the business folded, and as he left through those doors for the final time he was given $900 redundancy payment. He was stoked. Knowing one thing he didn't ever want to do again, he took his money and his belongings, and headed up to the Bay of Islands with his mate, Tom Burnett, another artist looking for work. They found a place to rent and started doing their own thing; Tony taught himself how to screenprint the landscapes and coastal images around him, in between surfing Sandy Bay and mowing neighbours' lawns to help pay the rent. He was free to do what he wanted, and it felt great.

It was here he did his first successful painting of Matapouri, where they were living. It was an image of the opposing headlands and beautiful crescent bay at the bottom, and above it the same Chinese windfish flying in the sky above the roof of their house. He also produced a screenprint of Great Barrier Island, where he'd surf every year. He produced a few surf-related images and put them up in Wayne Parkes' surf shop, but soon realised surfers couldn't afford them, so he ended up selling them to his friends instead. People warned him he'd be limiting himself and his market by focusing his work on a bunch of no-hoper surfers. Certainly from what he was finding, that was the case. In later years, he decided, stuff it; he wouldn't play to other people's expectations, their limitations of who he should be. He was a surfer, and it was something to be passionate about. If only surfers were going to appreciate his work, then so be it. With no pressure on himself and a clear vision, things progressed quickly; he found the purity of what he was doing crossed over from the surfing realm and into the non-surfing community. He made a couple of prints that showed a lot of promise, one a fictional place he called Pohutukawa Point, and another of Raglan, which he did while on a trip there, a piece, he says proudly, many non-surfers liked. Suddenly, people who'd never felt the raw energy of a wave surge beneath them or the disappointment of finding sand in their wax, were hanging his work in their upmarket homes.

A flash of red pohutukawa, the soft green of the shorebreak, that feeling of familiarity; you've been there before, just not where Tony has.

Twenty-five years later, Tony says that his art pieces trace periods of his life and places he's been. They are a storyboard of his life in some way. Even now, with his high-profile reputation and prolific output, he says he still gets great satisfaction out of people wanting his art in their lives. 'I guess they're not difficult pieces to relate to, I'm not ripping out my soul or trying to be "edgy" — it doesn't work for me. I'm trying to express what is special about it, what impresses me. It's only natural for me to do it. I don't do personal stuff like some artists, but there is going to come a time where I may wish to change my subject matter and even style, maybe do some portraits because I find people interesting. As of yet, though, I haven't had a chance to explore it because people keep asking me how's my next landscape coming along.' But it wouldn't stop at portraits. Tony's inspiration comes from the full kaleidoscope of the art world. It's no surprise to hear him talk fondly of someone like Picasso as an artist he aspires to, someone who could throw his hand at anything art related and pull it off. One day we may see Tony Ogle the draughtsman, the sculptor, the fine art extraordinaire, expressing himself through whatever medium, or period, just happens to take his fancy at the time. We discuss David Hockney, Stanley Palmer and Dick Frizzell. Sometimes he'll look at their work, or be browsing the many art books he has access to, and will acknowledge the diversity and quality of art and he'll become frustrated with what he sees as limitations of his own work. To him, the art universe is an infinite one, and his discovery of stimulating artists only goes to support that theory. It only makes him more excited about expanding his portfolio. And it seems that's where the beauty of surfing comes into it; surf art is already giving him an avenue to explore expansion in a small way. He can experiment with new styles and approaches, because landscape art will always be a constant. 'With surf art I can maybe free it up a bit more, that's why I'm excited about combining the two. As an artist you can get stuck in the same style because everyone expects you to continue that style forever. They don't accept it easily if you start going out on a limb.'

While we discuss his motivation, Tony tells me about someone special up north he used to visit on his way to the surf. 'Even though he was in his nineties, he was still this amazingly creative person. Ross Michie was such a hoot to talk to, his memories of the war and the stories of his life were fascinating. His knowledge of palms and native plants was extensive. Whilst his mates were sitting in some old age home, feet up on footstools, doing crosswords, he'd be sitting in his garage making pots, then painting them. He was so full of vitality. He'd built these massive pots that surrounded the entire property. I used to ask to use his bathroom just so I could go and check out all the interesting stuff inside the house. I did his portrait once, took a photo of it, and sent it to him. He wrote me a letter back before he died, which I still keep behind the painting. I never sold the painting, I never will. He was a huge inspiration to me.'

Tony still thinks his quality is evolving. While his experience and knowledge is driving the improvement, he says that's not always a golden rule. So many artists have warm memories of their original work, rather than feeling good about the one they just completed. 'Sometimes I think my work is too refined, that I should be a little more direct. I like the earlier crude work of some artists because it's less developed. Being an aesthetically motivated person I appreciate the sort of qualities inherent in art, but also how that translates to the world. So I enjoy that awkward-looking surfer, I enjoy watching someone get to their feet for the first time, or [Tom] Curren and [Kelly] Slater do things you think couldn't be done. I expect other people to sit through a surf movie, but not everyone can. They haven't experienced it. Maybe it's like someone getting excited about a golf putt, but for the life of me I can't — it's not quite as exciting as a spinning barrel — now that's a real hole in one! Each to their own though, I guess.'

It goes without saying that Tony's work is some of the most recognisable in the industry. His clever combination of vibrant and pale colours produces art that can excite a room. A flash of red pohutukawa, the soft green of the shorebreak, that feeling of familiarity; you've been there before, just not where Tony has. His style has evolved from the combination of his graphic design training and his love of rich, evocative colour. These days, his work still maintains a strong element of graphic design, something he reckons he'll probably never escape, especially where screenprinting is concerned; creating images with that in mind leads him to be graphic purely by nature, the colours have to stand alone, compared to conventional painting where colours blend together. He does the original work in his studio at home, then takes it to Artrite in Onehunga, Auckland, a specialist screenprinting business, who help produce the limited editions of each series. Tony will make 50 copies of his latest piece, *Te Pahi Beach*, here. To do that, the 21 individual colours he's used must all be painstakingly applied one at a time to each of the 50 prints in one specific order of application. They're listed vertically on a piece of cardboard, a dash of each colour and name beside them, like 'hill green', 'rock brown' and 'wet sand'. Using old-school print-making methods suits Tony more than using the latest technology to pump out limited edition prints. At the end of the day, what Tony does is pre-digital, and is the result of raw effort, skill and judgement. They may be old-fashioned values, but they are ones that have served him well.

Tony keeps an album of ideas and refers to it whenever he needs a bit of help. If something sparks an idea, he'll sketch it down on paper — a hangover from his adolescence — then stick it in the album. Sometimes he'll create something out of a combination of ideas he's recorded, something compositionally strong; a picture of a bach, headland in the background, footprints in the sand. He takes photos, too, if he has his camera handy, but never uses them to work from, just as a guide. Apparently, if you rely on a photograph, it'll look like a photograph. 'When all the pieces fall into place, and I'm looking at an image the next day and still feeling good about it, that's when I know it's coming together. It's that constant feedback from yourself that will assure it works on every level. Sometimes you can feel like you're getting it, try to get it at least, but never actually reach it.' What is working for him constantly though is his website, www.alohapiha.com, a special place on the net dedicated to his artwork. After seeing a few surf artists from overseas doing their own thing, he decided to give it a shot. A few people said it wouldn't work, saying surf art is too niche, but on a global scale, Tony's found the potential is huge. He's sold prints to California, Hawaii, the UK, Chile and Ireland, and to plenty of expat Kiwis. Elena looks after the administration side of it and helps make sure it's always evolving. He was recently picked up by Club of the Waves, a Californian website dedicated to surf artists and photographers. He's now part of an exclusive group of 60 well-respected artists selected from around the world, something of which he's especially proud.

There is something about a Tony Ogle print that highlights just how pristine and pure our beaches look; an image that can teleport the viewer to a New Zealand actually befitting the brand we project to the rest of the world. I ask him if there's an environmental message subliminally implanted in each image. 'I suppose implicitly there is in the beach scenes. I go to unspoilt parts of the coastline to capture that timelessness. I can't help but be drawn to it, it embodies the purity of our landscape. If it's got something manmade, it'll just be an old bach, or something else with character. I try to get people to appreciate the natural beauty.' Tony believes every surfer has empathy with the environment and can tell when it's being compromised. He sees the New Zealand coastline getting more pressures put on it every year, and worries we'll become too complacent, like in California where they've been used to the problem for so long that this generation of surfers has never known anything else. Our biggest advantage, he believes, is seeing it coming. 'We've just got to be aware every activity comes with a side effect. Obviously heavy industry and pristine surf breaks don't go together. Hopefully businesses are now a lot more aware of those implications than they have been in the past. We've reached a point where the environmental movement is at the front of their consciousness and we can mitigate the degradation that's already been caused. It's an easy thing to talk about, but it's a hard thing to convince other people of when people need economies to function. We've got to weigh everything up and be realistic, and hopefully the environmental voice will be a serious part of that. I want my children to experience the same surf I had without having to worry about eye and ear infections, or worse.'

Tony shows me a book he's brought with him to the café, a school exercise book with worn corners — with its faded cardboard cover it looks like every other notebook you would've seen in college during the 1970s. It once belonged to his brother, and still has 'French' written in the subject line, but he gave it to Tony after he failed to get past the first 10 pages. Inside, it's full of the writing of an 18-year-old Tony: notes copied from surf magazines, passages that inspired him or that he felt echoed his feelings about surfing. This is a collection of other people's words on surfing, words that articulated his own less developed feelings at the time. While a lot of it is classic '70s surf philosophy, it's also a prime example of how things can change, yet still remain the same. He reads out a section criticising competitive surfing ('who needs a gang of critical judges to run your life? It's too short to waste time on someone else's self-centred opinion. True self-confidence builds its own charisma'), then moves on to a letter to the editor that resonates true to this day ('no matter what you do, keep surfing. If you get depressed, keep surfing. If you get too excited, keep surfing. No matter what your excesses or problems amount to, keep surfing. Never mind your suffering, never mind about the person who rejected you, or the stereo you can't afford, just keep surfing. Keep surfing to look and feel better. Keep surfing to improve your surfing'). There's also some good stuff from films, like the classic, *Morning of the Earth*, and from renowned figures like Arthur C. Clarke, who compares the progression of humanity to riding a wave. This small exercise book, saved from the French class rubbish bin, has played an important grounding in shaping Tony's philosophy on life. 'Surfing inspires a literary response,' he says, 'and back then I admired those who were able to write about it. Rabbit Bartholomew sums it up really well in here, talking about the bullshit of society, seeing through it all, and defining what really matters to you. I think a lot of surfers will relate to that. In that sense of enlightenment, surfing has become a powerful guide in my life.' And it's taught him his physical and emotional limits; he admits being impatient at times has often affected the outcome. 'The ocean doesn't stop and give you a free pass. You have to go with it, there's no other way, it's always going to be bigger than you. You're a small component in the overall scheme of things, it's just letting you be a part of it for a tiny moment. It's a humbling experience, you're not everything, but it gives you a guideline of where you stand. You realise you've only got so much energy.' He relates knowing his limits in life to that of deciding whether to paddle out for one last wave in big surf, or choosing to catch the next wall of whitewater rushing in. 'I guess it's that philosophy of life, knowing who you are and what you are, understanding yourself. I realise now emotion isn't good for me, I have to calm down and take it in my stride. Don't be so impatient to get things done. Slow down.'

Surfing has given Tony some of the happiest moments of his life. Moments where life seems to be riding its own positive waves of energy. Special moments that can be relived with a simple closing of the eyes, or while sitting in a library-turned-café. Moments like the time Tony and a couple of mates scored perfect Makarori Point in Gisborne. After his session, he came back to the Holden parked above the break, flicked on the CD player, and as he lay on the bonnet feeling the warm sun and light offshore breeze dry his skin, Eric Clapton's classic 'Layla' and the remaining surfers below became knotted together in a stunning display of synchronicity. It was just a moment in time, but little did he know it was to become a permanent one. 'That's what life's about, I guess. Ambitions and dreams you come close to without really realising. Surfing's purity has led me to an awareness of what's really good and what really matters. A special consciousness of the world.'

> 'You're a small component in the overall scheme of things, it's just letting you be a part of it for a tiny moment.'

Rob Baker

Aaron Topp

CARVER
CHRISTCHURCH

In a very short period, New Brighton local Rob Baker has made a name for himself as a respected carver of that famous southern limestone, Oamaru stone. It's fair to say he was a late starter — he's had a string of diverse occupations, lifestyle choices, and an ongoing battle with a world that's tried to stick him in a box, all of which have played havoc with his desire to be creative. These days his work is prolific — he's making up for lost time — but only when he's not being inspired by the swell along the Canterbury coastline.

Surfing and art were both there at the beginning for Rob. His father, a taxi driver, would throw the family into the car and drive from their home in the Christchurch hills down to the beach, where he'd teach Rob and his siblings how to read the waves and skilfully propel themselves into the curves. Body surfing is a prerequisite for all ocean-based activities, and young Rob would watch the surfers out the back, fascinated by the sight of their silhouetted bodies gliding freely along the lines of swell. Art, on the other hand, wasn't so accessible. In college he desperately wanted to join the group taking French and their choice of art classes, but the education system at the time decided it was best he learnt to cut metal and shave wood, things that would help him in his career as a future factory worker. Maybe if you pass School Certificate, the system told him, and try a bit harder academically, then we could consider it. But that meant another whole year, and Rob didn't want to have to wait that long. Out of frustration he purchased a camera and taught himself how to use it well, as a way of satisfying his creative urges.

He dropped out of college and started his pre-programmed life as a carpenter, until it required him to work at height, when he settled for becoming a bricklayer instead. When he spotted an advertisement for a position for a photolithographer at *The Press*, Canterbury's premier newspaper, he assumed that, with a title like that, it was bound to be something to do with cameras. When he was successful in his application, he thought he'd just scored himself a role working with the glory boys of the media, the photographers. He knew it could likely mean something like carrying bags initially, but it was a start, at least, to getting his handiwork on the front page. On his first day he was taken to a large room and shown how to make zinc plates, then acid etching, and putting the dots in the photographs. It was as close as he was ever going to get to being paid to push a shutter button for the paper. He soon settled for leaving the camera in the car and accepted his role was office bound. It didn't matter, he told himself, he was in the heart of *The Press*. It would only be a matter of time before another door opened.

When he was 21, that door came in the form of a moonlighting job working part-time for a concert promoter as their photographer. He was there when The Boomtown Rats came to town to play a gig. As Bob Geldof began singing 'Getting My Picture Taken', Rob cruised through the mob of mauling press photographers vying for position and wandered out on stage. With his back to thousands of cheering fans and a body full of adrenalin, he began clicking away in the superstar's face. Rob knew the images he was collecting were front page material. He ran back to his house, got them developed and rushed them to the editor's desk, only to find the official photographer from the paper knew a faster route and was already discussing the final shot with him. When David Bowie came to town, Rob captured it all in colour. Then there was his favourite photo, a moody shot of the B52s' lady with the boofy red hair, swigging from a Steinlager bottle. Outside a bit of promotional work, none of them were ever considered and they became relegated to the tomb of a photo album on the shelf in his home.

He packed his camera and surfboard and travelled through Malaysia, Kathmandu, India and Bangladesh, taking time to experience Bali. He kept a diary of his travels, taking photos to complement his stories of exotic experiences and waves. He lived carefree, cruising wherever on a shoestring budget, taking in all that the eastern world could offer. When he arrived in London he found his old life waiting for him, and it quickly sucked him back into reality; he needed money, so he found a job at a bar. He met up again with his girlfriend, who had opted to bypass the Asian leg of his trip. He landed another job, tasting crap imported wine for local Kiwi pubs. He picked up a bit of photography work, shooting fashion and in the evenings he began compiling his diary into a story. It was enough to impress a few editors

> 'The whole trip with the boys in the car and the silliness and the anticipation of what we were going to find around that last corner . . . man, I'd missed it.'

and he started writing little travel blurbs for *Australasian Express* and for the Pentax travel magazine. He was finally being paid to do what he loved. He thought he'd made it.

He headed home with his girlfriend, got married, had two girls. He didn't want to be stuck taking photos of weddings and twenty-firsts, so he sold his cameras. He started producing pop art china from his own moulds and sold the pieces at his local art centre. Often he'd go diving, driving up to Kaikoura by himself on a motorbike, his dive gear on one side, a surfboard hanging on the other and his air tank strapped to his back. He'd stop on the side of the road, get some crays, then go for a surf. His wife didn't share his love of the beach, so they moved deep into the country, bought a few acres and horses at Oxford, and his surfboards were relegated to a shelf in the barn. He eventually sold the china moulds. He went back to his old role at *The Press* during the night, and in the day he took to restoring their old villa, or, when he had a bit of time, helping build the odd house or two out of Oamaru stone.

He began riding horses with the other locals, and took up other sports like polocross. He found he was watching the weather to see what would make the grass grow, rather than looking for indications of a swell. Onshore? Offshore? It didn't matter out there. No one in their new circle of friends had ever been a surfer, so he stopped speaking the language of surf. He became more and more distant from surf paraphernalia. Over time he did a fantastic job of convincing himself to ignore his boards that lay in the stables, gathering years of dust and fringes of hay and possum shit. When surfing finally became a distant memory, bored and with nothing else to do, Rob would take out horses for joyrides around the rural roads, then get in trouble for taking out one that was yet to be broken in. His had morphed into another life.

Rob was close to reaching 40 when he finished renovating their house and found he had a bit of spare time. It had been three years since his last surf, when an old surf buddy of his moved to Oxford. He was heading out with another mate the next day, so asked if Rob wanted to come. Sure, why not? He walked into the barn with a tingle he hadn't felt in a long time and began digging out the surfboards from their forgotten vault. He rummaged around for his old wetsuit and discovered something had happened to his waist since he'd last worn it. He didn't care; the feeling had turned to genuine excitement. 'By eight o'clock the next morning I was paddling out and it all came flooding back. The whole trip with the boys in the car and the silliness and the anticipation of what we were going to find around that last corner . . . man, I'd missed it. I spent that whole day surfing.'

The following day he went to the barn where he kept the building supplies, sold the kauri doors left over from the renovations, and bought a second-hand mini Mal. He hid it in the barn with his old board. He didn't want his wife to see it, she wouldn't understand and it was no use trying to explain it. And he didn't want it to suffer the same fate as his original boards. So he resorted to having a secret life. He'd drop the kids off at school, then go surfing. When he said he was popping out for the day to catch a bit more work, he went surfing. Eventually, his marriage ended. Twelve years later, and Rob talks candidly about that period. 'I wasn't a great communicator; I communicated well with a surfboard. When the marriage broke up I drifted back to the beach, back into surfing, commuted to work, and saw the kids often.'

He continued working nights and had the days off. He felt the country leaving his system. A friend of his from the paper left and started a boat shop, so Rob would hang around there during the day when there wasn't any surf. He didn't particularly like boats, but he had idle hands that needed work. He started repairing boats and helping import high-powered Thundercats, the Formula 1 version of catamaran that is designed for racing on pounding surf breaks. Rob even went so far as to help set up the first race events in Canterbury for these awesome craft. But once the glue and solvents began giving him headaches and neck pains, a naturopath recommended he stop going to the boat shop.

He began helping out another friend at the windsurf shop, who'd teach kids to surf in summer. 'I just loved it, helping kids in the water. I remember some wouldn't even stick their feet in, but I'd have them standing up in the end. Just helping them conquer their fear and getting their confidence up. It was going from that fear of crying and clinging, to the excitement of suddenly it was all right. It was a real thrill being able to show them the way the ocean can pick you up and propel you, seeing their faces as they felt the energy pushing them, experiencing the curl of the wave, even feeling themselves being tumbled around under water in a safe environment.'

A well-known sculptor, Bon Suta, ran a sculpture exhibition down at South Brighton beach for local artists. Rob had visited it a few times and been fascinated by what people could do with certain materials. His memories of the pop art he used to do tempted him to give it another go, but producing salt and pepper shakers and little china TVs didn't inspire him all that much any more. He had often carted off-cuts of Oamaru stone around with him when he was building with it, so knew of its soft, workable characteristics. He found an old piece and sat down one day and carved out a fantasy-like fish. He took it to the exhibition and showed Bon Suta his work. She was impressed with the finish on it, how smooth he'd made it look and feel. He thought he'd test the water, so he did a few more and set them up in her stone-carving garden in the sand dunes. They started selling. Another friend opened an art store in town, so he supplied some fish hook pieces and they went even quicker. Another artist friend suggested he should do it full time; in his eyes Rob was certainly good enough to succeed. The next week, after 20 years' service as a photolithographer, he was made redundant, technology having superseded his role at *The Press*. The timing couldn't have been more perfect.

When I met Rob for the first time, I was greeted by a 52-year-old who didn't look like the tortured artist type, more like a handyman who'd swapped his trade van for a convertible. He had a shy smile and his arm in a sling. He anticipated my imminent 'what happened?', and proceeded to let me know how it feels when you mistime a jump into the surf off the New Brighton pier. This is as self-tortured as the guy gets. He chuckles quietly at himself afterwards, and gets a dynamic, slightly crazed look in his eye, a look that goes well with the patch of facial hair under his bottom lip. He runs his good hand through his silver hair and the salty remnants from his last surf leave the strands sticking up. Suddenly, he's Einstein with a haircut.

> It helps people understand that the stone is something to treasure, a relic, something to be respected . . . It's his way of giving the fossils a rebirth, a new life.

'When I left *The Press*,' he says, 'I kicked back, adjusted my life, paid off the house and went to the lifestyle where it was my time. I decided I'd be a stone carver. I went on the Enterprise Allowance, a government grant for artists, where a small amount is made available each week. They sent me to a small business course for three weeks, I did a business plan, and became eligible for a full grant. It stacked up. It was feeling authentic. I was getting feedback. I like having surf relics around, but I always thought there was a huge hole in the surf art market. I started making these surfing picture frames, little surf wagons with boards on top. I thought I was in, but surfers didn't buy them and the surf stores weren't interested in selling art. Surfers would happily spend eighty bucks on a T-shirt, but not art.'

He didn't work with sculpturing clubs or seek advice from others working with the stone. He quickly learnt there was something very special about sourcing the limestone rock himself, straight from the quarry site where it had been lying for the last 40 million years. There are variations and different grades, he says, so the only way he can be certain he gets the best is to venture to the North Otago district himself. 'It's a kind of romantic thing. I love this idea that I've found this piece of stone from the ocean waiting for someone, and I've come along and found it and carved it into something from the ocean.'

Rob gets a kick out of that thought. The limestone was once living, more specifically, it was once a near-infinite number of microscopic and giant organisms that came to bathe in the warm shallow water in the area all those millions of years ago. Sometimes he'll come across a fossil in a perfect position and he'll keep it set in its resting place to add to the effect. It adds to the wairua of each carving he does, the unique energy being exuded from within its confines, which he uncovers with each passing of a blade or saw or piece of sandpaper. It helps people understand that the stone is something to treasure, a relic, something to be respected, and how such a simple thing can suddenly show the 21st century as nothing more than a pinprick on a giant time continuum. It's his way of giving the fossils a rebirth, a new life.

Rob focused on giving his work a much more generic appeal, with a subtle, yet deep, connection to surfing. The rough surface of the sculptures represent the land, while the smooth sections are the waves. His first pieces in this style were called Mataki — the name came from a surf trip where he was inspired by the scenery as he drove between two massive mountain ranges in the Mataki Valley. 'Everytime I carve, I'm thinking of the perfect curl. The first time I made the Mataki I had the two big waves coming into itself and another little wave, and when I stood back it was like this huge mountain range was there and another one there and another in the valley; it gave me a buzz. And usually there's a ball in them, a ying and yang thing, the wave is carrying the seed with it. People tell me they see different things, that's fine, I see a foetus in it as well, the birthstone for me with these waves and the seed, like the ones you see inside a woman's womb.'

The style was an instant hit, and now that Rob has galleries referring to it by name, he enjoys making something different every time. Some people naturally look at the curvature and expect it to have some reference to a koru or Maori meaning. 'I had a couple of artists tell me I shouldn't be carving korus because I don't know the stories and traditions, but the koru just happens to be a universal shape. It's in the pyramids, the Celtics, the Aztecs had it. I'm trying to be culturally sensitive, and in many respects I guess to a customer it does look like I'm influenced by Maori design, but to me it's really about the energy of the waves.'

After each surf, Rob takes the time to wander the beach looking for suitable pieces of driftwood, particularly the gnarly pieces found on the West Coast. He then takes them home and polishes them up, ready to become mounts for his stonework. 'So the stone has come from the sea, and been forced up onto land, and the wood has been forced from the land, washed down the river, tumbled around in the ocean for who knows how long, then washed back onto the land, and I've married the two together. That's the whole thing to me, the complete story. It's hugely inspiring. I love it when a gallery rings up and tells me it's going to somewhere like Germany, or the States, the Bahamas, or somewhere in England. Apart from someone liking your work enough to take it back with them, when you think about how those organic forms are still on the move, it's a real buzz.'

Each piece is produced at his home in New Brighton. It starts off as a slab and is cut down with a chainsaw to a usable state, sending organic dust into the air and onto the neighbouring lawns to help them stay green. Many of his newer pieces are designed to be placed outside, so he coats them in silicon to seal them and protect them from the elements. He supplies a dozen galleries, from Mangawhai in the north, to Raglan in the west, Gisborne in the east and Queenstown in the south. It's no surprise that most of the galleries are where the surf is at. Once a year he'll load his SUV with carvings and hit the road to supply the outlets. His first commission was for the South Island Women's Champs, a sculpture depicting a woman's face coming out of the wave. In 2007 he sold over 80 pieces. In 2008 he was invited to be an exhibitor at Gisborne's popular art festival.

Rob says he's inspired by New Brighton. Many people say it's scummy, too ghetto, too windswept, the sand's grey, the water's the same, it can be freezing while it's sunny in town, but he loves it. Despite its seaside appeal, the area is still one of the cheapest places in Christchurch to buy a house. Immigrants come over here and buy up, they can't believe it. It's a far cry from the 1970s, when the roads into New Brighton were thick with cars full of people wanting to go to the only place in New Zealand open in the weekends. It was a thriving village full of confidence and with a bright future.

But when the malls began opening closer to town and Saturday trading began, the place quickly became a ghost town. Rob's watched the local community and council try to give it a niche mall atmosphere in the last decade, making surfboards as chairs, attracting new businesses like cafés and boutique shops, and spending $4 million on concrete and steel to reconstruct a pier that was originally on the site back in 1894. These days, anyone coming to the township can walk through

'Surfing's taught me to live life for the moment. Too often we'll be busy rushing around and the moment can pass us by.'

the business area, grab a coffee, then carry on walking on the pier 300 metres out to sea, safely above the breaking waves. There used to be a pier warden, who'd warn the surfers they'd die jumping off the structure. Sometimes he'd even get a hand on a surfer's shoulder, but they'd just jump the 10 metres anyway. Since his last painful jump, Rob has resorted to taking advantage of the giant concrete pillars forming a rip through the grunty shorebreak and paddles out that way. Once on the wave it's exciting whizzing through the legs of the giant structure. Afterwards he might get mussels off the poles. It's a local's definition of surf and lunch.

But attracting people to unique landmarks and changing perceptions of the place is a slow process. Some of the beachfront housing has been bought to make apartments, but most of these ventures have gone belly up. The apartments are too expensive, in bad locations, and thanks to the sizeable sand dunes, they have no view. At one stage there was a big push from developers to get rid of the mounds and their vegetation just so their clients could watch the sea from their expensive condos. It was all going great guns until the tsunami hit Indonesia and suddenly there was no more talk about it. One of the best things in the area, Rob reckons, is that the sand dunes are actually growing and building natural protection, while also enabling local wildlife to flourish. One day he wants to do a sculpture for the place, a tribute to New Brighton's heritage and future, but in the current climate he knows it'll likely end up getting vandalised.

These days, Rob can fill in a whole day by not planning it. Some days he'll be so wrapped up in his art it'll be dinner time before he realises he hasn't eaten since breakfast. 'Surfing's taught me to live life for the moment. Too often we'll be busy rushing around and the moment can pass us by. There's a lot of waiting and patience and relaxation when you have to sit out the back and wait for the next wave, but in between you get these other cool things happening, could be a splash from a fishtail, a seagull gliding past, sometimes the waves are secondary. You're at one with nature, you're relying on that energy source, you'd have to be blind to go through surfing and not feel it. It gives your life back, when in so many ways it could easily take it from you.'

'I came in absolutely glowing. If I'd drowned that day, I would've been happy to do so.'

Now that Rob's based his life around the surf he's realised just how many others do the same. He laughs at the thought some people believed he was on the dole just because they always saw him at the beach. He once talked to a couple of surfers, an international pilot who used to keep what was effectively a fold-up surfboard behind his seat, and a lawyer, and they both envied the fact he could surf whenever he wanted. 'They had flash cars and nice homes and lived the life and they envied me? It was only because I worked at night. Being a photolithographer was one of the last bastions of the cool job; we had all these allowances and breaks during the night because we were working with acids. So during the day I was always out in the water.'

Now that he's a full-time artist, surfing still takes priority over how the day's going to pan out. He'll check the swell, the wind, think about whether somewhere is pumping or not. 'I either surf or get stuck into the carving. Once I'm into a carving I have to get it finished; it's like a nightmare I have to get out of my brain.'

Rob's taken up travelling again and had recently returned from his annual month-long trip to Bali. This time round things didn't go too well for him. He wanted to get the trip in before his shoulder operation; after that initial jump from the pier, then a series of falls from horses while in Oxford, and breaking it while snowboarding, the specialist told him for the sake of his carving it had to be opened up and looked at. Before the trip he'd been riding a Mal, so when he arrived in Bali and went to pick up his shortboard he leaves there, things became all too frustrating. 'I was surfing at Uluwatu. I was unfit and frustrated and falling off all the time. I was watching the young guys being far too competitive getting triple the waves than me. I paddled in, watched from the cliff and contemplated selling the lot.'

When he got back home he surfed Murdering Bay, near Dunedin, and the inspiration came flooding back. 'Everyone was friendly, they talk to you and wave; we weren't competing with each other, it was the best surf trip in years, just surfing your back yard and in perfect waves. It was a long right-hand wave, it had barrel sections, I wasn't falling off, there were seals on the beach, it was sunny. I realised I didn't need to go to Indo to experience surfing euphoria. Afterwards, I sat on the beach talking to other local surfers, listening to their stories, and when I checked my watch, a few hours had gone by, so I went out for another session. I came in absolutely glowing. If I'd drowned that day, I would've been happy to do so.'

While he was still at *The Press*, Rob met Dee, a graphic artist for the paper. She loves the beach, loves surfing, and loves travelling to exotic places to experience both of them. Despite his love of art, Rob admits he can't draw to save himself, so Dee taught him how to get his ideas down on paper. He acknowledges he wouldn't be where he is without her. They bought a bit of land at a bay in Moeraki, and parked a small caravan on it. It's a little fishing village, radiating spiritual energy from the local Maori history. Keri Hulme must've felt it too, when she wrote *The Bone People* here. After mowing the lawns in front of the site one day, Rob watched a series of waves pop up on the point and peel shoulder-height for a short distance, before closing out on the reef. He grabbed his board and paddled out for a closer look. He took off on a couple. 'When I made the wave, a wave no one has ever surfed before, I felt like I'd climbed Mount Everest. I was duckdiving in bull kelp, which was a bit sketchy, but it only added to that adrenalin rush and fear. It's such a buzz to surf the hidden breaks around there by yourself.'

But Magnet Bay, an hour from Brighton, remains his favourite wave. It was where he first experienced getting into a car with friends and hitting the road, anticipating that first sight of the swell conditions, the excitement of seeing perfect lefts wrapping around the point. Since that day he's decided it's where he's getting his ashes scattered. 'You see all the mountains and big lake, all this beautiful energy and feeling from the place; there's always something happening. It's where I've nearly drowned a few times, but it can have my ashes instead. I'd love to stick a carving there, a big Duke Kahanamoku-like statue. I'd mount it on the cliff there.

'It's funny how everyone wants to surf, they like the idea of being one. They see surfers and think, how do they do that? They all have a mate who is a surfer and recognise they're on a different level to others. It'd be nice if everyone got what we got out of surfing; the world would be better place. I just want to surf for the rest of my life, even if my daughters have to strap me to a board, I don't care what it is, I just want to be out there in the ocean.'

Jess Santorik

Aaron Topp

CARVER
RAGLAN

Jess Santorik has become a product of living at one of the world's most recognisable surf breaks. She's taken the act of riding waves all the way to an elite level, earning herself a healthy list of sponsors by brandishing her surfboard as she smacks another Manu Bay peeler. She could've been just another girl with pasty skin and corporate ambitions, but instead she's been raised by the ocean and her supportive parents to have a completely different outlook on life. When she enters the room she's a striking contrast to the winter rain on the roof. Her wispy, sun-bleached locks tell the story of her recent surf trip to Indonesia.

'When I was five Dad used to push me into waves on his surfboard,' she says. 'When I turned ten, Moreha [Roberts] moved in next door with his family and he was keen to get into it. He was a year younger, but we'd surf together every day after school. He's a whole lot better than me now.' At Raglan Area School the two students would talk their bilingual teacher into letting them have time off to go for a surf, with promises of coming back in afterwards, definitely by tomorrow. So he did, not all the time, just when the conditions were perfect. Perhaps that's more of a reflection of the Raglan culture, rather than the teacher. Her parents didn't know, and Jess wasn't going to blow a good thing by confessing, either. In fact, by the time she was old enough to spell and give a detailed definition of the word 'truancy' she was hiding in the bus shelter, waiting for her mum to drive to work, then running back up to the house, grabbing her board and wetsuit and going surfing for the day. Back at home, she'd make sure her wetsuit and hair were dry, then as her mum arrived in from work, she'd let her know she was just heading down for a surf, back by tea.

'Surfing was so much fun. You know when you love a sport so much you have to be out there doing it? It doesn't get perfect here all that often, so I didn't want to be in school looking at the bar thinking, oh my God, I bet it's so good. It's the most amazing thing to be out in the water, to be free, learning how to overcome difficult things. You can see how kids froth on it so much, they love it.'

Shortly after some neighbours spilled the beans to her parents about their daughter's extra-curricular activities, it must've been a godsend when New Zealand's first surfing academy started in her back yard. It was an impossible concept for the country's middle-aged population to comprehend — teenagers expected to surf every day between classes. Callers to talkback radio were aghast; what happened to surfing's cloak of disapproval? While they were out chasing a little white dimpled ball, surfing became a bona fide professional sport run off a billion dollar industry, that's what, and New Zealand just happened to have an abundance of waves as good as those found anywhere else in the world. Raglan's global surfing reputation and slightly alternative attitude were a perfect combination. Some would say a school for surfing was inevitable.

Each year a selection process takes place for the limited number of applicants accepted. Of course, you have to be at a certain level of competency in the waves; you have to be able to do the basics well, stand, do turns, have confidence when confronted with a heavy situation in the surf, things that are all very hard to tell from some kid's résumé. Each year, young hopefuls miss out; after all, it would be pretty pointless for someone of Larry Fisher's calibre to spend his time teaching someone where to lie on a surfboard. As for Jess, her position in her year of 20 enrolments was never in jeopardy.

The group of Year Eleven (fifth form) students was split in two groups of 10, both factions running the same programme in parallel. A typical day for Jess began with training in the college pool an hour before school. Under the watchful eye of their surf coach, she'd do a series of lengths, get out, run around the side, do press-ups, sit-ups, then get back in the pool for more lengths. Some mornings were spent running around the field instead. It was hard work and there were no allowances for her and the other three females. Jess would go to class, but at two o'clock would head out to the surf, whatever the weather conditions. They were being trained for competitions, for those times when they'd have to compete in sloppy conditions and do well. They'd come back and stay in class until four, with an extra hour to do homework before they were allowed to head home. There was heavy pressure on the students to succeed academically.

> . . . she was hiding in the bus shelter, waiting for her mum to drive to work, then running back up to the house, grabbing her board and wetsuit and going surfing for the day.

On Wednesdays they'd have surf competitions and at the end of term the winners would be awarded prizes like pizza supplied by local businesses. There was never a division between them and the non-surfing students, although for the first part of the year the academy students tended to hang out with each other; most of them were from other parts of the country and were billeted in the local community. But with the rest of the day spent in normal classes, it didn't take long to get to know everyone.

'A lot of people get in who aren't that good, but by the time they leave they're winning competitions. When I came I thought I surfed really well, until they played me on video and I thought, oh, my God. They're so good at motivating you and analysing your movements while you surf, it definitely improved my surfing. These days more and more girls are making up the numbers at the academy. Their talent is higher than when we were there because the standard has definitely been raised in recent years.'

Jess began competing more often. She backed herself and travelled overseas to compete in a few pro juniors, finding herself paddling out against the best female surfers in the world, like Sophia Mulanovich, and despite thinking her surfing wasn't in the same league, she still managed to reach as high as nineteenth in the world juniors. 'It was hard at first,' she says in her soft drawl. 'I was surfing against the best girls in Australia, girls in every magazine with all these sponsors, but most of them weren't actually any better than anyone else. That's the main reason why so many Kiwi girls freak out when faced with surfers who have been hyped up by their sponsors, but really our girls are better than half of them. That whole scene is crazy if you know the right people.'

With the support of her own sponsors and the carrot of making surfing a full-time career dangling within her reach, in her last year at the academy Jess decided she'd commit herself to the cause and consequently pulled out of school to chase the competitions. But that suddenly backfired when the surfing she had grown up with became a source of resentment and frustration. 'At that stage I was doing well in comps, but with that came more and more pressure for me to get better, so I kind of stopped. I didn't want to go surfing any more, it put me off the whole thing.' The mix of her successes in competitions, and being told what to do, meant she needed a break. 'That year was off and on, I free-surfed mostly, but I still did the comp thing over summer and I loved doing that, but being forced to do it the whole time was exhausting. I didn't like feeling I had to go surfing, we had to do it at the academy, if we didn't we'd get growled at. I want to do it because I love it, and I didn't want to be forced to do something I love. I was a stubborn little girl, I was like no, I don't wanna go out, you're forcing me not to like it. Sometimes I'd go just to keep them happy, but there were other times when I just didn't.'

But it wasn't to last. With more girls entering the competitions and getting better, competitions were starting to get harder to win. Now, at 21, Jess has gone on to win everything a female surfer can in New Zealand. She tells me this while she twists and plays unconsciously with the drawstrings dangling from her hoodie. When competitive surfing has been the essence of your life and you've been in so many comps, it's no big deal to talk openly about it. Ask her close friend Kelly Clarkson; she'll likely tell you the same. She grew up with Jess at Raglan and as teenagers the two of them would surf together all the time, pushing one another into the big stuff, telling each other they loved each other before duckdiving potentially the last wave of their lives. They surfed identically and for a while they'd share first and second places in comps. When Kelly stopped competing, Jess continued on her own.

'I like winning, like everybody else. I think surfing comps make you want to surf well. If I'm surfing normally, I'll just cruise, but in a heat you're concentrating on getting as many turns in as possible. You can be out there scoring a nine point five out of ten and laugh at the other girls, or you can be coming last and paddle around like crazy to get a wave. It makes you want to win if you lose, that's the good thing about it. If you win too many times you get blasé, it's not that much fun and you lose that high. That's what happened to me. This year I lost a few times, so when I won, I felt like I earned it.'

Travelling is a blessing and burden for the competing surfer. Jess loves the travelling side of it, seeing new destinations, surfing exotic waves. Sometimes she does it by herself, other times she's with a team, or friends and family. That recent trip to Indo was her fourth, just holidaying mostly. She's been with her family every time, but this year her boyfriend, Billy Stairmand, one of the country's upcoming talents, went with them. The family spent the first two weeks together, then Jess, Billy, her dad and brothers went to Sumbawa, surfing for six weeks. Competitive surfing has given her a very impressive-looking passport, with stamps from South Africa, Australia, Tahiti, America, New Caledonia, Fiji and Tonga. At the end of 2008 she went to Portugal to compete in the Open World Surfing Games.

Jess's sponsors — Billabong, Gallaz, Oakley, New Wave Surfboards and FCS — have been particularly supportive over the years. I imagine those guys get value from Jess's professionalism and her focused approach to competing, hence their longstanding support. Before a contest, Jess admits to just cruising, relaxing. She might get her boards ready, choose what wetsuit or bikini she's going to wear. She sticks as much to a normal routine as possible. If she's surfing in the first heat she won't eat, like some sort of crazy metaphor, starving herself makes her want things more. 'If I've had a meal I just wanna sit down and chill out. Sometimes I'll listen to music and dance around and be stupid, other times I'll watch others surfing, get down there an hour before my heat, read what the waves are doing. If you want to win, you need to get the best waves. I find if I surf really well in one heat I'll wear the same bikini and use the same board in the next.' After the comp she tends to cruise some more, leaving the other girls to go crazy.

I'm interested to hear she competes in the World Indigenous competitions. The blue eyes radiating from the tanned freckly face don't strike me as typical Maori traits, and she anticipates my confused look; it's something she's seen a few times in the past. Her mum is Maori, she tells me, can you tell? Jess learnt to speak Te Reo from the time she was five, thanks to a blend of bilingual classes and kapa haka teachers. Her hapu is Ngati Raparapa, based just out of Raglan. The indigenous competitions have been a personal favourite of hers; she's come second every time she's competed. But it's the Maori Nationals that stand out as the one to look forward to each year. The vibe is different; everyone still wants to win, but it's so cruisy that everyone just cheers each other on, it's a stark difference to other contests, she says.

It was a daunting scenario for any 16-year-old, to see their friend circled by a lynch mob on surfboards.

Jess surfs a lot with her older brother, Leon, the other professional surfer in the family. She chooses Manu Bay over the other two popular spots to surf, one because it's closer to her house and two because it tends to attract the tourist types, making it easier to pick off waves. Not that she gets hassled by the locals, she is one, after all — it's more the talent of the local crew as compared to the out-of-towners, who float in and don't know the conditions as well. 'But I still get guys who snake me on a wave 'cause I'm a girl, or the ones who'll sit next to me 'cause they think I'm an easy target, especially if I'm the only local out. But when I snake them back they suddenly realise. I like to surf with all the local boys, if I'm with them then it's OK, they share. If things get really bad with other guys dropping in on me the local guys will tell them off, although I'm not afraid to say something myself. There's no real staunch localism here, depends who's out and how good it is. I guess localism is everywhere. I mean, they won't chase you in to the beach and try to beat you up like in some places around the world, but if you're pissing someone off that much, maybe you deserve it. It's a pretty well-known rule — you don't snake the locals' waves.'

It was on a trip to San Diego that she experienced localism at its worst. Grown men were spitting in her face and offering death threats after a friend of hers accidentally dropped in on one of them, despite pulling off the wave as soon as he realised. It was a daunting scenario for any 16-year-old, to see their friend circled by a lynch mob on surfboards. 'I tried to step in and they swarmed me, calling me a bitch and splashing me, trying to push me in with their boards. But I didn't paddle in. For the rest of the surf they were going psycho at us. We were just trying to have a surf and keeping to ourselves, but they didn't even like that.'

A bit of localism is harmless compared to the beating an army of giant groundswell can dish out. Whenever a human chooses to take on the raw energy of climatic forces armed only with a surfboard, it's fair to say there's a pretty large element of risk involved. Australian great, Tom Carroll, once said if he wasn't feeling some sort of fear in anticipation of paddling out in big surf, then he wouldn't even get his board ready. Without fear, he'd be taking it for granted, and that's not how to approach something as unpredictable as the ocean. Surfing can be as much a mental battle as it is a physical one.

'It's almost like you're in a plane and it suddenly drops, that's how it feels, you're falling from the sky. It's crazy, it's exciting, it's frightening, you have all these emotions going through your body and you're shaking, but if you make it and start gliding down the face of the wave you're like . . . oh, my God.' She struggles to end the sentence. She looks at me like she's making no sense, apologises for talking gibberish, but I get it. 'How else do you explain that feeling to someone else who's never done it?' she continues. 'When I was little, surfing was different; it was a crazy feeling, things were much bigger, if you made it you were stoked. Later in life you don't think about dropping in, you're automatically looking at how you're gonna do a turn. It's only when I surf something big that all the initial feelings come flooding back, 'cause if you make it you're so happy.'

Out in big waves Jess admits getting hammered is always on her mind. But she has an escape plan tucked away in there too, and it's pulled her out of many a heavy situation. Staying calm as she's being digested by thousands of tonnes of water is the first step. Fighting or any form of freaking out will only consume what little air she has. Step two's a waiting game; let the ocean throw her around like a ragdoll for as long as it takes, she knows it will only do it for so long then get bored and move on. Of course, the size of breath at the beginning determines just how comfortable this part is going to be.

'Surfing has taught me to be calm and I take that calmness back onto the land with me. Even before I paddle out, I've got to be calm and just chill out. Be ready for anything. I couldn't imagine what those guys who surf places like Tahiti's Teahupoo are thinking when they paddle out — you can die out there, get pushed into coral caves. But if you didn't get held down and thrown around, then people would surf the biggest waves all the time. I would.'

Sometimes, deciding not to paddle out in big surf isn't an option for Jess. There have been times when she's turned up to a competition and seen waves well outside her comfort zone. People are watching, sponsors have paid her fare, other competitors are rubbing their hands in anticipation, so now's not the time to pussy out. Jess recalls a large session at Kuta Beach in Bali during 2005 when the sets were closing out up and down the beach. She couldn't even make the duckdives without feeling like she was going in and out of a washing machine. Once out the back she had to deal with sets that were just one continuously thick wave lip breaking in rugby field-sized sections. She paddled into one kamikaze style and managed to get a couple of turns on a face before the wave shut down. It was enough to get her second place.

Jess has brought a folder with her. Inside are photos of a series of carvings she's completed over the last couple of years, and they look vaguely familiar. The story is that the Kereopas and Santoriks have been close family friends for a long time. Jess, with time between competitions and a flair for art, hounded Aaron to teach her how to carve surfboard blanks. He didn't. She persisted, begging him to give her a chance. So he showed her some basics in the hope she might go away. But between heats of competitions at Manu Bay she'd arrive back at the studio and watch a bit more. 'He's so good at it,' she says referring to Aaron. 'He showed me some stuff then said, see ya, have fun. I show him my stuff, it's different. I purposely don't want to be similar to him, not that my stuff is, he does out-of-this-world crazy-good stuff.' As I flick through the pages I ask what tools she uses to carve, but I'm met with a short answer. Jess doesn't underestimate what Aaron's done for her and is staunchly protective of the knowledge she's been gifted. The craft isn't hers to give away that sort of information; it's Aaron's secret to tell. So, no, she's not going to tell me.

The pieces I'm looking at are remarkable, though, and it's obvious Jess's talents aren't only water-bound. 'I've always loved art and was lucky to have an amazing art teacher at school. She helped me so much. She was lovely. I always looked forward to going to her classes.' Her pieces are sold to local people through word of mouth mainly, which has led to the odd bit of commission work. One friend wants Jess to do a carving of a tattoo her deceased sister had, someone else is looking for a birthday present with a unique flavour. Her first piece was sold to one of her teachers. Some customers look through her book and get ideas. Others ask her to sketch ideas out for them, which can pose a problem. In a rush to get them down, Jess tends to scribble and things can look a bit rough. Some clients see this and question whether she's actually any good.

'It's almost like you're in a plane and it suddenly drops, that's how it feels, you're falling from the sky.'

Once they see the final product, though, the answer is yeah, she sure is.

Some days she'll work under the porch at her family home where she still lives. On a sunny day she might set up on the driveway. While it can be a messy process, her parents love it. They try to encourage her to try different styles or suggest other outlets to promote her work. Depending on the colours and details, each piece can take a matter of weeks, or maybe a couple of months. Sometimes one can drag on. 'I might leave a piece for a month. I'll walk past it until I finally recognise what it is and I'll grab it and change it. It's no use rushing it, you can't make mistakes. Once it's carved you can't put it back.'

Jess says life inspires her art, which provides her a place to bring her worldly experiences. Sometimes, though, she'll sit there with an idea but no design concept to carry it. Forcing it doesn't help, she says, so she just chills out some more and within a day or two she'll wake with a clear direction. Being free drives her creativity, confessing to be quite the cruisy person helps too. So does paddling out into the surf, or revisiting some of her ancestral roots. 'I was inspired by my teachers, who taught me Maori designs. I've since used a lot of Maoritanga in my art and incorporated the rhythm and technique I learnt from them. I put the same feeling into my art as I put into surfing. I guess it's your lifestyle and how you surf; you add in some flow and suddenly it's another love. If I'm not surfing, then I put it into my art. I've done plenty [of pieces] that have incorporated the ocean and waves. I like getting the movement.' Jess will often use plaited flax, straw or paua shell for added effect. She's currently exploring incorporating metal, looking to see where her art will evolve next. When the carving phase is nearly finished she'll stand back amongst the scribbles and chips of surfboard blank and take it all in; it's a time to reflect on whether it's going to work or not. It's her 'aah' moment. Then she'll reach for the paintbrushes. The fine detail and blend of earthy colours she uses result in art that looks like it's been part of the landscape for generations. A combination of mystique and Maori legend.

That's quite amazing when you take into account the medium was once used as a craft for catching waves. Jess understands the essence of working with a broken surfboard and the absorbed energy it brings from its previous owner. 'It's crazy, it's from somebody, it's been a part of someone else's adventure, so it's always exciting to use those boards. The surfboard changed their life, it's changed mine, now it's going to change the end recipient's. The wairua has flown through us all.'

This is the intimate relationship Jess has with the ocean. She affectionately calls it her best friend. A place to go to worship and feel alive. 'It's a part of your life, it's you, it's your family, you're going out to be with the one thing you love. Sometimes you come in from a surf feeling like you're on top of the world. You're free, you're surfing for yourself and it's all about you. It's the feeling you get from it, the flow and the turns, it's all incredibly exciting. There are some moves that are incredibly difficult and you work on them for months and when you get it right, it feels like you've been given some sort of gift to do that on water. It's the only sport where the ground is moving beneath you.'

Jess's future as a competitive surfer continues. She's preparing to have a crack at the WQS, the proving ground for the World Championship Tour; a holy place where the world's top handful of female surfers reside, including Taranaki surfer, Paige Hareb. She's well aware the reality of chasing the qualifying circuit is financially and emotionally draining. A long, rocky road ahead with few rewards. Her self-determination and proud record of outperforming some of the world's best are the only things she's going in to fight with, but they're both solid ammunition. The first year might be a tester, a time to get her bearings and pick up experience and places to stay, a time to plan and strategise her assault for the following year. While many girls travel with their mum or other family members, Jess prefers to travel alone most of the time, although she admits in some of the more expensive locations like France and South Africa an extra hand while travelling would be helpful. 'That in-between stuff gets to your head. You have to be able to relax, to concentrate, otherwise you won't do so well. It's a lot harder for those starting out. You get to surf some amazing places, but you'd never be home. I see myself on the WCT in ten years,' she says, 'or maybe helping out others in surfing or working with my sponsors to assist others at comps, that would be great. Could be anywhere, I'm that sort of person.'

Daryn McBride

ARTIST
MOUNT MAUNGANUI

I'm standing in the McBrides' house observing domesticity at its best. To my left, Ange McBride is in the kitchen preparing some home cooking, while her daughter, Willow, one of the 3-year-old triplets, is propped up on the bench shaking flour through a sifter. In the next room, Daryn McBride kneels in front of an open fireplace shaping kindling over screwed-up newspaper, as another triplet, Lennox, sits on his dad's exposed soles with a book. The third, Harper, is close by, pushing toy cars to his own sound effects.

Every so often he and his brother stop what they're doing and stare up at the television on the wall, where a Discovery Channel special on monster trucks is running. It's taped, and is apparently played often. It's a warm, tranquil scene, juxtaposed against the view directly behind me, where the ocean, not far south from the main beach at the Mount, looks violent and cold in the heavy winter rain.

There's not much in the house to show me I'm in the current national longboarding champion's home. OK, there's the brand-new black Hyundai parked out the front with the large signage telling the world who's driving, but that's pretty much it. There are a few surfing trophies on display high above the kitchen pantry and a stunning kaumatua-inspired walking stick with tiny engraved emblems showing past winners hanging on the wall, something I later discover is Daryn's pride and joy — it's an award for traditional longboarding, won by riding boards around 50 years old. Even 35-year-old Daryn, dressed in a worn hoodie and jeans, and blowing against the small flames to ignite the wood, looks unassuming. Just a family guy trying to create some heat for his three healthy kids and loving wife.

Ange is interested in the book I'm writing so we begin talking about it while she moves from cupboard to fridge to bench. Soon I make the comment that I'm going through a patch of overcommitment, and for the first time in my life I feel I'm discovering where my limits are. I hear the words come out of my mouth and suddenly I'm one of those tortured, self-obsessed writer types. Great manners, Aaron. But Ange stops what she's doing and looks back at me; she nods and motions her head to the next room. Apparently Daryn discovered the same thing not long ago. She knows exactly what I'm talking about.

Daryn has spent most of his life in the Tauranga district. When he was seven, during one of the family excursions to the beach, he was playing in the shorebreak on his polystyrene board when he noticed some older guys laughing and having fun out the back. They were taking turns on a big green surfboard in the bigger waves. The way they could ride the swell long before it broke, then control the vessel with a combination of body movements and balance, fascinated him. In his eyes they were absolutely ripping. He began begging his parents to get him a proper surfboard, but they got him a boogie board instead. While it was a step up from the foamy, where he could he'd borrow his mates' surfboards, which were the first of the modern, smaller, three-finned shapes exploding into the market and revolutionising an industry. An icon of coolness. It didn't take long for the impression of the green board to be left in the past; any old dunger of a surfboard wouldn't cut it, he wanted a proper shortboard. After more begging, his parents ended up giving him their friend's crusty old board that they'd cleaned up. He barely rode it. He couldn't stand it.

In fourth form at a college camp at Whangamata, Daryn borrowed a shortboard from a mate who was trying to sell it. The wave knowledge he'd gained made surfing it seem so easy; he'd watch his peers, study how they were surfing and he felt himself progressing. By the end of that summer he entered his first competition and won it, beating the guy he borrowed the board from in the process. From there things picked up momentum. He went through a series of his own shortboards trying to find that 'right' one that would become his soul mate in the waves. He began hooking up with the local talent at the Mount and started improving his surfing and competition results, which led to his first sponsorship. A couple of years later, on his way up the beach from a particularly bad surf, he started thinking about those guys with the green board again, and realised his surfing had become far removed from that vision of earlier years. 'I would watch other guys with the longboards while I was out in the water and they were having so much more fun. Shortboarders just seemed aggro, they were always getting blown off the back of waves, just struggling so much more,' he says.

During the 1980s longboards didn't exist, at least not new ones. The shortboard revolution had well and truly stamped its mark on the surfing community. Longboards were for hippies, kooks, old men. They were the dorky cousins relegated to their own table at the family function. Daryn had moved to the Mount permanently and started work experience at Assault, a local surf store. Out the back, amongst the rows of surfboards, a new longboard stood high and gangly above the more popular short versions, like a kid held back a year in school. Daryn could see it was little different to the traditional longboards; the rocker (the curve of its surface), its slightly shorter length, and its lightness gave it a contemporary look and feel. He borrowed it a few times on the small wave days and was amazed at how much fun he had. He surfed it some more, on bigger days, and each time relished how it was rekindling his love for the essence of surfing. It grew to be his favourite board; he desperately wanted to buy it; he would've slapped cash on the counter every time he returned it, but his lack of funds meant he was forced to settle for scrounging it. One day he went in to pick it up and it was gone, sold to a customer off the street. A few weeks later, still feeling a sense of loss, Daryn met Phil Griffin, who'd been picked to go to the World Titles as a New Zealand longboarder. Over time Phil would talk to Daryn about the fundamentals of longboarding and the discipline of competing. He let Daryn borrow his board, a massive nine-footer compared to the seven-footers he'd been riding, on which he struggled. But he persisted, and while Phil was out, Daryn would sneak around to his property, take the board from where it was kept under the house, and go for a surf. Phil would often ring Daryn asking for it back. Never mind, Daryn soon found there were plenty of longboards stashed under neighbours' houses; sneaking them back after his surf was the big challenge.

> . . . Daryn soon found there were plenty of longboards stashed under neighbours' houses; sneaking them back after his surf was the big challenge.

'The best surfs I had were on the longboard. The most fun was had on a longboard, so I went stuff it and traded my shortboard in for a new longboard, at least then I'd have fun everytime I went out. The first time I paddled it out a lot of the crew stopped talking to me, or gave me the odd funny look. Their attitudes to me changed.'

Daryn found a new group of longboarding friends, and within months they were all living together in a flat at the bottom of the Mount. They'd go on road trips to Gisborne, or head over to Matakana Island. Their antics in and out of the water were single-handedly changing the traditional stereotype of the longboarder. 'We started to get a bit of a reputation. The guys we were hanging out with were fishermen, and they'd always bring their rough mates with them. They'd come down and watch us surfing and drink piss on the beach, then afterwards we'd head back to the flat and join them. We had the first official longboard contest at the Mount and all these hardcore-looking skinheads turned up with a keg. The older crew at the contest were cringing, but when we looked, we discovered we knew them, so we ended up drinking with them for the rest of the comp.' Daryn continues painting a picture of a time when the flat was the epicentre for weekend-long drinking sessions, complete with fights, drugs, grommets, gang members and the occasional cop. He admits it was an out-of-control environment, and I sense I'm listening to a different guy today. 'I fitted in, but I wasn't like them,' he tells me, pausing to acknowledge what he was saying with a silent shake of his head, 'so I left that flat to go to art school in Rotorua.'

We continue talking in one of the bedrooms, mainly to move away from the children, who are eager for their dad's attention, but also to see some of the art that he's working on. Above the bed is a large piece of his artwork with the small title *Beyond the Blowhole* sketched along the bottom. Drawn in Daryn's unique, cartoonish style, two giant Hawaiian-sized waves are breaking, while in the top left corner a tiny surfer, only visible by the skinny legs and a hand holding a surfboard, waits on a rocky outcrop. His use of simple, smooth lines and earthy colours attracts and holds the eye. It takes me back to a time when comic books ruled and the worst thing to happen in your life was falling off your bike. In saying that, there's a mature connotation in every piece of his art, and that's why you'll find them hanging on any grown-up's wall. His love of art and this technique started out as small animations in the corners of his school books. He'd draw a little surfer paddling into a wave on each page then getting to his feet, so as the pages were flicked it'd become the one smooth movement. Years later, when he eventually moved out of his flat and found himself studying Fine Art and Design at Waiariki Polytechnic, he drew inspiration from that same doodling. By the second year of study he was approached to do a piece of art to acknowledge the new artificial reef going in at the Mount. He didn't say no to the commission, but inside he questioned if he was up to it. 'I never envisioned myself the sort of person who'd do surf art, I always found it to be tacky, air-brushed, fantasy-style art, especially back then, that's all you saw. You never saw any of the stuff that's around now that's amazing.' He was working with pastels a lot at polytech, and exploring depth with abstracts and faces. He did two pieces, one of a surfer, then another of the lifeguard tower on Tay Street, with a pohutukawa in the corner and Moturiki

Island in the background, with some waves coming through. He was happy with how it turned out, shocked really, he didn't think he could get something as clean and crisp as that.

His study took a break for a year when his first daughter, Paige, was born. When he went back to polytech the second time his competitive surfing was starting to take off and he had to decide whether art or contests were going to come first. Surfing won out. In 1997 he was picked to go to the World Titles in Hawaii as a longboarder. The results he got led to sponsorship from Classic Malibu Longboards, based in Australia. He packed a bag, caught a flight, and moved in with the owners. In 2000 he scored ninth in the McTavish Pro International, the globe's premier longboarding competition at the time. In between competing he worked in their shaping factory, as well as doubling as the brand's graphic designer. It was an intense time, heading into the factory at three in the morning to polish boards or stick in fin boxes. At lunch time they'd head to the beach, go for a surf, then head home, have a couple of beers, work on the computer doing design and be back up at three again. On top of this he was trying to concentrate on the competition circuit, and at times the two would overlap; once he had to juggle making changes to a design between heats of a contest. He felt himself starting to burn out real fast. I ask if there's regret there, but he reckons he wouldn't have changed a thing, it's all experience to him. He left CM and began an interim phase where art started to dominate.

'I moved into this flat at Yaromba with these two other surfers. We were all fully into riding different boards in different conditions and experimenting with expanding our minds by riding crazy boards in crazy states of mind. We were living the classic *Morning of the Earth* lifestyle. Life in the house became more about the connection between surfing and art; one guy was a writer, one a landscape designer, and I had my paintings. It was a super-creative phase.' At one point, struck by a serious illness and limited in what he could do, Daryn ended up getting a canvas, some pastels, and working on the floor of his room, picking up the style he'd used for the artificial reef job back home, this time featuring a series of Noosa surf points: the first one with its little stone wall, the second, Little Cove, with its shower on the boardwalk and pandanas with waves in between. And on it went. The style he's since become known for progressed from there, as he kept adding to and adjusting it. Later, happy with the waves, the rocks, and the how the water looked, he would start playing around with the trees. He began focusing on the Jurassic-like pandanas, putting in lots of knots and swirls and concentrating on getting their depth right.

Daryn was picked up by another longboard company and was paid to fly around Australia with 10 boards at a time, showing outlet stores the product. No competing requirements, just sales and the odd holiday on the side. It was a cushy job, he admits, but something never felt quite right. Nine months later there was a knock on the flat's door and the owner gave him a cheque saying it was all over. It was a slap of reality, and one that made him think hard about where he was heading: did he want to head home to settle down, or try to crack the world circuit?

He decided he'd play both out for now; he applied for sponsorship from another longboarding brand new to the market, then returned to New Zealand to wait for the reply. Back in town, he wandered into Assault and was recognised by one of the girls working there. Her name was Ange, she was a mate's younger sister when they were back in college, someone who Daryn would stick up for whenever she was picked on by her brother. He thought she was cute back then, but morally out of bounds. That didn't stop Ange secretly having a crush on this older guy in shining armour. Now grown up, and well within bounds, the two of them started hanging out. Daryn had almost left the thought of sponsorship behind when one day he received an email; the company were willing to sponsor him, but he had to move back to Australia. If he stayed in New Zealand they'd only supply him with product. He turned them down. He didn't care that much about chasing the circuit any more. He was in a good space with Ange, and all the boys heading back from their Oz excursions meant there was going to be a good local scene at the Mount. Their relationship developed even more. 'She used to take snowboard camps for women as an instructor. I thought I'd tag along and do the cooking. I had a mate who had a café and talked him into doing the main chef work while I'd be his assistant. He thought it sounded like fun, especially with the thought of a women's camp. Another mate of mine brought his partner and baby along, too. It was classic, because all the women would come back in from snowboarding all day, start drinking wine and having a good time, while watching these three guys in aprons preparing their meals in the kitchen, complete with baby in the arms.' Daryn admits hanging out with the baby made him get a bit clucky. Ange always wanted three kids before she was 30. She was 29 when they had triplets.

Daryn got back into his art seriously, adapting the style he worked on across the Tasman to suit Kiwi scenes. He produced a piece with a pohutukawa tree and a wave and it sold in a gallery within 24 hours. The gallery owner reckoned it was the pohutukawa that did it, so with a family to support, he started playing around with the native features, based on the fact they were sellable. 'A lot of the scenes I was doing were places no one else had seen, just places I'd venture to when surfing. One piece I showed, a person asked, where's that? I started explaining that it's halfway between Raglan and Kawhia, you climb down through this little valley, you jump off this little cliff, and they interrupted me to say, well, we'd never go there. I learnt if I did a scene people could relate to, then put in a pohutukawa, it become instantly more sellable. Artists all do it because we love it, but when you're dealing with art as a full-time earner . . . I had to take in that important aspect.' The pohutukawa started off as loose swirls and colours, but after a while he began emphasising each leaf and exaggerating the size. 'Then I started simplifying the leaves, thinking about a lead-light window, bold and simple, but at the same time trying to bring in more detail without losing that simplicity. That's what makes my art so unique I think, it's soft, simple, you can get lost in it, and it gives the illusion it's detailed, but it's not.'

Daryn's had around 12 pieces commissioned for features like foyers of expensive hotels, and plenty of gallery exhibitions based on that style. He's finding people are now coming to him for his uniqueness, while the computer design work he does for corporate branding has also taken off. A national company, Spaceship Campervans, has used his art as a backdrop in its stores and for its T-shirts. He made the cover of *NZ Longboarder* three out of the four times it was published, one as the artist of the image. He's had an article about him published in a German surfing magazine, and three inclusions in the annual art feature of US *Longboard Magazine*. It's fair to say that Daryn's work is getting great exposure, both locally and on the international stage. 'I like the fact my art has a real New Zealand feel to it, even though it's not that obvious. The whitewater coming down on the wave and swirling around, it looks like a koru. I like that feel they have. It can be as simple as the wave shapes of the foliage. It doesn't have to have a blatant New Zealand cultural significance to show that. Most of my art is generally coastal scenes, so I look at things as being environmental in that sense, because it's reflecting so boldly and clearly and passionately our coastline. I always try and portray it as like that, as somewhere where you're free to go, and anyone can get to. That's the whole vibe and feel I'm trying to get across. I'd never do anything that had a more modern, sterile feel to it. I like the fact that the water changes colour. I've always tried to get the feel of the water translucent and the water trying to swirl and flow. I'm trying to get that perfect day scenario.'

I ask him if there's any piece of work he wouldn't give up. He disappears out of the room and I expect him to come back with a finished piece in all its framed glory. Instead, he returns with a piece of scrap foam the size of a large notebook and hands it to me. It's a cartoon scene he's sketched of a woman emerging from the sea with a surfboard, while a guy sits in an open Kombi van playing a guitar as three kids hold hands in a circle, singing. 'It's a family portrait. The three kids are dancing, Ange has been surfing and I'm playing the guitar. I always show myself playing a guitar because even though I feel I've done well in surfing and art, I'd love to be able to play a musical instrument, but I can't play to save myself. So I always try and depict myself doing it, because I love

> He was only getting a couple of hours' sleep each day. He lived this disconnected life non-stop for a month.

listening to people who can. It's my chance of letting my musical skill out.' He tells me it will be made into a painting one day, for sure. Most of his work starts off as these sketches on scrap media.

I make the mistake of assuming Daryn's work is always positive, that he's a glass-half-full type of guy all the time; certainly, that's the impression I'm getting from him as we talk. But being a full-time artist has real challenges, as I'm about to find out, and sometimes the glass gets knocked over. After an exhibition at the Aotea Centre in Auckland that hadn't gone well, he was so angry he thought he'd create a storm scene instead of the 'perfect day' ones he'd evolved; a full grey painting, with the ocean stormy and bubbly. 'I sketched it on the wall of my studio. It had the whole family there, one of the kids out dragging a stick, Ange and I holding our hands in the raging sea. That was going to be the start of my new series.' We talk about his creative drive ('it never stops'), and whether it is a struggle to balance everyday commitments. 'Sometimes I'll get really frustrated and grumpy, because all I want to do is shut myself up in a room and explore all these ideas in my head, but I've got family duties and other roles to play. Every now and then I'll hide myself away for a weekend, and Ange and the family are really understanding about it. I think they know it's not good to not allow me to do it, otherwise I end up in that dazed state. When I get into it, it consumes me. Ange used to get frustrated because I'd sit in the lounge and be away with the fairies thinking about something art related and she'd eventually say, you're in art mode again, huh? Sometimes I'll notice her saying it, sometimes not. She's used to it by now.'

There came a time recently while he was preparing for an exhibition that Daryn was drawn into an exhausting routine where his art consumed him day and night. He'd start painting at nine in the morning, work through the day, have a couple of hours off in the evening for family time, then go back to work again. Ange tried to limit his habit by having a bedtime curfew of one in the morning, but driven by his desire to create and pressed by a deadline, he'd be going through to four or five instead. Then he'd be back up at six-thirty again, when the kids woke up. He was only getting a couple of hours' sleep each day. He lived this disconnected life non-stop for a month.

'I was a walking zombie. I was falling asleep at the easel, and I'd be trying to force myself awake because I wanted to get the work to a point. It was affecting my art — I don't even think it was coming out that great. All my art is done by blending the colours with my fingertips and I'd get to a stage where I'd be forcing it so much they'd start bleeding. There'd be little drops coming through onto the canvas. Or I'd be scratching the work because I'd get these calluses on the tips of my fingers, so I'd have to use my left hand instead of my right, or other fingers. Sometimes the canvas would be banging against the wall and keeping Ange awake in the next room. It was just ridiculous putting myself through that. I'd lose track of what I was doing, but I was just so into it. It took burning out completely to put things into perspective and make me realise I couldn't live like this — it wasn't reality.'

That happened at the end of 2007, leading up to the exhibition. For the last few weeks he'd been going for it full speed, drinking beer and smoking pot to help him stay awake. He was a complete write-off. He was so sleep deprived. He was good for nothing. He snapped. He got in the car early one morning, left his family still sleeping, and drove towards his father's place in Auckland. He'd had enough of life and was prepared to end it. His father informed Ange of the situation and Daryn was admitted to a psychiatric ward in Tauranga.

'It was such a hazy state to be in. You haven't slept, you haven't been straight, you haven't done anything for so long that you can't think properly. I used that time in the ward as a time to detox, basically. No smoking, no drinking. A time to re-evaluate my life. Things got put back in perspective. The most important thing was to be there for the kids and Ange, and to not put unnecessary pressure on myself. Don't set exhibition dates if I couldn't meet them. Don't put any time restrictions on yourself as much as getting the stuff done and delivering it. You have to be realistic with it. I went to Hanmer Clinic in Tauranga and they run an amazing rehabilitation programme for drugs and alcohol. You do a pre-treatment programme one morning a week, then an intensive programme for three nights a week for eight weeks, then after-care, which is one night a week for two years. I'm doing that now.'

Daryn hasn't touched alcohol or drugs since he went into hospital. 'Ange has been insanely supportive over the time. It was pretty scary for her to see me get to that breaking point and watch me get put into that ward. She didn't realise how much I was smoking because I hid it from her for so long. Back then I thought it was great working through the night, because I could smoke all night long in the studio without her knowing. To own up and be honest about it, it took a lot of pressure from me.' When people used to come around for dinner there'd always be some alcohol involved, but Ange has stopped bringing it into the house. 'It's been real cool for both of us. It's great to go out to some social event and waking up without a hangover. The next day you're feeling really good.' Daryn had a friend who would visit while he was in the ward. They'd talk about when they were young and how they'd joke about ending up there. It made Daryn realise he wasn't there because he was disturbed, he was there because of the substance abuse he'd put himself through. 'The more you talk to those people who are in there, the more you realise that they're a result of long-term drug abuse as well. So many people were in there because of it. It has such a massive detrimental effect on people. Since I've left, I'll often go back to visit a few friends I'd made, people who'd helped me out when I first went in, and it's a good way to remind myself of a place I don't want to go back to.'

Daryn had only been out of hospital for a week and half when he entered his first longboard event. He hadn't surfed all winter, just painted, smoked, drank. The waves would be pumping outside his place, but he'd turn his back on the window and go hide in the studio. Now, all of a sudden, he related doing art to getting high, or drunk, or both. 'I was scared of doing art. I was scared I had to be wasted because of it. So when I left the hospital, every time I wanted to do art, I went surfing instead. I ended up surfing non-stop for a week or two.' He mentioned to Ange he thought he'd give the competition a go. She was

'I feel like a role model for the first time in my life. Someone who can be looked up to because I achieved it clean and sober.'

cautious about it, fearful the pressure of competing, or the emotions from not doing well, would be a catalyst for a relapse. She gave it a tentative green light. Daryn entered and came second, a placing he was more than happy with. The next event up north, he won. Ange was happy for him, but remained wary of small steps, and the boozy environment of the prizegivings afterwards. But through her support, the counselling and visiting guys at hospital, Daryn was feeling really good about himself. He was finding the strength to put things behind him.

Daryn decided he'd take it a step further and do the national longboard circuit. He felt he needed an even bigger project to focus on, to distance himself from all that'd happened, all he'd put his family through. To clear his head and start again. He travelled with a close friend who understood the situation and who he (and Ange), could trust to keep an eye on him. His name was Lee Ryan, a British longboarder Daryn had met when they did the World Tour events together. In recent years Lee had met a Kiwi girl and moved permanently to Papamoa. When Daryn was in hospital, Lee would visit every second day and bring DVDs or hamburgers.

'He was really cool, really understanding. Super-supportive of me not drinking,' Daryn says. After the Christchurch competition a large social scene evolved and a lot of alcohol was being consumed. Daryn was inundated with guys wanting to shout him beers because he'd made the finals and surfed well, but he was getting sick of telling them he didn't drink any more. He realised once people start getting pissed, you can't tell them otherwise. Lee would check on him often, and when he saw Daryn give him the nod, he'd walk past, not stop and take the beer out of his hand.

'It's nice to have friends like that who support you, because you have others who'll try and tell you to just cut back, man. But they don't understand the complexities of it. If I could've cut back, I would've. On the circuit, I was leaving the parties at around nine o'clock and going back to the Spaceship campervan [they hooked him up], going to bed and reading a book. I'd be the first in the water in the morning, clear headed, not hung over. I remember one event in Kaikoura where I didn't do that well. I was angry, but I came in and looked at the other two divisions I was still competing in, the nose-riding division and old Mal division. I just thought to myself, well, at least the shortboard progressive part's out of the way, I can just focus on the two heats that I get the most fun out of now. Some traditional surfing. I walked off down the beach, had another surf by myself to chill out, and refocused. It was probably the first time in my competitive career where I've been able to turn it around like that. Any other time I would've been with the boys drowning my sorrows.'

Daryn successfully competed in the series and the sideline reward was being crowned national longboarding champion. Incredible for someone who was looking primarily for an avenue to focus his energy, although barely surprising; his personal motivation must have resulted in a level of commitment not normally seen in surfing. He acknowledges it gave him such a sense of achievement, doing it completely straight. And the extra bonus was being selected in the New Zealand Surf Team to compete at the World Surfing Champs in Portugal as the lone longboarding representative. 'It now feels real good. I feel like a role model for the first time in my life. Someone who can be looked up to because I achieved it clean and sober. And the reward on top of that is going to the World Titles, and the first time ever you couldn't give two stuffs if they ask you to pee in a cup because you know you're straight, you've never been this straight in your life. It's fantastic to feel like that.'

There's a definite sense of accomplishment, even an undercurrent of staunchness in his voice when he tells me he doesn't even think about using any more. 'I've got so much more patience with the kids. They used to go get me a beer, and I'd get three at a time 'cause they all wanted to get Dad one. So I'd drink them all. It's been a little while coming, but now they say, Daddy doesn't drink any more. I told them beer makes daddy sick, makes me do silly things. They've picked up the understanding of it and it's cool.' Smoking was the hardest to give up, he says. He's had people stick pot in his face since and that's been the biggest test. Smoking was a way of life to Daryn, he lived and socialised for so long in those circles. It was easy, he says, to get sucked into that cycle; he'd go to parties and get introduced to people who smoked, by friends who smoked and suddenly he was stuck there. 'It was the combination of surfing and the Hanmer programme that got me through. You need that programme, because you can't do it on your own. I've got a couple of good friends from the counselling group and we know we can text each other if the situation arises. It's amazing how I don't have the urges or anything, it's incredible. For so long I was thinking, is it ever going away? Within seven months I'd changed. To remain drug and alcohol free for your life, or as long as it takes to be in control, is a big challenge and the failure rate without doing a programme is above ninety percent. You need the education, the knowledge of what it's doing to your brain. The knowledge that physical exercise creates the same chemical that the drugs produce, the same rush, the same high. That's why if you have a heavy surf, you come in with that full-on buzz. I didn't have that understanding beforehand. Now I think I've got to surf, to cleanse my body and get myself right. Having the surfing there, you know it's helping me with goals and helping me keep balanced.

'Surfing got me through the time when I couldn't do art. It's such a good place to be, so clear headed. Being off the land, in an environment where everything's clean and pure and physical. I enjoy surfing any surf, but love those days when it's absolute perfection; we all do, it's that flawless perfection.' He points above the bed behind him to the piece of art showing the surfer and giant waves, 'Look at that one, it's got this intense feel to it, but you also get the feeling once he's out there it's going to be fine. It's a reflection of me as a surfer, because I've enjoyed riding smaller waves and the challenge of riding a longboard rather than larger waves. I'll ride anything, but the thing that brings me the most happiness is riding a heavy single fin and the challenge is mastering that board and putting it into places on the wave, rather than aggressively trying to belt the shit out of a wave. It's subconsciously just me reflecting my emotional attachment to waves.'

Surfing also brought him stability in his day-to-day wellbeing. After so many days of sleep deprivation, by the time he left hospital, his body, worn out from going cold turkey, still hadn't adjusted to a regular sleep pattern. Daryn found surfing took care of that issue. 'On the big days I'd get pounded by the waves and want to go in, but I'd paddle back out for a couple more, knowing I'd sleep so much better at night. Now I just go for a paddle, or get in my kayak if there's no swell, because it's a good

> 'Surfing got me through the time when I couldn't do art. It's such a good place to be, so clear headed.'

workout. Sleeping is one of those things that's so important. I was nervous when I had to stop taking sleeping pills. Now I read so many books, I've got a little headlamp I wear so not to disturb Ange in bed, and I just fall asleep, sometimes with it still on. Ange is stoked with the fact I've got into things I never had time for, like reading. She's forever saying how good it is now. It's an incredible feeling.'

To help Daryn reacquaint himself with his art, Ange cleaned the studio completely out and Daryn repainted it, turning it into a bedroom for Lennox. The garage became Daryn's studio and after a few more adjustments, the whole house began having a different feel to it. 'Now I've started my art again it's coming out better than it ever has. I'm not rushing it or forcing it, just doing a bit at a time when I feel like it. If it's not quite working, instead of slashing canvases like I used to, I'll just put it down, come back to it later, fix it up and carry on. It's all that clear-headedness. To be completely drug and alcohol free is just the best feeling. I don't miss anything about it.'

At a recent exhibition at a local gallery, Daryn got talking to a well-respected art valuer. Daryn was blown away when the expert told him he'd been watching his career, and how pleased he was to see Daryn stick to developing his own style, because that's what was giving his art its value. Daryn couldn't believe someone had been following his work like that. It changed how he approached his art. It gave him a sense of peace that complemented his new, clean lifestyle, an official stamp to say he didn't have to worry about proving himself. 'Sometimes I still think I'm trying to work out my style. It's taken me twenty years so far, and I'm almost nearly there. When I'm happy with how I've got everything looking I want to do one more piece that is huge, that's going to take me a couple of years to complete, life-size trees and waves, like you can step into it. A piece on that scale would be insane, because you could feel that you could reach in and touch it and pick a leaf off. Then I will start on the storms and skies and moving away from the waves, but keeping them still there. The drama is going to be in the sky instead. Once I get there I feel like I'll be able to happily move on to the next phase of this style. A different medium. Evolve again. I used to be in a rush to get there, but I'm not any more.'

Outside the rain is heavier than ever. The newsreader on the car stereo is warning of weather bombs and flooding and snow, and I think of the last few hours in the McBride residence. I think of Daryn standing silently at their window within the dry, warm walls of their house, watching a disturbed, grey sea and whitecaps battle squalls of cold southerly rain — perfect fodder for his art's next stage — and I can't help but think of the negative undertone involved in exploring a darker style. Then I think of that painting above the bed and the tiny surfer about to tackle the huge swell by himself, an almost impossible task, less than 10 per cent chance of survival, I'd say. But he does take it on, and not only does he survive, he's better off for it. He's done what many can't do, he's experienced how gloomy the bottom really is and how bright the surface can be. He feels empowered, in control, aware of his limitations. He's not afraid of the dark. I nod my head, that's why Daryn's next period of art is going to be so successful; his paintings may turn stormy and grey, and give the viewer the impression of disturbance, but behind the scenes he can laugh at that illusion now. Outside that studio door is reality, with its glassy surf and loving family.

Damon Meade

FILM DIRECTOR
GISBORNE

A few years back Damon Meade was enjoying a perfect day surf at his home break of Wainui. The sun had been unhindered on its westerly journey and the swell had retained a steady pulse throughout the day. His brother, the only other guy surfing with him, had just taken his last wave in. From out the back Damon watched his sibling's silhouette walk up the beach towards the trees. He faced the horizon, and waited in the stillness for the first sign of a fresh set. He didn't mind being alone, the ocean was company in which he was more than comfortable.

But within minutes he would be running in his brother's footsteps in the sand, surfboard above his head, and bearing a complexion as pale as the whitewater he'd happily caught.

I meet Damon at his flat three roads back from the famous Gisborne beach. Today the swell is a lumpy grey, with a cross-shore breeze making the peaks edgy at best. While it is surfable for us tourist-types keen on giving some integrity to the stories we'll take back home, as far as the locals are concerned the conditions are crap. A day to find something else to do. For Damon, I soon find out, that's an easy thing to do. I thought I was going to be talking to a guy with a couple of top-shelf surf flicks under his belt, but as we sit down in his lounge my eyes go from the surf movie quietly playing on the TV, to the large coffee table book about the impressionist era, to the original artwork hanging on the walls. He tells me he doesn't know if surf film is as creative as making art, and that he's currently in three minds, all with legitimate answers to that question.

Damon has lived his 29 years in a world of art in one way or another. He was always into drawing stuff. He liked painting the lighthouse off Tuahine Point and vistas with perfect surf. He favoured art subjects when he was at college. While he wasn't into science all that much, pseudo-science would later become something from which he would draw artistic inspiration. When he left college he painted for a year, exhibited locally and started doing a bit of work spraying cartoon pop art onto the LOST-branded surfboards shaped down the road. In 1999, he made a spontaneous decision to head south to Wanganui Polytechnic to take art further. He surfed the local breaks three times a week and appreciated the creative heritage of the small city. But once he returned to the scantily clad festivities of a summer in Gisborne, with its warm water, quality waves and party scene running constantly in the background, he decided home was where the heart is and never went back.

He took up spraying new surfboards at LOST again, refining his style and imagery and building a solid reputation in the process. His artwork helped make the brand iconic. The board's appeal was wide and their messages restricted only by the imagination. Want a board that complements your punk ethos? Sure, no worries. A bright seventies swirl to authenticate your new twin fin? In what colours? A large cartoon of a cute hula girl? Blonde lounging on a planet?

Evil Knievel for your big wave gun? Flames? How about a sweet Cadillac-blue design for your new Mal? Damon did it all and then some; in total, a couple of hundred unique designs of his hit the water. But after two years of relatively laidback work, between surfing whenever he wanted and doing his own artwork on the side, the desire to formalise his passion resurfaced. He applied for a three-year fine art course at the Wellington Art School and was accepted straight away.

'I was suddenly exposed to a whole lot of creativeness,' he says. 'I was taught how to present my work and think about it, explain why rather than just do it for the hell of it.' The course was totally open; he could do a painting paper if he wanted, a performance, anything went and he was free to explore and experiment with all realms of contemporary art in ways he'd never get to do again. His first project was on surrealism, an art form that originated in the 1920s and which explores the realms of fantasy and far-fetched imagination. To the artistically starved, it has connotations of hallucinations, dream-like principles, often a strong use of sexually charged imagery. Damon found difficulty in discussing such a detailed concept in front of his class, so he scanned a bunch of images, threw in a voice-over and presented it as a film. It would be his first introduction to video.

Film became his method of documenting progress, rather than the more conventional approach of photos. Having something the tutors could watch was easy. He moved into experimental art video, developing films with no story, no beginning and end, just movement. Who were the actors? No one was. I don't get it. He shows me some examples from that period. The surf on the television flickers to another type of liquid as pigment patterns and swirls move in sync with each other, creating tiny eddies and currents to great effect across the screen. He gives me a running commentary. 'Quite a lot of it required moving water, influenced by things like weather and the chaos theory.'

Wait a sec, I interrupt, the what?

The chaos theory describes the behaviour of a system, natural or otherwise, that evolves over time, and the use of pattern observation to predict the outcome of initial conditions. In a natural application, such as the weather, the laws of physics embody such an outcome. Apparently, it's got nothing to do with 'chaos' in the normal sense of the word. Damon understands the concept well and puts it much plainer. 'It's trying to predict things, but it's only predictable to a certain extent. I was using an artistic version of fluid dynamics to demonstrate. Fluid dynamics is a science that uses water to explain how weather works. Using dishes they try and calculate what it's gonna do, but there's still all these minute things they can't accurately predict. Meteorologists are the same; they can give you a three-day forecast but not get it exact. Some study water to try and explain how the great red spot on Jupiter works, which is actually a giant storm. It's the study of turbulence.'

He spent a lot of time making movies with moving pigment. He also spent a lot of time with dried-out pigment, making a series of patterns with the same methodology, but having a different result every time. The tutors were interested in the fact that he was repeating them and they'd turn out differently. 'Which is quite interesting when you think about it on a creative level. I was creating, but I had no control in the outcome, I was doing it blind. I could only predict how it was going to turn out. It's interesting to look back and draw the parallel to the fluidity of surfing and the ocean now, but it wasn't a conscious thing at the time.'

Damon was inspired by the idea after fluking a result using different types of pigments while he was researching ideas on how art relates to science. He points to one of the paintings on the wall above me, a picture I'd initially seen just as a silhouetted forest against a night sky. He created it one evening after playing around with a new technique. At the time he didn't think much of it, but the next morning when it had dried, he was blown away with the effect it'd left. That night he tried to emulate it again using the same methodology, but in the morning it didn't look the same. He gave it another shot, but still it didn't look anything like the original. 'It's a creative process. I always stress the process is the most important thing to get strong. The outcome will look after itself. That's where the video came into it to make it last.'

His interest in reflecting the relationship between art and weather evolved over the months into experimenting with the use of milk on a spinning turntable, inspired by a low pressure system. The class would drop pigment into the flow using eyedroppers and observe the patterns produced. He also filmed different currents of water and projected the film onto a giant ball made from lots of smaller balls wrapped in plastic wrap and fibreglassed, then left dangling from a ceiling. 'The process was exploring how water transforms and takes on forms any given time, including on physical appearances. I only got a B for that. I was devastated.'

His dad, a swimming coach, had taught him a deep appreciation of water. He entered Damon into his first swimming race when he was just five years old. Damon continued competing into his college years, training twice a day at the pool. When he was 14, his parents moved the family out to Wainui Beach, a decision Damon thinks helped to get him and his brother closer to the ocean. Soon after, he quit swimming for surfing, a decision his dad wasn't too happy about, but understood. He bought Damon his first board; Damon acknowledges his parents have been incredibly supportive of everything he's done. Once he had a board he had license to be out surfing every day, before and after school and in the weekends, regardless of conditions. For the next 10 years it was the focus of his day.

As for movie making, that wasn't anything he set out to do. When he left Wellington with a degree he'd inadvertently taught himself how to use a camera and edit to a professional standard. Filming surfing was a natural extension that just happened to involve all his passions. In the back of his mind, Damon knew a decent New Zealand surf film hadn't been produced in ages, but it wasn't until he'd shot a couple of hours of footage of his mates that he realised the potential of what he had. Heh, his mates. They just happened to be the same guys who were arguably the best surfers in the country; guys like Maz Quinn, who he grew up with, and Bobby Hansen, who resides just down the road,

'I was creating, but I had no control in the outcome, I was doing it blind.'

among others in an elite crew. They'd co-ordinate each other whenever the surf was on, and sometimes Damon would be woken by the chirp of the mobile beside his bed, but he never said no. Guys like Bobby are away for half the year, so he'd work extra hard to make the most of their time.

The end result was released in 2006, *Wolfskinz*, a name with nothing to do with surfing itself; something to do with a couple of the pros' reputations with the ladies, I learn, a private laugh between the Gizzy guys. OK, so the joke was lost on the rest of the country, but it's catchy and different and that's what Damon was aiming for in the market. With over half the footage based around the region, it could be argued the movie is a celebration of Gisborne's contribution to New Zealand's surf talent over the last decade. Damon filmed all year round in his back yard. 'Wainui is a beach break so it's always different. It produces long waves, short waves, hollow ones, all sorts, it's an amazing break. There's also Makorori beach, or off the island, even Gisborne Pipe has its day. There are a couple of breaks up the coast I love filming, but you've got to be conscious of exposing them. There's a right-hand point which is great, the surfers are only twenty metres away from you. Travelling to surf can be hard, but sometimes you just get it lucky.'

Yes, luck. Going out to fluke it time and time again. This is the amazing connection between his previous study and his new career. Sometimes Damon gets to control the angle when filming, while other times he's forced to set up the camera somewhere else. Either way, it's up to the surfer whether it works or not. 'When I try to make a film there's no way I can predict how it's going to turn out. There's only a certain amount of control I have. There's no way I can preconceive the end result, it depends on the time I spend with the camera and editing and with the people, and it's always evolving. You have to turn up every day for eight months and film, and you might get one moment per day, or sometimes a whole week will be spent shooting and you only get one clip. You're only looking for the top one per cent of what's available to you. I'm just there along for the ride really, there to help it come to fruition.'

He tells me of the trip to Matakana Island he took the day before on location for the 2009 sequel, *Skux Deluxe*. The swell maps had been monitored closely and by all accounts the waves on the island were overhead and perfectly clean. Damon met the rest of the guys there on the Mount Maunganui side, including Maz and Blair Stewart, and made the crossing on the back of jetskis, as arranged. While the surfers began paddling into the fresh sets of groundswell, Damon, still wearing a wetsuit, ran with his pelican case, tripod and his backpack, a couple of kilometres down the beach to position himself on a hill with the best vista of the action. An hour and a half had gone by and he was yet to take his eyes off the scene being played out in front of him; if he did, he risked missing that vital ride, manoeuvre, the special moment that was going straight to the top one per cent. While he can control that process, he can't control the fact a tall guy standing by himself behind a fancy camera is a magnet for anybody taking a leisurely stroll along the beach. 'I had a guy walk up to me and start asking me stuff. I resisted turning to him, but I had to eventually, to be polite. As soon as I did the wave of the day came in. Blair was on it, and I was thinking, don't make it, don't make it, and he did. And all the guy next to me could say was "Oh, did ya see that awesome wave?"' Damon was gutted.

Making a good surf flick in the 21st century is always going to be an ambitious task. Directors have done it all before, so the audience have seen it all before. Damon knows this; he understands the quality has to be at a global level, otherwise the viewer won't waste any time in activating the stop button. It helps, then, to have someone successful to help mould your strategy. 'I've always been a big fan of Taylor Steele and his movies. When I was a teenager I'd watch them everyday before I'd go surfing, to get amped. I've watched all his films hundreds of times. Steele is all about the performance. If I'm filming with my average camera and some guy does the best move of the whole film, I'm still gonna run that, whereas some film-makers will say, oh, you need a ten thousand dollar camera, and the sun's not out. That's kinda what Steele was all about. His first films were made on high eight cameras, not great quality, but he had the best surfers in the world to shoot and that's all that was needed. On a smaller scale, I've got the best surfers in the country to work with, so it helps a lot. I've sent footage from *Wolfskinz* to him in the past, and he's emailed me a few times.'

'Travelling to surf can be hard, but sometimes you just get it lucky.'

Probably the biggest challenge Damon has faced was unfortunate timing. The whole 'free DVD with the mag' thing has revolutionised the surf magazine industry and cheapened the film version, certainly the small, independent names. These days, only the biggest brands, like Steele or the goliath surf labels, can survive putting out a new movie thanks to the extra money they have to spend on launch campaigns. Damon had just finished *Wolfskinz* when the first of the plastic-wrapped mags was attracting wide-eyed grommets at the book stand. Over time, some of the quality of these throw-away flicks has been questionable, but some have obviously taken just as long to make as Damon spends on his productions.

Aware his market was slowly dissolving, Damon decided to jump on board the trend. He secured an agreement with *Kiwi Surf* magazine to distribute the second movie he produced, *The Motive*. It also helped increase the odds of attracting potential sponsors, due to the guaranteed number of copies to be sold. And he needs sponsorship. Damon works with limited resources (his editing suite takes up most of his bedroom) and he's self-employed, having started up the company Undergrown Productions Ltd. Things need to be organised before he starts; often he'll have to create half the film with no financial backing before he can approach a company and show them that he's using footage of their sponsored rider. With a bit of luck, it's enough to get some coin in the coffers and he can go and finish filming.

'The sponsors in this country don't put a lot of money into the films. Sometimes the sponsors don't really quite know what's going on, sometimes they contribute, sometimes they don't. At the same time, I kinda feel if I didn't do this it wouldn't be done. I've made three surf films in a three-year period, but I'm not too sure if I can make a fourth one. That last time wasn't a nice experience, juggling the sponsorship gods. When I started out I thought there'd be good money from the surf companies, but they're doing it quite tough too. New Zealand isn't a big country, so there's not a lot of spare cash to support projects like mine. It helps having a seasoned pro like Maz as a friend. He's the backbone of my movies in a way. He understands what I'm up against.'

There's also the music involved.

'Finding all the bands to contribute to the music is a massive process. I can't pay them, if I make ten grand then that's a pittance of what I've put into it. Thankfully, a lot of bands are really understanding of that, which is great. Things have become a bit easier, I've gotten to know the right people, and I know how things work.'

As mentioned, the creative side of filming is something over which Damon has little control. Sometimes, when the moons align, like someone gets a crazy barrel and he manages to film it all perfectly, then he'll know, but apart from those rare moments, he doesn't start getting excited until he's in the editing process. 'Some segments, you can't see the forest through the trees. Sometimes it's good to distance yourself for a day, go surf, do some more filming, come back and look at it with fresh eyes. I'll show the surfer and gauge their reaction if I have to.' The performance of the surfer, how it's filmed and wave quality are the three biggest factors Damon puts down to a successful shoot. 'You can have performance, but if you don't film him well, like he does an air and goes out of screen, then I've blown it and the shot's wasted. Waves are best with a bit of size, something head high or bigger, to make any manoeuvre look the best. Lighting is important, but not essential to me.'

Rounding off *Wolfskinz* was some footage in Teahupoo of big wave charger, Doug Young, riding what is highly regarded as the biggest surf ever ridden by a Kiwi. Damon didn't film it himself, but managed to buy it off the guy filming the insanity from the boat in the channel at the time (Damon was stoked, he was allowed to release the footage before anyone else). He also went to the Gold Coast with Maz and stayed at his brother, Jay's, place for three weeks of good surf and filming. In *The Motive* he travelled with photographer, Cory Scott, around selective New Zealand surf breaks, and with the help of some successful sponsorship pitching, to Bali for a month with some pros. In *Skux Deluxe* the location schedule has meant travelling further abroad within the country, this time including the deep south, but that all comes at a personal cost. Between the days when he's not on call, his reputation as a skilled cameraman has meant he's been able to pick up extra work getting promotional footage of the concerts and bikini competition at the Rhythm and Vines Festival, and Rip Curl call on him to film their sponsored competitions around the North Island. While he says other film companies could easily charge $1000 a day to capture those events, Damon shakes his head and laughs at the likelihood of getting work at those rates within the surf industry.

Damon's art background has also helped him create his own motion graphics to complement his films and create a much-needed uniqueness in what is a saturated market. It's time-consuming stuff, doing things like making names that move to special effects. He even bought an old typewriter and used a macro lens to make the graphics come to life on the screen on *Skux Deluxe*. He shows me the stacks of tapes piled so high they lean precariously. There's well over 500 gigabytes of footage in them and not all have been sorted. He pulls out one and shows me a random barrel ride; he makes a positive murmur, it's a potential one percenter he forgot he had. There's still time to stick it in the final cut. He'll work right to the end of the deadline to make sure the final feature is as perfect as it can be.

Personally, I think Damon deserves a beer from every surfer who's ever got any stoke from one of his movies. Think about it. While the rest of us are living the surfing ethos, enjoying the sensation of being immersed in the ocean, the smooth motion beneath our feet, the rush of dropping into perfect opal walls of liquid, one guy is standing on the dry sand under a blazing sun capturing it all for us to enjoy later when we're all surfed out, or in need of a surfing fix in-house. And don't think just because he's hanging out with pros that he gets to surf all the time, either. It's as close to self-inflicted torture as one could possibly get. Look at those perfect waves, but don't touch. You're taking one for the team, brother. He has been for the last five years. That's the tenacity of the guy. As torn as he is, he's dedicated to the cause, dedicated to the rest of us; he's doing a job and it's not gonna get done by itself. He knows if he decides, just once, that he's leaving the camera at home and paddles out, then that air Bobby Hansen does in his face will be the move that was required to finish his section. It's just not worth the risk.

'It's a metaphor for life really; you have to make the best of it, work with what you've got, and not force anything.'

So what does he miss the most about not getting into the surf when he wants? 'There's the whole fitness side of it; if you're active every day, there's something in that. You work that out if you stop doing it on a daily basis. When you surf, you sleep better, you feel better, it's good thing. Surfing is a good feeling. Barrel riding, there's nothing like that in the world. You never think about the problems in life, kinda like time slows down, I don't think I hear anything when I surf. There's something there, but you're blocking out everything when you're on a wave, you're in the moment, it's really nice. I think Kelly Slater might have said you're tapping into an energy source that's already there. It's a metaphor for life really; you have to make the best of it, work with what you've got, and not force anything.

'It's rewarding, it's not like it falls in your lap, you have to work for a good wave. That's why I think surfers are so happy; if it was easy, I doubt we'd be like that. Especially for the non-pro surfer. I might make a barrel five times a year and I'll be stoked, whereas Maz might make one and he'll be like [and here he drops into a low, monotone impersonation], oh, it was pretty small. Those guys look on it as a job, the rest of us don't.'

There was a session where Damon was filming at the southern end of their local break, when Maz came in looking shocked. A storm water run-off from a new subdivision had eroded and was spilling massive amounts of brown liquid into the ocean and creating a big pond of mud on the beach. 'He was all slimy, he'd never seen anything like it before. Surfers notice changes like that. If there's litter on the beach, it sticks out. When you go to places like Bali, they just throw their rubbish on the ground and it's definitely different to here. The guys who drive you around finish their Coke and throw the bottle on the ground and laugh, and you want to tell them it's wrong, but it's how they live. Twenty years ago they were eating out of banana leaves and dropping them, it's the same with plastic bottles. Surfers definitely have a valid voice on coastal issues. We know what the coast is all about. Surfing is a bit of a paradox, though, in sustainability; surfboards aren't exactly environmentally friendly, but apart from that we're not using a lot of non-renewable resources. If an environmental solution turns up in board design and doesn't affect the performance, great, but that's a big call. It depends on the level of growth surfing has; the bigger it gets the more serious the industry will take it.'

Damon's affinity with the environment, and in particular the weather, will always play a large part in his life as long as it continues to produce swell and great filming conditions, and not the effect it had on him that perfect day at Wainui. When his brother had gone in, things got a little strange. First, the swell stopped to nothing, then it went really quiet. From the south the sky had begun to darken to black, bringing with it a shift in wind direction and chop across the surface of the water. When the storm was directly over the top of him it seemed to pause, like it'd found what it was looking for. That's when it happened. 'I actually saw it strike. It's like I was an ant and someone just stuck a giant camera above me with the flash on. The image in my mind is fork lightning with a tiny thread creeping towards me along the water. It created rings on the surface near me, like it veered in my direction, but never reached me. It all happened in silence, then the loudest thunder I'd ever heard roared down on me. I took a few seconds to work out what happened. I was in shock, maybe I'd been hit, I dunno. I started paddling in as more lightning and thunder broke above me. My heart rate was up, I was freaking.' Damon ran up the beach, sheltering under his board over his head, but stopped halfway after thinking how ridiculous that must look.

Perhaps one day we will see that moment emulated in an original piece of art. Damon's philosophical about the future. He doesn't see himself making surf films in another 10 years. He tells me about an even more ambitious and innovative plan in the pipeline, but for now he's keeping things close to his chest. Suffice to say it'll get him back in the water twice a day again. Even if it doesn't work out, he's determined to do things he enjoys for the rest of his life, not end up in a cushy nine to five job just for the sake of it. Exploring his art further is definitely on the table, taking the time to continue being inspired by the impressionist era and creating his own tributes, such as the starry night-inspired painting of his that hangs in the room where we are sitting. New ideas, he says, are quite common.

He certainly has the means to do it.

Peter Lambert

Aaron Topp

ARTIST
OKATO

There's a popular surf break on the Taranaki coast that owes a lot to Peter Lambert and a few of his surfing buddies. Before they came along, Rocky Point was like a gawky teenager. It was a barren piece of coast with rocks protruding like bad acne through years of discarded rubbish and grazed farmland. It would get bullied by the howling sou'wester as it roared up the Surf Highway, turning the break into a scene of grazed sea chop and spray. This affected its personality for decades, making it the bane of local surfers, who were forced to read the conditions carefully before heading up its gravel driveway.

On the ugly days, it'd never answer the door. But on its good days it had that goin'-on look for which model agencies would happily cage fight.

There's no doubt the long, shapely left-handers of Rocky Point have driven myriad surfers into ridiculously high peaks of ecstasy behind their dashboards. Did for me on my first visit, I admit it; after an outburst of pointing and hooting at wave after carbon-copied wave grinding its way down the point, I was left tripping around on the grass while my wetsuit's limbs were navigated in record time. If Stent Road is the undisputed centrefold pin-up of the 'Naki, then since the 1990s Rockies has claimed the titles of 'most improved', 'brightest future', and the 'wave you'd most like to take home to meet the parents'.

> One of Peter's great strengths as an artist is his ability to observe and capture an active moment and portray its emotional significance.

So what exactly did a talented resident artist and his mates do to transform the place from brass band upstart to bona fide solo artist? Peter and a crew of 12 others, including local surfers, Roy Olley and Ernie Innes-Walker, set out to turn the sterile area into a patch of nature that could match the beauty of the waves on offer. It was an ambitious task, to pimp a wave, but doable. Funny thing was, it was a fluke it ever came about, for if it wasn't for Peter's inquisitive streak, Rocky Point would still be a wave of chance to this day.

Let's step back for a moment. Peter's name may not be household status in many places, but his artwork sure is. His paintings, in particular his collection of limited edition coastal screen prints, are some of the most recognisable in the industry. He's featured all the main Taranaki surf breaks: Stent Road, Graveyards, the Kumara Patch, Arawhata, Waiwhakaiho, and of course, Rocky Point. Even if you aren't familiar with the names, you'll likely know someone with an affinity to the West Coast who's got a copy of one hanging in a frame on their wall. His studio in the relaxed village of Okato is just how I imagined it'd look. Colourful. Disorganised. Creative. Walls used to showcase his brilliance. A sink surrounded by dozens of containers half full with water, paintbrushes sprouting from them like they're growing there. Rows of canvas stacked against one another, each one harbouring some piece of art we all wish we could one day produce, but don't have the time, or obvious natural talent, to do so. And across the far side, a window with a view of the neighbour's dairy cows happily chewing grass under the watchful presence of Mount Taranaki; perfect fodder for a moment's musing.

Peter sits down at a desk while I look amongst the chaos for a seat myself. He stands and clears a plastic chair of his painting tools, and offers it to me with an apology. Understandably; this is an artist's studio, not an art gallery. Want to talk about fine art over a latte or wine in a cosy environment? Peter's work is in at least two galleries in New Plymouth that will welcome you at the door. This room is different; it is, after all, a working environment, where all the magic takes place. As authentic an experience as you'd get. The plastic chair will be fine, thank you.

'Art was my love and passion,' says Peter, 'but I was heavily talked out of pursuing that by teachers and parents who were more concerned with the respected professions of the time. So I did three years' full-time study at Canterbury University, graduating with a BSc in Pure Mathematics, and drew a bit in my spare time. After that I wanted to get into something visual, so I applied for the National Film Unit.' Peter scored a role in TV that he describes as 'playing around in the studio'; this eventually led to a promotion to studio director of some of TVNZ's local programmes. He took a course in studio production and film, but the far-away call of a swinging 1960s London had started playing to his romantic spirit. The temptation was too much. Peter packed his bag, a sketchbook, and left the world of television behind him. 'I went through the States on the way. Worked in London for a while but got sick of all the grey, so hitchhiked to Morocco, where it was warmer and very different. I met many young Americans trying to get the Vietnam War out of their system during travels through France, Spain, and Germany, and experienced first-hand the anti-war demonstrations taking place. It was an interesting time to be overseas.'

Peter carried his sketchbook everywhere. By that stage he'd decided he wanted to pursue art seriously, but had no idea where to start. One way was to keep an abstract diary of his journey through quick sketches. He'd give away many of the drawings to the people he came in contact with, and he certainly did plenty of that, even if the other person didn't realise it. One of Peter's great strengths as an artist is his ability to observe and capture an active moment and portray its emotional significance; a certain look, a feeling, a millisecond of gloom, a lifetime of happiness. 'I always liked the quick little drawings, so I'd just draw what I was seeing from where I was sitting. I've still got a few copies of what I did over there.' He starts flicking through one of the rows of canvas and pulls out a sketch of four people in a car, beautifully framed and ready for a client; its simple, cartoonish style carries a fascinating undertone from the four big-headed occupants. 'I did this over in Vancouver while my friend and I were sitting in a café next to some traffic lights. It's of some Americans on a Sunday drive, you could tell that by the flags on their car. I drew it while they were waiting for the green. I've always been keen on satires, and when I look at that sketch now I still think it says a lot about Americans. Here they are, cocooned in their air-conditioned vehicle, looking out at the world wondering what's going on, protected by their own American way of life.' He shows me the original drawing done at the café all those years ago; it's a much smaller version, almost palm sized; it had to be, it was important he remained incognito to his subjects. The amazing thing is, he's still selling copies of this sketch, proving that Peter's knack at capturing that certain look in his subjects is a gift that defies time itself. He takes me over to another picture in the same style, of three men sitting around a table and having a drink. Again, it's just a basic sketch; it looks like it was done in a hurry, yet you can see the mood of the room, the emotions of the individuals. 'I drew these guys in a café over in East London, who'd recently immigrated to England, along with many of the others in there.' He'd sat across the room from them, and from behind the safety of his coffee, he'd used a few short glances in their direction to capture the scene. 'It was a new world to them, one of uncertainty and dislocation. I guess I wanted to capture that moment in history.' Then it was gone.

Peter's love of art thrived on that trip. He was surrounded by the work of the greatest artists in the world. He spent a lot of time going through the galleries of Europe, experiencing first hand a flourishing time for visual art, in particular the arrival of the American work found in New York, and the pop art culture of the 1950s. The art scene had traditionally come from Europe to the United States, but by the 1960s it began returning with a distinctive American flavour. It had a resounding effect on Peter. 'I remember seeing a stunning collection of pop art and abstract art in a German gallery in Cologne that collected this stuff. I didn't know it was there, I just walked in off the street. The colours were amazing. I'd always liked American art, so it was refreshing to see it after all the old classical art in the other galleries I'd been to. It was so new and sacrilegious. America was hated because of the Vietnam War, yet at the same time the hottest music and art was coming from there. So Europe was loving and hating the culture simultaneously. They were funny times.'

Once back in New Zealand, Peter, fuelled with inspiration, started as a professional artist. His trip had cemented that desire well and truly. In the early eighties he started doing some screen-printed pieces of work that sold quickly. Soon, he worked out he could probably sell enough to make a living. He bought the old chemist's in Okato and turned it into his first studio. Between him and a few other artists in the area, they managed to collect enough skills and resources to put together successful exhibitions in town. Twelve years later, Peter and his wife, Rene, moved a couple of hundred metres down the road and set up his present studio at the back of their house.

Peter was 40 years old when he decided to take up surfing. That makes him a traditional late starter, but still too early to blame on a mid-life crisis. Peter wasn't unfamiliar with the pastime; he'd previously made Taylors Mistake his hangout during his time of study and television work in Christchurch. And on his travels, he'd found a place in Cornwall that hired boards and proceeded to take on the cold waves of southern England. But he never pursued it seriously until the day he woke up and found himself in a new age bracket. If he didn't do it now, he never would, or could. Helping his cause was the fact that he had a bit more spare time. And just to sweeten the deal, Rene decided she'd join him in the waves, getting a bodyboard for herself.

'Wayne Arthur had a surf shop in town, so I painted his portrait and he gave me a wetsuit. Then I got an old board from a friend out here. That first time I stood up properly, I was blown away by it. Those first sensations of riding waves were great, feeling the energy of the wave behind you. I think anyone who chases the surf gets in tune with the natural rhythms of how things are, how the planet works, the way nature functions. In a spiritual sense, you have to get in tune with these things, get your head in a right space. These days, when the creative reservoir is empty I go for surf. They kind of go hand in hand.

'It can be pretty egalitarian, surfing. How much someone earns back on land or who they are doesn't count for anything in the surf. We're all the same when we're out there. I like the feeling you get afterwards, total wellbeing that can last for three or four days. Apart from it being a healthy sport to be involved in, I think from a societal point of view it does a hell of a lot of good for young men in their teens and early twenties to have raw challenges to face that the ocean offers, and gaining the confidence from that experience. I've seen these guys change from just a few sessions out in the surf. The ocean is always the boss, it always wins. It's a great place to overcome your fears. Sometimes you do that just putting on a wetsuit on a big day.'

Before the surf-specific prints appeared from his studio, Peter would sit at Rocky Point and use that amazing skill of his of capturing a moving subject, painting the watery scenes on site, à la brushes and easel, despite the elements,

' . . . it does a hell of a lot of good for young men in their teens and early twenties to have raw challenges to face that the ocean offers . . .'

and of course the threat from the southerly. 'I've never gone out and taken photographs then brought them back and painted from them. It's all off what I see at the time. As an artist I seriously believe the work should be based on the skill of observation and drawing, so that's what I do. It's far more satisfying.' Yet despite the work he did there being stunning examples of the rugged coastline, he admits back then he wasn't looking at the place from a surfer's perspective. But as soon as he started getting out in the water with his board, his perception changed dramatically. 'In terms of art, I wanted to have a view of the land from the sea and capture it from a surfer's point of view. To make the screen prints authentic there was no choice but to get out in the surf. If I was going to do a wave from out at the different spots, then it had to be an authentic wave.'

The first surf screen print Peter did was of Rocky Point in 1992, then afterwards Stent Road, which was the one that took off with the public. 'I'd always liked comic book cartoons and storyboards, you know, frame by frame. I partially got the idea from a Sam Hunt poem on the radio about the trips he made in his dinghy and the thoughts going through his head. It was all about the journey for him. At that stage, I was regularly going down all these roads

224

to check the surf and I thought about doing a little storyboard sequence about the journey to the surf break, the view of the waves from the shore, and at least one image of the view from being out in the water. It's part storybook, part comic. It connects to American pop art in a sense.' Peter hadn't been out in the water for a few months and was feeling a little unfit, so he left the surfboard on the rack and took Rene's bodyboard instead. Once he was out in the surf a new door suddenly opened in Peter's world — having his face mere inches away from the ocean gave him a view he'd never seen when riding a wave. 'I began trying to capture that curve, and to work out the relationship with why it broke that way on the reef. I tried to draw the waves out in the water by sticking paper on the bodyboard. I thought if I got good-quality watercolour paper and wax crayons it would probably handle it, but I wasn't really that successful. Then I thought I'd draw straight on to the bodyboard and scrub it off afterwards.'

If you've ever checked out one of Peter's surf prints, the thing that really makes it stand out from those of other artists is how he's captured that curve, that precise moment of anticipation. I couldn't help but draw comparisons with his years of secretly capturing the human spirit in a matter of seconds, and whether it all led him to this? Capturing that final second in a wave's life? Perhaps. It's that curve in the wave that draws any surfer in the room back to his work, even if it's just for a second or two to mind-surf the wave hanging on the wall. 'That's the most exciting bit really, isn't it, the sight of the wave about to break? It's the promise, it's coming up, it's coming, it's coming. That's the biggest rush when you're surfing. Do you take it? Do you leave it? I think the photos in the surf mags miss that point a lot, that moment in the wave all us wave-riders cherish. You hardly ever see them show a wide shot of the lines of swell building up. It's often far too close in at the wave. In the studio I was trying to catch that bit of spray you get just before the wave breaks with a toothbrush and Indian ink.' To demonstrate this, he gets a small jar of black ink and a scrap bit of paper, places them on the floor, and with a brush begins flicking the liquid against the white, leaving the effect of an offshore on the wave. 'There's something about when you drag the brush and you get those lines. Those lines are like the movement of the wave while the larger particles from the bristles are the splash.' Like I said, an authentic experience.

Looking around the different landscape paintings in the studio, and the shape of Mount Taranaki featured in some of them, I wonder whether he feels he has an intimate relationship with the iconic land form. 'In some ways I feel like I know the mountain like the back of my hand, especially the profile. You can never satisfy the public's hunger for mountain images.' But when it came to doing the print for Arawhata, it took on a whole new dimension. At that stage, Peter was having trouble coming up with a fourth image. It wasn't until he was out in the surf at the break, watching the waves to the right of him surge along the reef, that he saw it. 'I remember thinking, of course. The wave goes past, and for half a second it's in line with the mountain in the background. That curve of the wave has echoes of the mountain as well, because that line is very similar to the silhouette of the mountain. And it's a view most people wouldn't see, something only the surfing community gets to. It's a great perspective out there, so it's a shame for others not to experience it.'

Peter's eyes widen and his voice picks up tempo when we start to talk about the conservation work done at Rocky Point, work that began in 1992. He's kept a scrapbook of the developments, all in chronological order. 'We've got a programme going where we've planted Rockies with native trees. It's a strip of coast that runs one and a half kilometres and was surveyed off in nineteen eighty-one as a public reserve. Back in those days, if the land around the coast changed in size or ownership then the government could take a twenty-metre strip for preservation.' He flicks through the pages, pointing out specific photos and important faces like a proud parent showing their champion kid's album. That may sound over the top, but what they've achieved is damned cool. Photos from the 1990s don't do it justice though. He closes the book and reaches for his hat and scarf. Looks like I was off for the grand tour.

On the way there I wanted to know how they first got on to it. 'No one knew about it until I was having a nosey through some old Lands and Surveys maps and I realised this favourite place for surfers was actually a public reserve. At that stage I was thinking, wouldn't it be great to have trees to protect the surf, and have a place for me to paint out of the wind. I got a dozen locals to rally together and we got a meeting organised. Surprisingly, we had some people tell us it would never work, that we were wasting our time. But the council came on board with us and basically said, if we do all the work, they'll supply us with the materials to fence the reserve.'

We pull up at Rockies and park beside some wooden steps specially built into the farm fence and a cabbage tree marking an entrance. We walk into the reserve and Peter makes a point of showing me the 'office', a large burrow inside a couple of fully grown taupata, with a plank of wood tucked at the back for sitting on; a place for a pre-surf check, a post-surf debrief, or just somewhere to chill and wax lyrical on the view and how lucky we are. It's features like this that have been extra satisfying to Peter and the rest of the group, not so much the physical presence of small seats, but how the surfing and local community have adopted the place as their own. The group not only planted and nurtured vegetation, but they managed to create a culture to go with it, which is no easy feat at all. Peter tells me the rubbish they had to clear from the land before anything was planted was horrific, but in my time of walking around the reserve I didn't come across one piece of litter anywhere. Surfers and visitors acknowledge the work that's been done, including the addition of a public toilet, and now make a conscious effort to keep it that way, despite the lack of any signs telling people not to litter — a ploy the group purposely integrated into the project to retain its natural aesthetics. Even the hundreds of campers that park up for days at a time to enjoy the world-class surf and breathtaking sunsets, leave their patch of grassy real estate exactly as they found it. It seems Rockies is a prime example of how empowering people to do good is far more effective than trying to get them to confine to a bunch of orders on sticks. City councils take note.

'I began trying to capture that curve, and to work out the relationship with why it broke that way on the reef.'

We continue walking the strip of pathway between the growth. A father and his two children walk past us, the kids running ahead with looks of adventure on their faces. Apparently it's not only surfers who are enjoying the transformation; people now come to just enjoy the atmosphere that's been created. 'The transformation from just bare grass to this has been very satisfying for me. The whole length has now been fenced and planted with natives such as hebes, karo, flaxes, pohutukawa, some karaka. The local farmer has been very co-operative and done more planting himself, while we've had further

227

support from the Treetrust and South Taranaki Forest and Bird. It's improved the surf break, especially in a howling sou'wester; it takes the raw edge off the wave and, of course, it's now easier to paint. I love seeing these trees planted.' As we're walking through the long strip of head-high vegetation — the coastal side having periodic gaps for people to enjoy the view of the waves peeling a few metres away — I turn to talk to Peter, but he's disappeared. I start backtracking as he springs out from within the vegetation. 'I planted a nikau in here somewhere,' he tells me, before morphing back into the green. 'Here it is,' he calls out. I push my way through the branches and find Peter crouched down beside the two-foot high tree, hiding in a sheltered clearing between the natives. 'It's an experiment,' he tells me. 'They said it wouldn't grow in these conditions but I thought I'd give it a go anyway. It's already grown since I planted it,' he says with a satisfied smirk.

I wonder if Peter sees this reserve as a visual, interactive piece of art he's played a part in creating. Something that's here for generations, for the community to enjoy. It's obvious that art can transform a surf spot the same way it can transform a room; that might sound strange to some people, but it'd make perfect sense once they saw the connection with Peter. I ask about his thoughts on the environment and whether surfers have greater empathy with it than other strands of society. 'I think surfers have become a lot more conscious of being clean. If I was going on a camping trip, despite my love for surfing, I would stay at surf spots, because surfers look after their own areas. Surfers should always be listened to where the coastal environment is concerned. We're always seeing things happening, because we're out there in it. I remember we were trying to get a protection order on the Stony River, and a surfer in the group who mainly rode the waves at the Kumara Patch situated at the mouth of the river, spoke of the difference of the water quality there compared to the other surf breaks. That's a valid view. We're not taking a machine out in the water. We're not taking anything from the water, just good times.'

When we arrive back at Okato we head into Café Lahar for a coffee and to check out more of his work. We sit and talk longer about his art, his love of surfing, the story behind each piece of his work on the wall. One in particular stands out; a lady serving behind a bar — her vibrant red hair and expression of modest beauty is striking. It's done in the same style as his other secret portraits.

Peter tells me he and Rene recently returned from a trip to Melbourne where they were having a drink at a sidewalk café. Peter made Rene sit in his view while he quickly drew the attractive woman in his sketchbook. When he returned to Okato, he made an etching of her and sent it back across the Tasman to the restaurant as a way of thanks. He chuckles when I ask him how he thinks she'll respond to it. He shrugs his shoulders lightly. He's not expecting a reply. He never does.

I bet she'll be stoked.

Andrew McAlpine

Aaron Topp

FILM DIRECTOR
AUCKLAND

*There's this thing I've been doing over the years that
I'm not all that keen on sharing. But for the sake
of this intro, I'm gonna come clean. See, I've got a
closet secret — I tune the car stereo in to Solid Gold
FM. To be completely honest, it takes up three of my
preset buttons on the tuner. Don't worry, I don't
tune in all the time — ZM, The Rock and Radio
Hauraki are there too. Why am I telling you this?
Because I like to explore the wonders of music in all
its various forms and evolutionary stages.*

With a push of a button I can invite the sounds of the fifties, sixties and seventies into my world whenever the mood surfaces; it's my way of paying respect to those forefathers who paved the way for the other three stations. A musical journey, like discovering a tomb containing three decades of hieroglyphics in stereo. It's the soundtrack to the longboarding and twin-fin eras. It helps me understand my parents. It helps me understand anyone over 50 for that matter.

When a very good photographer friend of mine, a guy who's still comfortable living in the longboarding phase, received a DVD copy of the 1968 surf movie, *Children of the Sun*, he was stoked to be reminded of the surfing world that was; the same one he'd almost forgotten existed. For the same reasons I tune in to Solid Gold; I wanted to see where modern surfing was spawned. I eagerly borrowed the DVD from him and that following Sunday arvo on the couch I was transported 40 years into the past to a New Zealand that seemed all just a little too perfect. A place where the weather was permanently sunny, the wind offshore. The waves were always shoulder height and only a handful of crew ever went out. Guys invited others to share their waves, while dames, as organic as a peach from the tree in your grandparents' back yard, bathed unprotected on the sand, basking in the ultra-violet rays. Everything was clean, pristine, untouched. Carefree. Teenagers didn't mope, they weren't reaching into their fast food bag, pushing tiny buttons and looking at tiny screens, hiding their egos behind a tattoo or shutting the world out with loud music played directly in their ears. New Zealand teenagers floated in the breeze; when they weren't surfing, they were goofing off, leaping from sand dunes, strutting bronzed, athletic bodies in front of the other sex's equivalent, roadtripping to some other pumping surf break, while the party followed to ensure the fun never stopped. And all to the narrative of some guy with a really deep voice and a penchant for breaking into psychedelic prose.

Was 1960s New Zealand really the surf utopia a 19-year-old Andrew McAlpine captured on film, or was it all just a clever illusion created in an editing room?

I had to find out.

Over the summers of '66 and '68, Andrew borrowed his dad's 16 mm camera and took it everywhere him and his mates went surfing. He made his

own waterproof housing out of Perspex and developed a suction technique to
fix the camera to the front of the surfboard, so the viewer could be as close
to the wave as a possible without actually getting wet. He filmed the crew
at their home break of Piha, and at other beaches
like Gisborne, Whangamata, Shipwrecks, Raglan,
Kaikoura, even across the ditch in various North
Queensland locations. He captured pioneering
surfers like Bob McTavish, Russell Hughes, George
Greenough, and Wayne Parkes. He left the camera
rolling during chill-out sessions at sunset, and nude
swimming ventures. He explored innovative angles
and new possibilities to make sure the journey and
the lifestyle were given as much attention as the
surfing. Not once did he actually think it was going
to be used as anything other than a bit of a laugh
during home movie evenings. Although later, I
found, in the back of his mind he had toyed with
the idea of making a proper surf movie, but had no
idea how to go about it.

New Zealand
teenagers
floated in the
breeze; when
they weren't
surfing, they
were goofing
off, leaping
from sand
dunes, strutting
bronzed, athletic
bodies . . .

He arrived back from a three-month trip
shooting his buddies surfing perfect Noosa. The locals there were saying they
were the best waves they'd seen in decades, perhaps ever. He looked at all the
cases of film he'd accumulated and thought about the potential. Could he
have a movie somewhere amongst that footage? Would people actually like this
stuff? Was it a lot of effort for a limited audience of mates and a society that
looked at them sideways?

'We didn't consider surfing to be a culture back then,' Andrew says, reflecting
from a couch in his Remuera home. 'Overseas it was considered a culture, but
we didn't have enough people here to warrant it. Here we were called beach
bums. I'd always thought, people go snow skiing, but they're not called snow
bums. They're just going down a mountain, so what's the difference? I suppose
we were onto something new, something different.'

It's hard to picture a New Zealand surfing scene like that, but I guess that's
testament to the rapid explosion of popularity the pastime experienced through

the seventies, eighties and particularly the nineties. With so few people around, Andrew had been quite selective in the shots he'd taken. It was a tight-knit group of friends he was with, and while he may have hidden the fact back then, Andrew admits some people were more photogenic than others. Every weekend was another opportunity to film the story of their lives, but only if the weather was sunny and the waves were pumping. Andrew wanted to capture surfing in all its perfection and that required good old-fashioned guesswork, the most highly advanced technology of the day; an almost impossible task, I find out, when so much of New Zealand experienced grey, dreary days. Yeah, even back then. 'It was traditional to have a big party on the Friday night, decide where we're heading to, then get going about two in the morning. We usually had three or four cars. There wasn't much traffic on the road in those days. My mother wasn't so keen on the whole routine.'

There was camaraderie and fun from start to finish. On the way there and back, they'd be talking about stupid things, funny stuff, getting into mischief with egg fights and stealing road signs. It was all about the lifestyle to them. Chasing the waves, the sun, the girls. Simple cotton shorts were the surfing attire of choice by default, whether they were in the warm waters of the north, or doing a three-hour session below the snowy Kaikoura Ranges (to thaw out they upped the ante in misdemeanours and were arrested for throwing rocks at power insulators. Forty years later and Andrew shakes his head sensibly at the thought; it would've cost the taxpayers a lot of money to fix those, he tells me). The fun was reflected out in the water; with so few people to shoot, he'd endeavour to capture as many bodies in the surf as possible to make it look good. Even in popular places like Whangamata — a particular favourite place of his to film — he'd only be dealing with a dozen surfers at the most. 'Even though there were always plenty of waves to go around, it wasn't uncommon to share as well. There is actually more skill in riding a wave with others compared to surfing it by yourself. You wanted more people to join in, you were looking for the company. When we were filming we were trying to capture the fun factor, and the more people we got in the shot, the more fun it looked. You don't see that focus any more, modern surfing has gone the opposite way. There was a purity to surfing back then. Young people these days don't get a chance to see that side of it, the commercial and modern stereotype gets trampled into them early on.' Andrew shrugs his shoulders; he's philosophical about it all, 'but you can't expect things to stay the same'.

When Andrew sat down in the editing room for the first time in 1967 ready to tackle the hours of footage, he was asked by a friend what the storyline was going to be. Just two years earlier the American film director, Bruce Brown, had released his surf hit, *The Endless Summer*. It had gone on to well and truly set the bar for surf flicks of the day. While Andrew never went out to emulate the plot, the idea of two surfers travelling the world for a year following the summer season to an entertaining voice-over certainly helped inspire a format. It was the dry, light-humoured commentary that had helped make *The Endless Summer* such a big hit for surfers and non-surfers alike, and even now Andrew acknowledges Bruce Brown is the undisputed king of cinematic storytelling. As for his own feature, the script was written by another of Andrew's friends in advertising, and cleverly read out by Peter Telling, at the time a radio announcer for Radio Hauraki. And just like it did for Mr Brown, the narration used in *Children of the Sun* put the sugar coating on what was already a masterpiece of surf cinematography.

Speaking as someone who never experienced that period, the poetic style of narration used, the rich, energetic tone of Mr Telling's voice-over, and clever use of cheeky wit, is all a fantastic, candid example of what I missed out on, and only adds to the experience:

> The brain never stops thinking, the days never end, time is as brief as a flickering eyelid.
> Involved with the sea, surfing is communicating with nature,
> Understanding our own small part and how we fit into the scheme of things.
> We sit and watch and life goes by, even if we don't fill every second with action, we're still a part of it
> If we think.
> Don't stop thinking.
> Don't stop.

Andrew repositions himself in the chair and chuckles uncomfortably. He speaks quite openly about how that must sound now; the times have changed. Much like fashion, just because it felt right in the 1960s doesn't mean it's going to fit comfortably into a contemporary world. 'Some of it was OK, but other lines were a bit corny. I used to be very critical about it, very embarrassed about how it sounded. The way the commentary was all edited together. It was all a bit too flowery, but that's what the trend was back then, to write flowery stuff about surfing.' He chuckles again, and I almost get the feeling he accepts the language used has some legitimate historical significance for anyone wanting to remember, or as in my case understand, the time.

> As the waves splashed against the wooden side and the land thinned to nothing, he didn't worry about anything. He knew he was safe from harm out there.

Andrew grew up in Remuera. As a kid he used to spend hours sailing at Whangaparaoa, steering the boat miles out to sea, far beyond the horizon. As the waves splashed against the wooden side and the land thinned to nothing, he didn't worry about anything. He knew he was safe from harm out there. His father always said he was born with a caul over his head, and according to Scottish beliefs, he would never drown. His love of water continued when, as a teenager on a day trip to Piha, he found a row of pop-out foam surfboards for hire in front of Peter Byers' surf shop. 'I paid the ten shillings and took one out. I thought it was fantastic, it was so much fun. I suppose surfing is something you always try, and once you experience those initial sensations you always want to go back to capture the thrills again. Moving along through the water and the sensation of travelling along in the green of the wave. I remember surfing Shipwreck Bay early on; there were these big waves, like lumps of green. I was flying along.'

His father had set up McAlpine Refrigeration, one of the biggest names in the industry, but passed away when Andrew was only 13. By his late teens, Andrew had begun the process of following in his dad's footsteps by enrolling in a refrigeration apprenticeship with Fisher and Paykel. 'I started working in a factory, but deep down I never really wanted to get involved, I just wasn't that interested in it. My main attraction was thinking about my next surf. It was so much more colourful and nice going to the beach. In the end, the camera became the catalyst for change.'

With the final cut ready to release to the world, Andrew secured backing from the Rialto chain of theatres. *Children of the Sun* ran for three weeks in Newmarket, its advertisements sitting alongside those for the likes of *Gone with the Wind*, and attracting punters with the strapline, 'the surf scene swinging in New Zealand and Australia'. While he had good reviews and a lot of interest from the general public, who were curious to see how successful a film on surfing could be, the financial reward was meagre; his skills lay in being creative, not in negotiating fair deals. After a small period of hype, things died down pretty quickly.

After it screened in black and white on TV1 and Australia's ABC channel, the movie almost spent the rest of its existence buried in an archives cupboard. That was until video came around and suddenly *Children of the Sun* was doing the rounds again, this time in people's VCR machines. Five hundred tapes later, and it's now available on disc for the new generation to put into their DVD players. Like surfing itself, the movie has evolved over time. Andrew laughs when I ask him if the New Zealand market has played its part in securing his financial future. Forty years have passed and sales for the film are still consistent in America, Australia, Japan, even in France. OK, so it's not private helicopter material (sales average about one a week), but how many other Kiwi directors can claim international recognition on their 40-year-old movie? Americans love the timelessness of it; they like to reminisce about the days when there weren't any crowds and before the alpha-male wannabes began paddling circles around them. All up, Andrew reckons he would've sold around 2000 copies of *Children of the Sun* over four decades.

Is that enough to make him somewhat of a household name in industry circles? He was exiting the surf with his son in Australia back in 2007 when an American surfer started making a fuss after he found out who he was. Andrew thought it was hilarious. Andrew's a quiet guy who doesn't like to talk too much, preferring instead to keep things simple and short. He ends each sentence with a smile. He doesn't see himself as anything other than a guy who played around with a camera once upon a time. That's a big call from someone who received a letter from Bruce Brown himself, stating *Children of the Sun* was the best film he'd ever seen from a first-time surf film-maker, going on to give it high praise for its originality and its crisp use of photography, stating he'd started watching it with a 'ho-hum' attitude, like most of the films sent to him by upstart film-makers, noting that after a few minutes of viewing he was impressed by Andrew's obvious talent and passion. What advice did Bruce give him? Pound the streets of New York until an American television station or film buyer notices you. But Andrew never bothered to show me that letter, let alone talk about it during the interview; it took his wife, Cathy, to let me read it as I was leaving. Andrew shrugged my amazement off with a light-hearted comment and smiled again. He makes out it's not that big a deal, really, although he acknowledges it was great getting some technical feedback from the legend himself; he was always asking questions to make sure he was doing the right stuff.

I ask whether he took up the advice and roamed the streets of the Big Apple, but he shakes his head, 'Shortboards were suddenly coming in and I guess I missed the boat there. I had to keep up with it and I couldn't. I wasn't that great at the selling side of things. I think I've learnt a lot more about that side of business later in life. The skills I've acquired since would have made things a lot different then. But if you look back you'll go mad.'

Since the 1980s, surf films have focused on capturing every second of the sport's rapid progression by chasing the Slaters of the world, who headed the charge with their radical moves and professional attitudes, in far-away locations, the more exotic the better. The narrator was out, the underground punk band was in. The market became swamped with movies that portrayed a tightly packed collage of every groundbreaking manoeuvre, all set to a soundtrack that tested the TV's speakers. 'These days, surf movies have too much surfing in them,' Andrew says. 'If you give people too much of a good thing, then they're going to get blasé. Starve them of it and they'll want more, I think that's what made guys like Bruce Brown and Jack McCoy's films so good, to them it was also about capturing the journey and experience.'

After doing another surfing project, *Beautiful Day* (a 30-minute feature destined for the television networks) produced in collaboration with a mate, John Cassidy, Andrew decided he'd start focusing his lens on land-based projects. He created McAlpine Productions, a studio dedicated to television advertising. Still absorbed by the surfing ethos, he went to his first job meeting at a corporate advertising agency in jeans and jandals and listened to guys in suits and ties explain the creative brief for a new drink, L&P. He knew it was a little unorthodox to be sitting there in a T-shirt and tapping his toes, but the times, they were a-changin'. 'Film was starting to become a lot more creative in those days. That's probably why they used me, because my techniques and alternative approach were different to the norm. I didn't like the corporate dealings very much, it was hard going from filming stuff I wanted to do, to doing what they wanted me to do. The creative side was much better.'

There was also the Pizza Hut ad in the 1980s; who can forget that image of the kid sitting in the restaurant's booth, pulling a slice of the Hut's finest from his mouth as steaming mozzarella refused to separate? Or the iconic English Muffin ad, with the little girl and cream on her nose? 'We used to use the wide-angle lenses a lot and get in close so everything became a lot more vivid. I used to like filming people without any practice, otherwise they get too formal. Get it on the first take. With surfing you've got to do that. Even when they jumped around in the sand dunes in *Children of the Sun*, it was all just the one shot. I s'pose that explains a lot of its vitality.'

'There is a sense of enlightenment when you surf. Your senses are heightened. You're in the moment at the time, constantly aware of what you're doing.'

Andrew's clients included shirt manufacturers like Crimplene, a job that required him to try to make something out of a handful of models standing in a paddock in the rain ('I filmed a seagull at a rubbish dump and edited it into the shoot. The whole ad looked fantastic in black and white'). There was also his own modelling job for Summit Shirts; he wouldn't tell you that, of course — he hated every second in front of the lens — but Cathy would. His biggest recognition, though, came from a promotion he did for Suzuki motorbikes. It went on to win the advertisement of the year, as chosen by Brian Edwards. To pull it off, he used everything he'd learnt from filming surfers. 'We didn't know what we were going to do, so we went down to Rotorua with a group of guys from the agency and got shots of the bikes going through the mud. We used a long telephoto lens, which was unusual for the time, and mounted a camera to the handlebars of the bike and to the forks so the dirt sprayed up. No one was doing that sort of stuff back then, exploring different angles and techniques, it was all still very formalised.'

Just before 1990, McAlpine Productions stopped. The fun factor had left, replaced by a highly competitive market. Andrew's swansong was a sailboarding feature featuring Barbara and Aaron Kendall, *Wavesailing Down Under*. He'd filmed it during 1985 to capture the rise in popularity of yet another water sport. He took it into Amalgamated Theatres, who just happened to be looking for a short film to play before the release of a new film, *Crocodile Dundee*. They decided the music and imagery was a perfect match for the Australian-based blockbuster. This time round, Andrew's film was shown in every movie theatre in the country.

Andrew got into the real estate profession not long after and it's been his day job ever since. He enjoys it. It's much easier, he says, selling someone else's product than trying to peddle his own. I could imagine he has a lot of return business out there; he doesn't strike me as the intense, pushy type of person the industry tends to attract, and I didn't recall seeing any whacky, self-promoting vehicle parked out the front either. While I assume he's retired the jandals and jeans to the drawer when meeting a prospective client, he's still retained his laidback attitude. When he was 25 years old and studying at the Auckland School of Philosophy, he saw an advertisement for Advaita meditation classes. Something about it intrigued him, perhaps the thought of empowering himself. He took a class, then another. Now, at the age of 62, he still meditates twice a day. 'Advaita means "all one". The teaching is a combination of different eastern cultures. Meditating gives you a broader acceptance of it all, that's the result of it.' Is there a connection between surfing and meditation? 'There is a sense of enlightenment when you surf. Your senses are heightened. You're in the moment at the time, constantly aware of what you're doing. When you're in the curl of the wave you get a deep sensation. When you speak to surfers you can tell when they haven't surfed for a while, there's a sort of cleansing in that. Like meditation, I guess, it teaches you flexibility to handle different situations, to go with the flow.' He pauses and recalls his younger years, 'yachties are similar in many ways'.

In 2009, during its 41st anniversary year, *Children of the Sun* will get another lease of life in a new international film depicting the evolution from longboards to shortboards. Ironically, one of the star surfers in the original movie, Bob McTavish, is co-producing it with surfing powerhouse, Rip Curl. Andrew was approached after they found no one had filmed anything decent during the period of 1966–68, except some Kiwi bloke and his mates. They're spending a fortune on making sure they create an authentic historical account of the day, before premiering it at a major contest at Noosa. Afterwards, it will be released around the world. Andrew laughs at the reality of having a film that was so old, no one wanted to watch it, but now has a historical element that makes it important. I ask if he ever thought, just once, what he was capturing was going to have such significance in the future. No way. In fact, a lot of the film he shot was thrown in the bin.

After all, it was just him capturing his mates doing fun things in the sun and the surf.

Who would wanna watch that?

> This is Piha, a rather picturesque place and we love it,
> We go for fun, we've often thought about it enough.
> Fun.
> Every ride is a gift to be treasured and remembered.
> You know, there's freedom out there,
> More freedom than you've ever felt before.
> You feel it as soon as you get out of the car,
> You see it and you hear it.
> It's the surfing time and you can't wait.

Matt Hishon

Aaron Topp

ARTIST/GRAPHIC DESIGNER
HAMILTON

Back in 2005 Matt Hishon was standing at Hamilton Airport watching a plane come to rest on the tarmac. His instructions were simple: greet the guy who was flying in, drive him out to Raglan, take him surfing and hang out for a few days. He fondled the keys to a borrowed Holden as the man, a person who Forbes *magazine had recently recognised as America's third most influential athlete, walked from the plane. Tony Hawk had just finished demonstrating at Vodafone X Air; two days of top athletes competing in the disciplines of BMX, freestyle motocross, inline and skateboarding, while the country's hottest bands of the day supplied the live soundtrack.*

It was up to Matt to make sure he was looked after now the event was over. He subtly wiped the sweat from his palms as he reached out to shake the Californian's hand.

When I rang the doorbell at Matt's home in Hamilton there was a period of silence, then I was greeted by a man with a tall frame, extended hand and explosive smile. The same reaction Tony would have received at the airport, I'd imagine, although this time round Matt was probably a little more relaxed. He apologised for keeping me waiting; he was busy pushing work through before a deadline, but was contemplating chucking it in for the day and heading out for a surf. Yesterday he did the same thing. There's always tomorrow to work that little bit harder. Matt's a self-employed graphic designer, a very talented one, working under the business name, Anomaly Creative. If you've been a consumer in the surf industry you will have seen some of his handiwork. He's worked with many high-profile companies, both in the surf industry and further afield. He's currently working on rebranding one of Europe's largest surfing hardware suppliers. He also sells his skills to other creative companies who are looking for that special touch for a client. At the moment, he's a guy in hot demand.

As far as chaperoning goes, it's not something he's trained for. Matt's always believed opportunities present themselves through people you know and if the work is there it will inevitably find him. He wasn't surprised, then, to get a call from a mate's older brother asking if he'd mind looking after someone for a few days. At that stage, no names were mentioned, but Matt agreed to it anyway. He was just happy to help out.

And to start, it was a smooth run; he met Tony on time and got him out of Hamilton unscathed. Everything was going well until they stopped at a supermarket in Dinsdale to get supplies and Tony insisted he used his own card to pay for them. 'The chick behind the counter looked at his name, then looked at him, then looked back at the card,' Matt recalls. 'When we left we were suddenly swamped by all these kids asking him to sign their rugby ball, their shirt, whatever they had on them. I was freaking about what I should be doing, but Tony was sweet about it, he just signed everything. A couple of days later I took him to the Raglan skate park and you could tell he was just cruising but still absolutely ripping. The whole three days people would just bowl up to him non-stop and he was super-nice to everyone, giving all his time to anyone who wanted a chat. On the last day, he, his manager, and I surfed Indicators by ourselves while Tony's fiancée videoed us from the rocks. When they got home they sent me the footage. He gave me some T-shirts and stuff. I should've got him to sign them in hindsight, but he was just a normal down-to-earth guy, it didn't seem right.'

While there haven't been any further special minder jobs, Matt has since been busy with the promo artwork for Vodafone Homegrown, a musical extravaganza of the who's who in the New Zealand music scene, set on five massive stages on the Wellington waterfront. For the 2008 event, Matt designed a pohutukawa tree with fantails and speakers to carry the concept of a purely Kiwi sound. In 2009, he took it a step further and created an old-school ghettoblaster made out of traditional kete weaving and paua shell trimming, with a couple of sliced kiwifruit for speakers. While he admits it was a labour-intensive process, he enjoyed being able to retain a lot of the creative control. 'I left the world of agencies as I felt I was compromising quality too much for the sake of getting stuff out the door. I want to focus more on a high-end, quality product. Sometimes you get someone who will trust you and let you have free rein, then other times you'll get a situation where it's design by committee, and you have to please ten different people all putting in their ten cents. That's the difference between fine art and design; art is purely an expression, observation or commentary, where design is more for someone else's purpose and function. I want to get to the stage where I can blur the line between the two, that's the direction I'm trying to take my artwork.' His fine art is just as impressive, by the way. He uses predominantly acrylic and spray stencils to draw the two worlds of graphic and freehand together. Fine art is laborious, mentally draining, much more physically immersive. He uses exactly the same thought process for design and fine art — a computer is just another tool, the same as a paintbrush. The difference with digital art is that it's more instantaneous, it's as contemporary as you'll get. Here today, gone tomorrow.

'We might all see the same thing, but we all see it differently, have different interpretations. It's what makes us who we are.'

It's no surprise art was Matt's strongest topic at school. He loved writing too, but in a cruel, ironic twist he was so rushed to get the ideas down, his hands couldn't keep up. His printing looked like a bunch of hieroglyphics. His teachers banned him from using a pen until he was in Form Two. By his own admission, his writing remains atrocious. It's a fascinating anomaly when you consider the detail those same hands can create with a tool twice as long as a pencil. In seventh form he took three arts — painting, sculpting and design — and enrolled in a media arts degree at the Waikato Institute of Technology. 'If I'd majored in fine art I wasn't sure if I'd come out with this huge debt and no way to pay it off. I was a bit young and didn't back myself. But this way I appreciate the time I do get to paint.'

'I remember surfing there alone once. Every wave was perfect. Even though I stayed out for six hours, time seemed to stand still that day.'

Matt's love for the ocean and the surfing ethos are both sources of inspiration for him. He aims to articulate his experiences in the form of something visual to share with the viewer. 'We might all see the same thing, but we all see it differently, have different interpretations. It's what makes us who we are. I did an exhibition about ten years ago based on seascapes of Raglan and how light on water reflects and refracts and changes. With these paintings I wasn't too concerned about it being photo-perfect, it was more about capturing the spirit of the place and that feeling when you're paddling out. The whole sensation of how the light's reacting to the water. I'm always looking and remembering how things appear, figuring out how I'm gonna put it on canvas. Capturing those *Morning of the Earth* moments when a wave's in slow-mo and you're like, wow, check that out. There are so many different angles you can look at things, I'm always inspired by what I see and experimenting with ways to translate that into something people can relate to.' His latest efforts take his art a step further towards the abstract; looking at how light works on the surface of the canvas, coming up with different depths, textures and patterns that alter as you walk past. In the morning the angle of light will give a piece a certain appearance, but that completely changes by the time afternoon arrives.

His last few pieces have been sold through friends. He's yet to again achieve his goal of getting a large enough body of work together to warrant an exhibition, and it's not going to happen while people are buying pieces before he can horde them away. With his daytime commitments, it's a matter of putting enough time aside to focus on getting an exhibition done. Probably only need to dedicate a day or two a week, he reckons, and it'd be a piece of cake. He thinks about that, and mentions he's got some time coming up in a couple of months that he might keep free. But it's a big call to turn away work when it's there. And he's not that keen on compromising his trips to Raglan when the urge calls.

'That's where I'm my own worst enemy. There'll be a number of things that come in the next day and they ask for crazy deadlines and the rest all compounds. Some days I'll work twenty hours a day, other times maybe two hours a day. That's one thing I haven't found yet, the balance; it's about being disciplined. I'm getting better at sitting down and not rushing things. I don't think my creativity is ever low, a strong coffee might help when I'm tired, but the actual act of creating is what I always enjoy. I still want to do it, it's never a chore. People ask me how I come up with different solutions every day and not be repetitive. It's a reaction to the pieces of puzzle put in front of you and your brain just fills in the gaps, it's a natural formula to solve it.'

What drives him to paint in his spare time? Instead of some standard answer involving creative urges that need releasing, he tells me how he did a painting of a panoramic vista looking from Manu Bay, across Whale Bay and through to Indicators, the main surf spots at Raglan. It was 40 hours' worth of work. He wanted to keep it for himself as a centrepiece. After showing it to his friend's mum, though, and seeing how much she loved it, he sold it to her instead for a third its worth. A year later she passed away from cancer, but according to her husband that painting kept her spirits up until the end. 'That's what I do it for, the enjoyment others get from it. When I'm gone, I want to leave something behind to be enjoyed. That'd be nice, given the grand scheme of how little time we're on this planet for. Leaving some sort of resonance of who we once were.'

Picked up a copy of *New Zealand Surfing* magazine lately? That's Matt's work in your hands. Not the photography or the copy (although he has reported on the odd surf trip), but the layout, the fonts, typography, the special effects, the colours used. Aside from the cover shot itself, it was the reason you were subliminally attracted to it while it sat amongst dozens of other magazines in the rack. After hearing they were looking for someone to give the mag a fresh new design, Matt flicked his portfolio through to the editor. From the mag's point of view it made good creative sense to use a guy who was as keen about surfing as the person reading it, so he got the job. His role involves talking with the photographer and content director about the feel of each image and determining how much of a creative influence he should bring to it. They give him a loose layout of where the shots go, Matt reads the story and thinks about the tone and what's been said and how he can add value to it with layout and graphic elements. Basically, Matt's job is all about flow, making sure the pages work with each other so the reader can be as immersed as possible. He shows me some of his work on the latest issue, a few comparisons of before and after shots and the amount of minute detail involved in each of the 80 or so pages. For each edition he does the prep work in Hamilton and then heads up to Tairua, where Kemalu Publishing is located. He sets up, gets comfortable, and for the next six days works through day and night to get it finished, the last three with no sleep. The approaching deadline and lots of coffee are the only two things that keep him functioning. Then he crashes and burns. He has no complaints, though; that's pretty common where a deadline's concerned. He laughs and shrugs his shoulders, and mentions the promise of a work balance again. 'And anyway,' he continues, 'with the current workload I've been feeling one step removed from surfing, but now with the magazine I feel a little more connected again.'

When Matt was a toddler, his mother couldn't get him past the sand dunes; he'd be screaming; the sight of the roaring white monsters was too much for him. By the time Matt was five, his father was pushing him and his two older brothers on a board into the whitewater at Mount Maunganui, or Whangamata, or Hot Water Beach. Before Matt got a licence he'd sweet talk his mum into driving him across Tauranga to the beach, but once they built a bridge he biked across, one arm holding his board while the other attempted to keep the handlebars straight in the wind and traffic. By the time he was 14, he entered his first competition. 'I still really enjoy it, if you lose you lose, whatever. I accepted long ago I was never gonna be Kelly Slater. I've always been competitive on a certain level, but never in other sports, it's something about getting out there and getting a couple of waves and beating someone. I lose more than I win, but whatever, it's still good times.' I absorb his modest comments at the time, but a few hours later, with the sun setting over Manu Bay, I watched him paddle into wave after wave, drawing smooth lines across the green walls like he was painting with one of his brushes. It's the same style that's seen him win the over-28-year-old division at Raglan club contests, and continue to compete at national level.

'It's thinking about the pulses of energy and what's made them. Thinking about how that little problem you're festering over ain't all that big in comparison.'

While he says he was once obsessed with South African surfer, Martin Potter, going as far as getting the same flames on his first custom board, Matt's main inspiration came from surfing with his brother, who was a few years older than him. The two of them would surf together all the time at the Mount, until the day his brother met a girlfriend and suddenly Matt was left watching them drive off without him. He's still envious of the amount of surf time his brother gets and is proud of the fact he was instrumental in the establishment of the Raglan Surf Academy.

Occasionally these days Matt will go on a solo mission out to the coast. There are moments in the middle of winter when he'll drive around to Ruapuke and no one will be there; it's a time to embrace the elements and appreciate the surroundings. 'I remember surfing there alone once. Every wave was perfect. Even though I stayed out for six hours, time seemed to stand still that day. I came in and sat in the car and was gonna go home, but went back out instead, it was that good. Anytime when the light's right and everything's vivid and crisp and reflecting off the water and you notice how it affects the colour of things, how water can look pink and other subtle tones of red, or blue, or warm and cold, those are the moments when surfers are truly absorbed in what nature can offer. I think we have a better compassion for the environment. You can't be somewhere pristine and see some rubbish float past. New Zealand is so sweet. Everything is so much easier here on every level compared to somewhere like Bali, yet they're so happy with what little they have. To be able to put good food on the plate, climate-wise, we're a lucky country.

'I find it frustrating to see small-minded people getting angry over small stuff like traffic. I'm super-guilty of it, too. When you live in the city, you're living in a box and it's easy to become isolated from the big picture, I think, more sterile in that respect. Once you feel how much energy there is in the ocean, then you start to appreciate how small and insignificant we are. I think in society it's great to be around people, but if you're always in that environment, you risk getting caught in a downward spiral, because you get so caught up in your own junk and small issues and you don't look at the big issues so much.'

For a while I sit on the couch opposite him and listen. Matt's an easy guy to listen to. We start to explore deeper issues, and after 10 minutes I realise I haven't seen that designer beard of his move much more than his sincere talking allows. 'I think we humans can feel self-important. Even when it comes down to stuff like religion, it's us trying to explain what our tiny brains can't comprehend. Even the motives behind the green movement, it sometimes feels like it's more for the survival of mankind; we can be stupid and wipe ourselves off the planet, but the earth will shrug us off like fleas and eventually come right again. Maybe surfing helps us think about these things more, I dunno.' And with that he allows himself to laugh quietly. 'There's just so much energy there, a cubic metre of water weighs a tonne, and you think how many cubic metres of water there are in a four-foot wave. As it gets bigger and bigger it's exponentially more violent, more powerful, more energy. It's thinking about the pulses of energy and what's made them. Thinking about how that little problem you're festering over ain't all that big in comparison.'

'Surfing helped me build blocks on top of each other, from being really low to looking at the small things and thinking about how lucky I am to have this . . .'

He nods faintly, like he's agreeing with himself. He likes how that sounds.

His green eyes glance down towards his feet and after a pause he goes on. There was a point, he continues, where he found himself at the opposite end of the spectrum; everything seemed too big in life and he went into a period of meltdown. 'It lasted for a couple of years,' he says. 'They were real bad times. I didn't understand what I was going through, so through that period I felt really lucky I could go surfing.' Matt was studying at the time in Hamilton. Prior to that, he'd been raised in a Christian environment, went to Sunday school as a kid, felt comfortable with his brother's strong religious beliefs. But by his early twenties, Matt's own values in religion, his understanding of what was right and wrong, were being questioned every day. Matt admits he tends to overanalyse things, break them down, scrutinise, rearrange them, look at them from different angles in an effort to find a meaning. Ultimately it came down to him having a faith, then it disappearing. 'I started seeing other things, other ways of doing stuff, other ways of thinking. I realised I wasn't happy with life at the time and eventually me and that state of mind parted ways, a shift in direction. It was a time in my life when nothing made sense. I was always waiting for something to come around the corner, rather than being happy with what I had and where I was at. It got to the stage where I'd walk around the supermarket and I couldn't make eye contact with people. I didn't feel good enough, and being who I was I didn't talk to friends about stuff, it was pretty heavy.'

To help him express his feelings, Matt turned to blank canvas and produced a series of paintings that now hold special significance for him. One, done in oil, was of an old house — owned by his parents at the time — painted as though the viewer is looking through a fish-eye lens and in dark, moody tones of blue with a touch of orange for light. Across the road is the periodic detention centre which exposed him and his brothers to society's rebels on a daily basis. Outside the house next door is his flattie's car which he smashed into a power pole. Nearby, a person walks past with a dog on a leash. Also in the picture is a house that later burned down and the place where the guy who smashed the America's Cup once lived. It's a picture of well over a thousand words. 'It sort of summed up my existence for a couple of years. I did a few like that. I did one inside in the same style, three figures of the guys I was living with at the time, all blues and really dark. It was a reflection of my state of mind at the time.

There was another one, a triptych of a guy walking along, a painting about missed opportunities and letting life pass you by.

'I appreciated having the ability to go surfing at that time, too, and just always being able to feel at home in the water. I couldn't feel like that on land or around people. It was my sanctuary, I guess. When you're sitting out in the ocean it makes you feel so small; it can be violent, yet a lot of us find an unexplained peace out there. That's my best thinking place, out the back. Surfing helped me build blocks on top of each other, from being really low to looking at the small things and thinking about how lucky I am to have this, then just building back from there. These days, if I feel any relapses I can recognise it for what it is. Now I can look at my life and instead of comparing things and wanting something more, I can compare myself with someone less fortunate. It could be better, it always can, but you know what? I'm lucky. I think in that respect, surfing's taught me to get in the right headspace and stay there.'

Matt says it's cool having the paintings he did to look back on and understand what was going on at the time and remind himself where he's come from. Since then he's realised that heaps of guys went through the same thing at that time in their lives. He asks if I ever saw it? Yeah, damned right I did. It's rampant in every male's journey from young adult to manhood, but the psyche of the Kiwi bloke doesn't make allowance for it. He agrees.

We talk about that more, a couple of guys who've only known each other for an hour or so swapping theories. 'Maybe it's a human condition, a recalibration stage in your life,' he says. 'Maybe it's that time where you've been living through your youth and you get to a point where you're not comfortable or understand who you are, then suddenly everything clicks and you're sweet.' In retrospect, he's philosophical about what he went through. 'I think it's a cool thing now, it's an amazing thing. I've learnt to appreciate things more and never take them for granted. My only fear these days is going through life without living, to not experience things. If you want to do something, who's not to say you can't do it?'

That explains why he took up karate a couple of years ago. It was something he always wanted to do and when he woke one day and realised he was 30, he figured he wasn't getting any younger. A mate of his takes classes, so he hung around to have a play. He ended up getting the bash. While he says it's got a great crossover to surfing, another reason is to retrain his body after a life of injuries. Matt's list of misdemeanours makes for impressive reading: he's blown both his ankles skating, he received a bad back injury while playing basketball at school that's just one relapse away from surgery, he's had stitches on over 20 different occasions, he's had each leg have a turn in a cast, and both his arms, for that matter. And there's a metal plate holding his foot onto his ankle after he broke his fibula and shredded his ligaments when a skateboarding stunt went horribly wrong. He was 21 at the time. Now, at 32, he doesn't skate much any more. He shows me the movement that he's got back. The flexibility and physical components of karate have helped him overcome some of the consequences of these injuries.

'There's a lot of balance conditioning and stretching, developing all your main muscles, and getting core strength and balance back. I notice if I go for a surf after training everything's too sore, you don't have the energy to generate speed, but a couple of days afterwards it's wicked.' He's worked hard on it, remaining as disciplined as work commitments allow. After two years he's still at the start of the journey, but adamant it's now a permanent part of his life. By all accounts, black belt is just the beginning, the learner plate if you like, and that's still a year or two away. 'It's definitely mentally challenging, requiring drive and mental focus. Nowadays, there's not many times when I can't get myself in the headspace in whatever I'm doing, whether it be surfing or karate, fine art or graphic design. Karate also gives you a good structure and teaches respect for people further up the hierarchy than you. It's great for kids to learn that. Grading for each belt is exponentially harder; when someone receives a belt they truly deserve it, you understand how hard they have worked to get there and they deserve respect for that. I've just had to start doing press-ups on my knuckles; it sucks now but I know it'll get easier. It's funny, the young kids in class have the attention span of a goldfish when they first come in, but they quickly learn that if they're not being good they're gonna be doing a whole lot of press-ups for punishment.'

While karate gives him a focus on land, he admits it doesn't give him the same feeling surfing does. 'Surfing is an unknown quantity. You can't explain the effect of getting a really good barrel to someone, it's a hundred per cent contentment, but it's also so much more. Sometimes you're looking around the water and thinking, wow! When I came in from the surf that winter day at Ruapuke, it was freezing cold, getting dark, really low tide. I was walking down the beach by myself, soaking wet. But I was out in the elements and appreciating every second of it. I felt energised. I was stoked for days. I don't know many other sports where you get that buzz, no matter what level you're at.'

Fran Kora

Aaron Topp

MUSICIAN
WELLINGTON

It's five days before Christmas and the Boiler Room in Whakatane is living up to its name. I was told to get here early and it was good advice. I've been in the same seat for the last hour, watching the town's population of 18- to 40-year-olds flow through the gaping front doors like water entering the Titanic. *It's getting damned hot in here, and my bladder's stretched at the seams, but with the bar at a resting elbow's reach and the stage directly in line . . . well, it's way too late in the game to give up my piece of prime real estate now.*

Whakatane is a sweet place. There's a vibe here that reeks of nonchalant attitudes, where jandals and smiles are the first things put on in the morning, and where, at least for the crowd around me, it's customary to end every sentence with 'bro'. It's big enough to be easily self-sufficient, but small enough to keep an untainted heart. I can see it around me; these people are proud of their town, proud of its culture and judging by the atmosphere that's very quickly encompassing me and my bar stool, these people are proud of their local brothers. It seems everyone wants a piece of their hometown heroes, KORA.

Apart from being here to check out a band whose self-titled debut album, leapfrogged the rest to claim national number one spot, I'm in town to catch up with one of the four Kora brothers, Fran, and talk about his surfing. At the moment, though, I'm trapped in a four-team rugby maul pressed against the bar, and feeling like a 40-year-old virgin amongst the locals. One of the Kora brothers, Laughton, is doing the rounds through the crowd like he's on a campaign trail. He gives an equal amount of smiles and thumb handshakes to every new group of familiar faces. He's nervous, he tells me; playing to tens of thousands of strangers is easy compared to a few hundred family and friends. That doesn't stop him jumping up on stage, grabbing a spare guitar and jamming with the acoustic pre-act. I spark up a conversation with the guy next to me — I may as well, considering he's already well within the realms of my personal space and practically sharing my seat. We talk about the band and before I know it, others are joining in. It seems everyone in this venue can pull out a personal story about one of the brothers when prompted, bro.

The house lights fade and a beer is placed in my hand. Fran, Laughton, and Stuart enter from the edge of the stage, instruments in hands, mikes positioned, sharing the limelight like knights around the round table. The remaining brother, Brad, is already behind the drums. If anyone had any doubt these guys were related, the acoustic harmony that follows leaves no question — they all possess the same genetic make-up. They have me, and the other few hundred present, in a trance, stunned. In complete awe. Their instruments suddenly spring into life, the stage lights up and the Boiler Room's roof pulses a foot or two in the air. The crowd goes into a euphoric state and my beer suddenly wants to move to my lips more often. This is going to be one hell of a night and I'm in the best seat in the house.

Six months prior to this evening I met Fran at his flat in Lyall Bay. He was hung over — a result of just arriving back in the country from a whirlwind tour of Eastern Australia and an all-nighter involving Final Fantasy on his PSP. We'd headed to his favourite local café overlooking the waves for some breakfast and a strong coffee. I forgot the names of all the people he introduced me to in the short walk from the car park to the table.

Francis Kora, born in 1979, first walked into the Ohope surf with a board under his arm during the summer of '89. 'I had a lot of mates who were already surfing at that stage, so it was only natural that they'd introduce me to it. I'll always remember the first time I went across the face on a green single fin. I didn't turn or anything, I didn't know what was happening, but I was buzzing out. A mate showed me the ropes, old school styles, single to twin to longboard, body surfing. I learnt all the different styles at an early age. I've been a surf junkie ever since, taking every chance I can get to enjoy the waves.'

This early passion, however, had its share of obstacles. School was an obvious one. But another, just as significant, was the fact that Fran and his other siblings were born into a family that valued music at an almost religious level. His father, Tait, whose love for music knows no boundaries, ensured

'He made us practise hard when we were young. At times I hated it because all I wanted to do was go surfing.'

Fran and his other brothers were fed a combination of chords and notes and band practice daily. 'He'd make us sing "Soldier boy",' Fran recalls. 'Man, I hated that song, I hated it big time, but he'd force us to do it. We'd be at home by the piano singing it all the time, Jackson Five-style, you know.' Fran suddenly breaks into the chorus for me, giving me a small example of his smooth vocals, 'I'm a little sooooooldier boy . . .' He shakes his head. 'Hell, no.' He chuckles. When he was about seven, Fran and his brothers made their first public performance, taking part in a Telethon event in the Whakatane Little Theatre. His dad tried to make them sing 'Soldier boy', but Fran refused. 'Looking back, it makes me laugh. I can see what he was trying to do, trying to teach us, but at that age I was way too cool for a song like that.' Instead, they played 'Black magic woman' and Garry Moore's, 'I just want to be your loving man' (he sings that line too). They were the first songs he learnt on the bass. We look at an old photo from the night — Stewie on the keyboards, Brad on the drums, their dad on lead guitar and at the front but staring backwards to watch his dad for timing is Fran, with a bass guitar almost as long as he is tall. It's a scene that still continues; the word around me at the concert is that Tait and two of the sons were indulging in an impromptu acoustic jam on the street only a few hours ago.

'The old man was hard but fair on us. He had a dream of having a family band and wanted to teach his kids and that's what happened. I had no choice but to play music. He made us practise hard when we were young. At times I hated it because all I wanted to do was go surfing. He was always teaching us stuff. When he reffed our rugby games he'd be pushing us on the field. He was getting into his fitness the same time we were discovering sports so he was leading by example. I was right into sports but I'd find interests in too many things and found I couldn't do everything. I still play the bass now as my main instrument, but I wanna play everything, become a jack of all trades, master of none. The others are like that in their own way; we were a big pool of talent, all wanting to be like each other. I think that's followed through our musical journeys and onto KORA itself.'

While at Whakatane High, Fran and his brothers kicked national Rockquest butt twice in the early 1990s, when they were known as Auntie Beatrice and Poostance, and were asked not to enter in their third year. They also won the East Coast Battle of the Bands three years running, earning a record release for their efforts. Afterwards, the brothers went and did their own thing for a while, with Fran and Laughton heading south to Queenstown and recording a four-track demo. In 2002, the brothers reunited again and, with the inclusion of Queenstown muso, Dan McGruer (affectionately known as 'the fifth brother' of the group), KORA was officially formed. 'I'm so thankful now for the old man's persistence though. I'm playing in a band with my bros, touring the world and having a good time.'

And watching him on stage, you can see it; his fingers command the bass strings, his body exudes an energetic presence, the vocals are in sync, and he stares out across a sea of raised hands and battering eyelids. It's hard to imagine these guys have spent a sizeable chunk of the year playing in foreign venues.

The first time they went to Britain was during the 2007 Rugby World Cup where they found themselves in Scotland at the same time that the All Blacks were playing. The majority of the crowd were black-wearing expats. Cracking the British market is on KORA's things-to-do list. The next time they'll be there, it will be for eight gigs in 10 days and they'll be fighting jet lag the whole time. But Fran says they just want to get over there, get their heads down, do the work and get home. It was on their first trip to London that the album was mastered. There they were, a band of brothers from a secluded seaside town of an isolated country, in the presence of the same guy who'd worked with the likes of Bowie and Madonna and Queen. 'He's got all this old analogue equipment, but he's got the golden ear and can hear all these quips. We'll look at each other and go, how the hell can he hear that? But he'd open up the file and spread it out and sure enough, there it is. We were all buzzing out.' Their big break came through their British-based agent, who managed to get the group's foot in the door, bringing them the ultimate bonus of a listing in the largest booking agency in the world, ITV; they take care of everyone from Pearl Jam to Christina Aguilera. Look up KORA and you'll find them between KISS and Korn. They're one of only two Kiwi artists on the agency's list. Hollie Smith is there too.

Back home things are a little harder. With the band members living in three different cities (Wellington, Whakatane and Auckland), rehearsals can't follow the typical spare-room-after-work model like in the old days. Driving or flying to get to rehearsal makes it an expensive proposition, and with six guys, one car and all their gear, it can get pretty hectic. But now, with the musical world at their fingertips, practice has become even more important. 'It's got to a level where we have to rehearse. We never practised before, we knew enough about each other. Now we have to make time to do it, because it's really important to keep in sync with each other,' Fran says. The best place to do this is in a large warehouse they've found in Edgecumbe, 20 minutes out of Whakatane. It's a prime spot to set up their gear, get the boys back into it and keep away from distractions; in town, Fran says, everyone wants to come in, which is cool, but not much gets done. This way, if anyone wants to see them, they have to travel. It's served them well; they recorded most of the album there.

'When the creative reservoir is low I go for a surf to completely clear my mind. Every surfer knows if their head is somewhere else, then they'll have a shit surf, but when you're on, man, you're at one with the elements. Sounds spiritual, but it's true. There're no worries. It's peaceful. I like that. Surfing makes me feel like me. I would've been a different person if I hadn't had the experience of the beach. It's my time to check myself, see where I'm at. It's like meditation, that's the truth; if things aren't working it's my place to meditate and focus my mind on something else.'

Recently, Fran has been learning about the Magnabrain principle. It's based on the concept that we only use 4 per cent of our brain, the conscious part that controls thoughts and our creative side, where our ideas come from. The other 96 per cent is all the unconscious habits we develop. 'The conscious part comes up with all the ideas, but it doesn't last because it has a short memory. The unconscious has a memory that lasts forever. Early on, if you're told you can't do this or that all the time, then you learn that for life. If you're driving in your car and you get home but you can't remember the trip, that's your unconscious brain taking over. So at those early ages, you're learning all the habits, they're automatic. But you can train your conscious brain to learn new ones. Most people have to go out of their comfort zone, but that's the secret.

'It's like meditation, that's the truth; if things aren't working it's my place to meditate and focus my mind on something else.'

All the stuff I've wanted to achieve, I've accomplished most of it. I've learnt a lot about myself on the way, accepted my old habits. Some people don't do that, they live in the past. But once you accept the past, you're free to move on. I'm way more enlightened these days, almost to boredom. I've always tried to stay positive in life, focusing on the fun factor, but I've become even more [positive], I think, since I've learnt that stuff. We humans waste too much time being negative.'

To emphasise the concept, while we are having breakfast he tells me to raise my finger in front of my face and focus so it's in sharp detail. I'm aware of everything going on behind my digit, but it's blurry, it's my finger that's most important. Fran keeps me in this position for a while. I ignore the random stares from other tables and do what I'm told, hoping his sense of humour doesn't involve piss-takes. He wants me to imagine I've had a shit sleep and while getting out of bed I stub my toe, which has a snowballing negative effect on the rest of my day. 'So if the bad sleep and stubbed toe is only the finger, look past it, look at me, look around the room, look out the windows. Look at everything available. How many options have you got now, bro? You have your own ability to focus on whatever you want. That's how your mind works. I taught that to myself, to remind me of what's important.'

Funnily enough, my next breath is deeper and leaves me fresher than I've felt for a while.

If you don't believe me, try it for yourself.

KORA's music draws its inspirations from an eclectic mix of genres, ranging from funk to metal to reggae to Motown. From these, they've created a sound they've claimed as their own, cleverly developing a musical point of difference from anything else in the industry. Watching them on stage, you can see they're good; blow-your-mind, scull-your-beer, groove-in-your-bar-seat good. They instinctively know how to draw in the crowd and form a symbiotic relationship with them, matching them ounce for ounce in the sweat-loss stakes. A large part of this vibe stems from the fact that Fran and Laughton trained at New Zealand Drama School. Most actors strive to get a place on stage anywhere they can, yet the brothers figured that with all the stage time they were getting as musicians, they could make the most of it with their drama skills. 'The audience is a mirror image of what performance is given to them. We've learnt how to feel the audience out first and change things if they aren't working. The rest of the boys have picked up on that too. When you can sense the crowd has a playful energy, it's time to play. That's the best part about doing theatre; you're trying to manipulate the audience, take them on a trip and have fun. Feeding off each other; the more fun we're having, the more they are. We may not be the greatest minstrels on the instruments, but the boys are good. We had a few rehearsals based around fun and it went well right from the start. We'd even surprise ourselves by coming up with a riff before we went on stage and playing, using spontaneity, taking the risks and flying with it. The biggest kick is playing to an audience who've never seen us before and [knowing] we've got them. That tells me it works.'

This is best demonstrated in the song 'Flow', a personal favourite of Fran's, which starts off with a classic laid-back Kora brothers' harmony in the chorus — on par with anything the Finn brothers can produce — but morphs into a combination of heavy power chords and theatre sport-like antics. 'Music has a universal connection with everything,' Fran tells me. 'Einstein once said "Energy equals MC squared". So within a human body, everything vibrates with energy. When you play a major chord, then major vibrations within a human body will occur. Major chords associate with happiness. Minor chords will vibrate sad, angry. That's the worldwide connection to humans. It doesn't matter where you are in the world, it'll affect humans the same way. That's why it's the universal language. You have groundswell and sound waves, it's all energy. If you look at a recording programme, you have lines like swell. It's a written energy.' Throughout the breakfast, Fran has periodically been wiping his left ear. He perforated it while out surfing, and this, combined with the common condition known as 'surfers' ear' (where the ear canal grows extra cartilage to keep out the cold), means his ears are a concern. He had it drained recently, but now he's got a hole in his eardrum and it's still dripping. He's on a waiting list to get a skin graft to fix it, but the surgeon has already warned him he'll lose a couple of frequencies once it's healed.

While surfing may be responsible for that threat to his music, like any successful relationship, there has to be compromise at times, and the times he's successfully married the two together have far outweighed what's in store. Instead of leaving his musical consciousness in the car on the beach, he takes it out with him into the swell, to let the two activities work off each other. To foster enlightenment. 'I worked out years ago that surfing and music complement each other. To me, a wave is something that you must feel your way through, because every wave is different. You're out there, constantly adapting to an ever-changing environment. If you know how this works, then the transition to music is automatic. Every skilled musician knows when they are in sync with each other; they can change and adapt musically while jamming. Jazz musicians are a great example of how musically this can be just like surfers on a wave.'

Back on stage, and it's obvious Fran is in his element. He's a big guy, and judging by the amount of stoke he's throwing around like confetti, he's someone who obviously places an emphasis on fitness. But it's only been in recent times he's been able to take his stage performance to this level, thanks to the new art form he discovered. Since 2006, his love for music and surfing has been shared by a third passion, Brazilian jiujitsu. He was introduced to the sport by Lyall Bay surf store owners, Sacha Jackson and Hemi Pou, after talking to them one day about suitable training for surfing. It ended up being a life-changing discussion. 'Surfing and Brazilian jiujitsu are the same thing, but in a different art form,' explains Fran. 'One involves natural elements, and the other a human connection. For me, surfing is a better feeling than things like skateboarding, snowboarding, or wakeboarding, because the surface is constantly changing and moving, which means the rider has to change and adapt to whatever the wave is doing. BJJ is the same. Your opponent is constantly moving and changing his or her every move, which means you move and adapt to your opponent. It's no coincidence that most BJJ guys surf. Someone who surfs a lot will pick it up way quicker than non-surfers; the transition is a natural one. It's the perfect training for surfing: endurance, flexibility, strength, balance — it's everything you need for surfing to a T. I've noticed a huge change in my surf fitness because of it. The more you do, the more you see, and you can read the game ahead of the opponent, like surfing.'

There is an obvious link here that can be traced back to Tait Kora's strong emphasis on teaching Fran and his brothers the importance of a disciplined attitude to life. BJJ requires consistent dedication and an acceptance of its holistic philosophy. 'I have four classes a week that are around two hours long. The first hour focuses on techniques, while the second involves competing to apply the new moves learnt. The best thing is that it's so much fun, you don't realise how good a workout it is.' Fran has already had success in the sport, placing second in the Wellington GSW tournament, involving local and national BJJ clubs. He recently went to Auckland to compete, and whereas in class there is time to do rolls with his mates and joke around if they beat each other, he found the competitive environment attracted the guys more interested in a fight-to-the-death style. This posed a problem for Fran. 'I'm not that competitive any more. It was an interesting experience to discover that at the competition. I'm keen to train for comps, but I know the difference now. It was like comparing a soul surfer to a competitive one. They do it for different reasons; one's there to love it, the other to win. I'm definitely there to love it. If it's not fun, I won't do it.' That didn't stop him convincingly winning his division, then having a crack at the Auckland Open. He was stopped by an opponent 30 kilograms heavier than him. 'I try and move like water when I'm doing physical stuff. I did some training when I was at drama school — elemental training. I found out my strongest elements are earth and water, so I'm either really solid or fluid. I adapt between the two. When I'm surfing I'm really watery. In jiujitsu I'm really watery too, that's why I didn't do as well as I wanted in the comp, 'cause everyone else was like rock.' He laughs. 'I got shut down by a bunch of rocks.'

Brazilian jiujitsu and surfing have shared a connection for a long time, although not necessarily for all the right reasons. It's a well-known fact in the wave-riding world that if you intend to surf in Brazil, then you have two options: one is tape a massive searchlight to the front of your surfboard and hit the swell somewhere around midnight. Or two, spend years learning the art of jiujitsu to give yourself a slim chance at competing for the waves. Like many coasts around the globe, surfing in Brazil is a highly competitive pastime. However, the population-to-wave ratio intensifies the sport so much that physical fights are about as common as the waves, meaning that only the fittest, most highly skilled surfers, suvive. And jiujitsu is the fighting technique of choice. They even have a Black Belt Surf Tournament each year, where competitors have to have a BJJ black belt just to enter. It may be a culture that sits way outside the realm of the traditional surfing philosophy, but it's their culture. It's how they surf.

Jiujitsu, which ironically means 'gentle art', is known as the oldest form of martial art. It originated in India around 2000 BC amongst a group of monks who were looking to protect themselves from attack by barbarians, without the need for weapons. It soon spread to China, then eventually Japan. In 1914, the Japanese jiujitsu champ, Esai Maeda, migrated to Brazil and set up camp, helped by a local scholar, Gastao Gracie. As an expression of his gratitude, Maeda taught the Brazilian's oldest son juijitsu, and he taught his four brothers. One of the brothers, Helio Gracie, who was the smallest of the family and in poor health, went on to experiment, modify and enhance the basics of jiujitsu, thus developing a new form of fighting, Brazilian jiujitsu. Helio's newfound skills allowed him to defeat the world's best fighters, establishing himself as a global legend.

Although the monks couldn't have possibly foreseen that their art would become connected to riding waves, it was Helio's son, Rickson (pronounced Hickson), who cemented the two codes together. Rickson, the Michael Jordan of BJJ, has always been affiliated with the sport of surfing, which perhaps helps to explain the way the BJJ phenomenon has spread along the South American coastline. A dedicated surfer, Rickson once said that if he lost his two legs, he wouldn't lose his sense of life. While he'd question his ability to fight, he felt he'd never lose his ability to surf. Once, he walked into a major BJJ championship already thinking about the waves he was going to catch afterwards. Inside the stadium, he marched up to the officials' stand and asked to compete in all three of his fights one after another. The judges eventually gave him permission to do this and the rest is BJJ history. According to one of his pupils at the time, he kicked the ass of all three fighters, bang, bang, bang, just like that. Then he went for a surf.

'You're out there, constantly adapting to an ever-changing environment. If you know how this works, then the transition to music is automatic.'

Sharing his love for surfing, it's natural that Fran draws inspiration from this unparalleled sportsman. 'Competing is just like finding a new surf break,' says Fran. 'I'm constantly thinking about new techniques by watching a heap of BJJ DVDs, UFC, and YouTube. I loved watching the movie *CHOKE* where Rickson demonstrates the connection between surfing and jiujitsu. It's hugely inspirational.' Even surfing's nine-time world champ, Kelly Slater, was influenced by the ancient martial art after meeting Rickson out in the surf one day. Slater has called Rickson one of his heroes, maybe the most dominant athlete in any sport of all time and said he's been a huge inspiration for him in the last few years. Like Fran, Slater has used the knowledge passed down from Rickson to improve his overall performance on the world stage, including aspects of his diet and the way he approaches competitions. In an expression of his gratitude, Slater had some surfboards made for Rickson, and as payback, he got to have a private training session with him at his home.

Fran Kora is mastering the art of life. Through his three passions, he's managed to mould a lifestyle that encompasses a sense of wellbeing. In this crap-on-the-little-guy society we have created for ourselves, it's refreshing to find people like Fran, who still treasure the small-town values of family, community and fun. In fact, I don't think it's any coincidence that these same values are found in the heart of every surfer on the planet, even somewhere deep within hyped-up Brazilian surfers.

'Surfing has always been there for me. Things change over time, but I've always been able to grab my board and go catch a wave. It's such an awesome feeling, being able to immerse yourself in the environment like that. I often think us surfers are the custodians of the shoreline; we're not hurting anyone, we're not polluting anything, we're respecting the environment and appreciating all that nature provides. Surfers are in that space more than anyone else. When the swell is pumping we can be paddling around out there for hours. That's why we're normally the first and loudest to speak out against anything that's gonna threaten our beaches. New Zealand is the place where we're driven by the environment. We're known as the clean green place, middle earth, dedicated to preserving nature. Surfers fit into that picture. Surfers have a better empathy. If they didn't, we'd be surfing around shit like overseas. It's about respect. A lot of stuff gets dumped out there. We're always aware of rubbish, aware of others doing stupid things like flicking their cigarette butts.

'I don't wanna be seventy years old, retire and then have fun. I wanna do it now. I decided at an early age that surfing would be one of the things I'll never give up, so I've based my life around that. It's the greatest addiction you can ever have, where you can see how balanced you are physically, mentally and spiritually. It's a way of life that cannot be described, only experienced. I think surfers in general tend to live a lot more than the nine-to-five desk jobs. Surfing gets people out there in the elements and being physical. All the surfers I know, if there's a problem, it ain't that major. That's the big difference between surfers and non-surfers. We're free and easy. Too many people just think about money; they've lost the spirit of life and become slaves to the mortgage and chasing the dollar. As far as they're concerned, if you surf then you're a bum. But I tend to think you have to have a balance. I'd rather base my work around my lifestyle, not the other way around. A lot of people don't understand that. Music has helped free my life up. I'd rather do it now and worry about the consequences later on. Take your pick man; it's the finger, there's plenty of other things out there.'

The band plays their last note for the evening. The brothers put their tools down, and leave the stage to hang out with their still-cheering extended whanau. There are plenty more sideways handshakes and smiles to be shared. I contemplate getting one last comment from Fran, hot off the press, so to speak, but considering how the maul has moved from the bar to the band, I figure I'll pass. I doubt Fran will be hanging around long — tomorrow night the brothers will be playing at the traditional Christmas concert, allowing the rest of the town's population to get another snapshot of how the town's favourite sons have grown in front of their eyes. The Heads is meant to be pumping with six foot of northerly swell tomorrow anyway, so I know where I'll find him. For now, though, I finish what's left in my handle, take the opportunity to finally stand and head towards the bathroom.

Dave Jenkins

Bob Barker/RovingEye.com

SURFAID FOUNDER AND CEO
MENTAWAIS

September 2008, and Kiwi doctor Dave Jenkins is in a crowded room in the upmarket area of Southern California's La Jolla. He's surrounded by the who's who of the billion dollar surf industry. Iconic surfers like Kelly Slater, Taj Burrow, Lisa Anderson, Rob Machado, Greg Noll and Rochelle Ballard are all there enjoying themselves, as well as CEOs and other high-profile business leaders from powerhouses like Billabong and Quiksilver. They're here for the Liquid Nation Ball, an annual event held by the Surf Industry Manufacturers Association (SIMA) as the main fundraiser for their Humanitarian Fund.

The fund is a chance for SIMA's 300 industry suppliers to support needy surf-based, not-for-profit organisations. It's a night of live music, great food, dancing and of course, the main event, the charity auction, which will ultimately make up the biggest chunk of the A$230,000 raised that night.

The host for the night, and co-founder of Reef, Santiago Aguerre, announces that a very special presentation is to be made and asks Dr Dave, as he's affectionately known, to join him on stage. Aguerre bestows on him a large, glass-encased wooden plaque, complete with miniature hanging surfboard, and the words 'Humanitarian of the Year' engraved into the plate on its front. It's recognition of Dave's tenacious commitment, the role he has played in attacking the Goliath-like aid problem, his success in helping to improve the lives of others, and his ability to cast his organisation's net wide and to raise awareness of it and its issues far beyond the tightknit surf community. It's also the first time SIMA has ever given out such a prestigious award.

Jump forward to 3 January 2009, and I seem to be the only one on the road heading into Gisborne. In the other lane is a stream of cars bearing sleeping 20-somethings and their weary drivers. Yesterday was the last day of the popular Rhythm and Vines Festival and the Poverty Bay city is draining like someone just pulled the plug on it. When I meet up with Dave at Wainui Beach where he's staying in an old caravan tucked behind the back of a friend's house he's walking around in a pair of boardies. Like the rest of the city's population, he went to the music festival, but the sound of text and email chimes ringing out from the makeshift office at the family dinner table state he's still very much at work. Even while he's having a well-earned fortnight's holiday back at home, it seems Dave's conscience never rests.

The SurfAid story started back in 1999 on a regular surf trip to the Mentawais, a chain of islands off the coast of Sumatra. The region is home to 70,000 people and some of the most perfect reef surf breaks the world has to offer. New Zealander, Dave Jenkins, a career-focused doctor working out of Singapore, had arrived with the aim of gorging himself on the buffet of tropical waves on offer. He wasn't disappointed. However, late one afternoon, on what should have been a harmless tourist venture inland to one of the villages, his beliefs in what was important in life were changed forever. What he saw was the indigenous people, mainly women and children, dying from malaria, malnutrition, inadequate living standards, things his medical background told him were easily treatable. The scene haunted his subconscious for the rest of the trip and followed him back to Singapore. He began questioning his life. Did it have meaning? Were his skills wasted chasing some corporate carrot? What if he could make a real difference to these people? The thought of more children dying drove him mad with frustration and helplessness, yet, at the same time and in some strange way, it filled his soul with inspiration and empowerment. He couldn't just walk away from that memory. Fellow humans would help, if they knew about it. He vowed to return to the Mentawais with people and supplies.

That Christmas, in another tiny coastal Kiwi village called Makorori, situated in a small country thousands of kilometres away from the Mentawais, a small group of business-savvy surfers met at a barbecue to listen to Dave's vision. One of the people present, Dr Steve Hathaway, volunteered (along with many others) to assist in this highly ambitious idea, and so began a journey that would take hundreds of hours as they sought to turn the vision into a reality. Ten years later and Dave is staying in Steve's house and caravan. Steve is currently juggling the role of Chairman of SurfAid with commuting three days a week to Wellington, where he works as director of the New Zealand Food Safety Authority. He also makes a great coffee. 'We were just a garage band back then,' he tells me, 'with no formal business model. It created its own momentum and craziness. It was unstructured, driven by passion. It was just people with no money having a go. Whoever turned up, we'd use their skills and we grabbed who we could.'

> He couldn't just walk away from that memory. Fellow humans would help, if they knew about it. He vowed to return to the Mentawais with people and supplies.

Their first big project involved having a little stall at the national surf competition in Gisborne — à la school-science-fair presentation. Dave talked his daughter into running it. They quickly found surfers didn't want to spend money on anything but beer, boards and the occasional girl. They followed the Big Day Out circuit and tirelessly tried to convince teenagers, hyped up on party pills and attitude, that they should be helping malnourished babies.

A year or so down the track, and while supplies and resources were starting to filter into the villages, their total capital was still no more than $30,000. They had doctors working for nothing and living in villages; SurfAid management had no money to ship them food, so the volunteers were forced to live on chickens and rice supplied by the local families. But still they persisted. 'In a way,' says Steve, 'without a business model, it's been the core passion that's played the biggest advantage. It's been an organic thing.'

Today, SurfAid has become a truly international organisation. In 2002 it established an American division, and in 2004, set up in Australia. They have developed a heavyweight board of directors, who oversee the six different programmes involving community-based health, emergency preparedness, improving water and sanitation, reducing malaria, introducing permaculture techniques and the successful schools programme that heightens global awareness to the plight of remote Indonesia. They have the support of numerous top-level surfers, like Tom Curren and Kelly Slater, and musicians, like Jack Johnson and Donovan Frankenreiter. They get individuals willing to donate tens of thousands of their own personal wealth to the cause. Individual groups throw fundraisers for them. They get so many people asking to volunteer their services that they've had to develop a standard rejection letter. In 2007, SurfAid won the World Association of Non-Governmental Organisations Humanitarian Award and the esteemed Rainer Fellowship for three years, a programme supporting leadership in improving other people's lives. Currently, Google coughs up over 380,000 links to SurfAid.

'Everyone was saying, who are these guys? . . . look at their reports and look at what they're doing . . . we were just a bunch of surfers in the right place at the right time.'

With such fast and monumental changes in a relatively short period, how has the original vision changed or evolved since that first meeting? 'At a macro level there's been some real shifts,' Steve says. 'But what hasn't changed is that level of responsibility. We were just having a go because it was so dire. We thought we could save some lives from malaria, stop some diarrhoea, bring some worm pills in, whatever. That was achieving something. Now the enormity of doing it right is what drives us. Dave has this beautiful vision in his head, and at one stage that was enough, but we have a significant amount of public money, significant responsibility, we have to deliver on promises, so we have to look at scale.' Dave and Steve show me some of the marketing material they use. There are pictures of perfect surf blended with appreciative smiling faces of some of the thousands of children who have benefitted from the foundation's work. It's refreshing to see it all put in a positive light rather than the shock tactics some other appeals use. While it makes it easy to get caught up in the romance of what is being achieved, by the same token, it's just as easy to think the SurfAid crew are working in a cruisy environment. That couldn't be further from the truth; the isolation and the unpredictable environment they work in is a constant challenge. This isn't the sort of place you can just rock up in a Range Rover with a UN sticker, meet with the head man of the village, then move onto the next.

But it was Boxing Day in 2004 that would snatch Dave's vision from him and challenge it far beyond its capability. When the 9.3 earthquake struck deep under the Indian Ocean, it sent a giant tsunami towards the Sumatran coastline and straight into the history books as one of the most devastating natural catastrophes of modern history, killing 225,000 people in 11 different countries. Before it struck, SurfAid was well into its malaria-free programme. Workers had seen their initial success, and the organisers were trying to expand the foundation with what little money they had. Within hours of the tsunami, they went from a small team focusing on community health, to an emergency response organisation — a monumental shift in direction. Almost four years later to the day, Dave says it became the turning point in SurfAid's life. 'We didn't know what we could do or how we could help. We didn't back ourselves as the people to do anything huge, we didn't have the finances or the experience. We thought maybe we could assist other organisations, people equipped for this sort of thing. But when Quiksilver rang us to ask if we could be their agency, then Billabong, then the New Zealand Government, we realised there was no one else. Suddenly we had upwards of a million dollars to assist. We were like, OK, now we can do something.'

They began contacting the owners of surf charter boats, who were already responding individually. The captains said the problem was huge, but no aid was getting out there. Dave knew supplies were on their way, but with no knowledge of the hotspots, the area, or how to charter boats, the support effort was coming in blind. Dave and his team knew there was a vacuum of information to fill. They packed up and got out to the worst hit area. What greeted them was a sense of bleakness, but each member of the team remained focused and they got to work setting up a station. 'It became very obvious we were the only ones with ability to supply need to the isolated island villages. Things like packs, food, water, medical care, you name it. Most importantly though we were feeding the information back to the United Nations, because without us there was just silence.' If you look back on the UN website, you'll see daily reports from SurfAid, written by two of Dave's volunteers, who luckily had experience in that area of work. They set up the communication system and with that a co-ordinated flow of supply and aid began streaming in. Tens of thousands of lives were saved. 'Everyone was saying, who are these guys? They're not World Vision, but look at their reports and look at what they're doing . . . we were just a bunch of surfers in the right place at the right time.'

When another earthquake hit Sumatra just three months later, it sparked a tsunami scare across the still-recovering region. While the wave that eventuated was small in comparison to the Boxing Day tsunami, it was still deadly, killing 1300 people, mostly on the island of Nias, home to one of the world's most renowned surf breaks. After proving itself to the world, SurfAid was thrown an open chequebook so its members could get to work. Dave contacted the charter boats out there already, but within hours he'd also organised another 18 boats and a helicopter to assist with the rescue work. SurfAid went from 22 staff to 155 in six weeks; every team member was committed to assisting and had a results-orientated attitude. They stayed to help repair communities. So effective was SurfAid, not only in response, but also recovery, Dave was asked to speak at AusAID and NZAID about making the shift from emergency response to rehabilitation. 'That's how the tsunami changed us [SurfAid], because it built our reputation to the point where others could see we were the only agency who could work the islands. No one wanted to take on that logistical nightmare. We were left being the only agency who could work in the remote marine environments.'

Looking at Dave, lounging back on a plastic deck chair beside his bright orange, two-wheeled accommodation, I was interested to know how such a dramatic period changed him on a personal level. But something I learn about him is that he's so focused on where his vision will evolve to next, his replies are always SurfAid based. It's like he and it are one and the same. Even the energy of words, it seems, is better spent on progressing the cause. 'It changed the possibilities. We were no longer a garage band, we were suddenly doing concerts on the world stage, and we couldn't miss a beat. It also meant our opportunity to fulfil our vision was now feasible. That's how it changed.' But surely, back in 1999 when he was pitching the idea to a small group of people around a barbecue, he never envisioned himself being thrown under a spotlight in one of the worst natural cases of human suffering ever seen? He takes a moment to think about that. If there was any doubt they could do it, he finally says, it showed what they, as a team, were capable of. 'You have to have that confidence and optimism that you can achieve what the vision is. It would be easy to lose that motivation simply because the work is so hard. If you didn't have successes along the way, it wouldn't work. It was very rewarding from that point of view.'

> 'The thing I would like SurfAid to be known for more than anything else is that we're brutally honest. You have to be, there are children's lives at stake.'

Dave's childhood was a wholesome Kiwi one. He was one of four children in a typical middle-class family. He grew up in Wellington, then Auckland, before being sent to boarding school in Nelson. Did he ever envision himself as a leader? No. But he liked improving things. After practising as a MD, he bought a general practice, turned it from a one-man outfit to a 3.5-doctor practice, then expanded it, opening up clinics around the region, all the while focusing on improving the time patients had with doctors. That's always been his emphasis, trying to create win-wins and improvements in whatever situation he finds himself. SurfAid, he says, is just another example of this. I ask how he'd describe himself and he naturally asks for clarification — SurfAid or myself? The human version, I say. 'Unreasonable.' He laughs. 'Unreasonable people are like that because they're unqualified, and that's how it felt for us. You need a mix of people to succeed. I was a guy who was a part of this core team. When we said let's have a go, we really meant it. I represent the scene publicly, get the interviews, but it takes so much to get organised. There should be stories on guys like Steve, or Phil [Dreifuss] our lawyer, or any of the others. Steve donates thousands of hours, while Phil has spent all the time behind the scenes.' More than anything, Dave admits he has plenty of grim determination and will. In the early days he twice had to go back to work to keep bread on the table. Shutting up shop just because they didn't have money wasn't an option. Issues that arose were simply new opportunities in disguise.

'If I was a big donor, I'd say right, who are the key management people, how much time do they spend in the villages?'

So he's the eternal optimist then? The laughter coming from Steve states I'm off the mark. 'Dave's got to be the most stubborn guy I've ever met. He's a skittle, you knock him down and he gets back up. He's gone way beyond optimistic. He's a visionary. If it was just optimism, he would've failed.' Dave agrees; he's not that optimistic about mankind and the degree of collective wisdom from our political outcomes. He is, however, optimistic about what SurfAid will achieve, and acknowledges that as an organisation, they're gaining rapidly. 'But despite the successes, we've made mistakes. To me that's fine, though. The thing I would like SurfAid to be known for more than anything else is that we're brutally honest. You have to be, there are children's lives at stake.' He tells his staff they're not going to get it right straightaway. There's no university degree that'll teach them how to do what the organisation is doing. 'The only way is to go out with the right heart and listen to people and find their stories. You have to be curious and talk to the mother who believes she shouldn't exclusively breastfeed because that's what she was taught, and find out why.' He counts the following on his fingers, 'Curiosity and brutal honesty and striving to get a great result — you have to put those things together, and that's where I'm optimistic SurfAid is on the right track.'

He says the basic motivation behind SurfAid hasn't changed, as the job is far from done. 'There's still a huge amount of childhood and adult suffering that's completely preventable with low-technology solutions and behavioural changes,' he says. 'It feels outrageous to me that on one level there's all these little graves and on another there's the solutions and they're not being prioritised.' The infant mortality rate in the Mentawais is 93 per 1000 live births (almost one in every 10 infants). To put that in perspective, in your average industrialised country, the rate is only around 6 per 1000. Somewhere between 13 and 18 per cent of under-five-year-olds' mortality can be reduced if everyone exclusively breastfed until the age of two, he says. Hundreds of billions of dollars are spent on childhood mortality, yet he doesn't see even 5 per cent of it being spent trying to work out how to do it on a big scale. He's frustrated. He sees it in best practice; he'll read about it in public health protocol, it may even filter down to local community health, but it doesn't get any further. It never gets prioritised. That's the opportunity, and outrage, he says. 'It's like saying to a room full of entrepreneurs, here's the franchise for McDonalds to China, you can have it for a dollar. But no one takes it. That's the size of the issue here.'

SurfAid does not give handouts. The donations don't go straight into forcing change on these proud and spiritual people in remote tropical villages. Dave can't stress this enough. It's not even primarily weighted towards education, I find. That's only a small part of it. The real challenge SurfAid faces is empowerment through behavioural change and on a scale where it makes impact. 'Emergency response to the tsunamis, as hard as it is, isn't nearly as hard as facilitating behavioural change,' he says. 'While that period was tremendously challenging, it's only a fraction as hard as changing someone's behaviour.' Dave has dwelled on this for a very long time and it would be fair to say he has become a global expert on what it takes. 'We need to start with the end in mind and work backwards. What do we do to get there? Training systems. But there's no training you can do for this sort of work. It's outside-the-box creative thinking. We have to train people from scratch; that's why working from an isolated area challenges everything we do.'

Dave has recently read William Easterly's book, *White Man's Burden*, about how the western world's 'big brother' aid efforts can actually do more harm than good. And he agrees. He's seen the results for himself. 'That political incentive has been the dominant incentive. It's not aimed at creating lasting change that's cost effective and at scale. No one's thinking, how do we do this in a business-like way. If that question had been asked at the beginning, we'd have very different effectiveness right now. If you use a business-like model, like [Bill] Gates is using with his foundation, you'd say, OK non-government organisation world, I have twenty billion dollars to deal with kids who are dying from household behaviours in the Mentawais. Mum delivers baby on dirt floor and cuts cord with bamboo stick and kid dies a week later from infection. Or child gets diarrhoea because they don't give it coconut juice, despite thousands of them above their heads, and the mother doesn't feed it properly and supply fluids and it dies of dehydration. Or there's smoke in the house from the cooking and the child gets pneumonia from smoke inhalation. In one of our villages we have a seventy-six per cent rate of malnutrition in a tropical paradise with wild spinach and coconuts and fish on their doorstep, so there's a dislocation between food and health. Something you think a caveman could work out, but it's been instilled in them for so long. The business model would be focused on behaviour change, because there's a difference between education and behaviour. Education is just phase one.'

New Zealanders who die from heart attacks as a result of smoking all their lives no doubt know well the dangers of smoking. They were educated. It's not the end once the education process has been implemented, Dave says. Afterwards you need to work out what environment people need to create in order to generate a behavioural change that eventually becomes the cultural norm in a society. Right now, back in the islands, the cultural norm is not to exclusively breastfeed for the first six months of a child's life. Changing that, he says, is the single most powerful way to save a child's life. Unfortunately, he is dealing with a culture developed over thousands of years. 'They breastfeed, but they don't class it as a food. So if you said aid was now a business, and you now have to prove to me you're going to get the biggest profit, then you have to give me a return on my investment, you have to prove to me what you're doing and the results you're achieving. This is SurfAid's approach.'

Despite relying on donors, Dave believes the responsibility for how well the money is used falls heavily on the donors themselves. They're not demanding enough. They're too complacent. Too submissive. Recently, Dave was interviewed by a guy who was doing a PhD on NGO effectiveness, post-tsunami, and the student said Dave was the only CEO he knew who wanted to go to villages. It's that attitude, Dave says, that needs to change. 'If I was a big donor, I'd say right, who are the key management people, how much time do they spend in the villages? If you want my money, you have to spend twenty per cent of the time in villages. I want to know what you've changed, learnt, what you're doing about it. I want the interviews from thirty randomly chosen households. It's a fundamental shift in attitude to the donors who say build some toilets, or some new water tanks. The box gets ticked, then it's sent back to the thirteenth floor in some CBD. Donor happy, we did a good job.'

But a lot of the time this sort of impact is small, often negligible, or in some cases, even harm's been done. Dave tells his staff all the time, they could hurt these people and waste millions of dollars. In their current living conditions, villagers are vulnerable to the concept of a gift rather than a reward. 'The African countries experiencing the biggest GDP growth are the countries with less development from aid. That's a macro-example. While it's not black and white, as a broad statement it's true. What does that mean? It means developments have done the countries harm, it's hurt them. A micro-example is the Nias earthquake and multiple NGOs coming in with aid, the biggest most generous act in mankind's history, hundreds of millions of dollars raised, and suddenly you have pressures, sometimes conscious, sometimes unconscious, to spend that money. Talk to some local person at Nias and they'll tell you it's the best thing that's ever happened. There are now more motorbikes than ever, more jobs been created, but when the NGOs start to leave, as they are now, the culture becomes used to and dependent on the handout model, the charity model. Improvements now become dependent on an outside source.'

'We really like it when donors make the time to come out and see the partnership in real time. They can sit down and make sense of it.'

Dave and I talk about the word 'empowerment' and how it has become the buzzword in modern aid. Taking such a simple concept and seeing a village community put it into practice by saying, you know what, let's fix that ourselves, we've done it before — remember that SurfAid programme, when we got together and changed our eating habits? Well, we can do this too. That's what's tickling Dave's fancy more than anything else at the moment. He says: 'That's empowerment — when they realise they know how to assess the problem and find the solutions themselves. The question of power is fundamental to what we do and it should be fundamental to the incentive structure for development, but it's not. We're experiencing more examples of our large water-sanitation programmes where we've had to pull out of villages because locals have come in and wanted a handout to help. We've had a wharf built, the government paid locals to do something essential for the village, now they want us to pay them to help, but we're not paying them. The reward system is wrong. There should be more of the money given for prototyping and finding out what's working in this behaviour change aspect.'

'If you regularly participate with a sense of awe with nature and a sense of camaraderie, then that combination is the building blocks of happiness.'

Dave says the best thing a donor can do is take the time to come out and see for themselves where the money is being spent. SurfAid's two biggest donors, NZAID and AusAID, do that at regular intervals. 'We really like it when donors make the time to come out and see the partnership in real time. They can sit down and make sense of it. A lot of donors never leave their air-conditioned offices in some high-rise, they sign cheques for millions of dollars for aid and development, but they've never been out in the field. And that's one of the fundamental flaws of the development sector.' One businessman from Sydney journeyed out to the Mentawais for a week and was shown the villages and what Dave and his team were achieving with the help of his money. He went home and increased his support by 1000 per cent to AUS$200,000.

Dave's creative mind has helped establish five villages that are used for prototyping, such as reducing malaria and growing vegetables and looking at behavioural changes over a three- to five-year time frame. Once the data shows an approach is working then they will look at replicating it in another village. A typical village is small, with an average of around 300 people. They are extremely remote and for the inexperienced westerner, dangerous. Most have no roads, so travel is by boat, foot or canoe. Nias has some motorbike tracks and slightly bigger villages. One of the projects in the pipeline is looking at what it would be like to create the infrastructure to enable people to ride a motorbike between each village.

The prototype set-ups are not expected to be perfect; mistakes help in finding solutions. 'Part of our vision is experimentation, prototyping, trying to work out what works, what doesn't. If you had a business incentive structure, you'd be asking your NGO what mistakes have you made so far? What do you mean, none?' Part of the prototyping is about embracing technology, not ignoring it just because locations are remote. SurfAid was the first to use long-lasting insecticide nets to keep malaria-carrying mosquitoes at bay. A recent NZAID report described SurfAid's work in reducing malaria as 'working at the Ground Zero of malaria prevention in Indonesia'. They piloted the work in one village, expanded it to six, and now, based on the success of a 90 per cent decrease in parasite activity, and empowering the Mentawai people by helping them to understand the benefits of using a net, they have tackled the whole 206 villages. These days, they believe 90 per cent of Mentawai people are sleeping under a net and have access to education and anti-malarial health supplies. 'The malaria programme has been very, very effective. It's been a good start. Once the villagers see quick results, they then ask what else can we do.' But Dave's also conscious of rushing the accolades without having the complete programme data in support. It's part of that honesty he talks about; there's way too much money at risk, and even worse, lives to be lost, to be basing decisions on preliminary results. In the meantime, he's constantly trawling the Internet to pick up new stuff. He's recently found solar-powered cells that charge during the day and are four times more powerful than kerosene lamps. Each one costs less than $10. His eyes widen as he talks. He's clearly excited at the thought of literally turning on the lights in the islands.

It's amazing to think that if it wasn't for the act of surfing, lives would continue to be lost, good-willed people would be searching for inspiration and

I wouldn't be sitting in a back yard talking to Dave. He calls surfing an 'enabler' — it's enabled him to create SurfAid. Despite most of the donations coming from the non-surfing community, the catalyst has definitely been boardrider based. Just like World Vision has the churches, Salvation Army has its people, surfers are SurfAid's infinity group, they're the visual currency. I ask him what makes surfing so special. It's not like you see SkiAid, or RugbyAid, or other activities giving something back. He looks like he's never thought about it, most likely because he hasn't had time to. Sir Edmund Hillary, he says after a while, is the only other example of a tourist in the world he knows of who's managed to do anything at scale, who's wanted to give back to areas that have given so much pleasure to travellers. Perhaps it's a reflection of the Kiwi attitude, he says.

I'm surprised to hear he doesn't have a steady stream of travelling surfers willing to pay a visit to the prototype research centre beside the world-famous break, 'HTs'. I'm even more surprised when Dave moves in his chair and tells me not everyone in the area backs SurfAid's cause. 'We have a relationship with some of the charters, which is great. But it's very hard for us to get the local surf industry to consistently embrace communicating to the travelling surfer. There's certainly an equation; the more you know about us and the facts and the challenges we've overcome, then the more people tend to support us. But if you aren't a member of the group who are embracing what we're doing, then you could see us as something different, or something they don't understand, or even something they don't like.' Surely the travelling surfer would take the opportunity to add value to their week-long trip by observing a couple of hours of aid work? Dave draws a long breath. He's given up waiting for that to happen. 'That's frustrated me in the past. The hardest thing is there's a lot of surfers who would be willing to donate — the region sees over three thousand travelling surfers there every year — but very few actually do. We make a lot of effort to communicate, but if you're a captain of a surf boat charter, generally we're not going to be in their consciousness. Those who've made the effort, arrived and been shown around, have really enjoyed it. But to everyone else, it's about going hard and getting the most surf for their buck.'

Dave spends between 40 and 50 per cent of his time living at his home in Bali, where the main office is, and the rest of the time living out of his green backpack. His job has evolved hugely since those early days. These days he juggles keeping up with what's going on, with representing the organisation. While at the moment he's sitting here with me, a week ago he was having lunch with a lobbyist who knows the Australian Treasurer, who's a surfer. In two days' time he's flying to America to talk to the television network, ABC, then he's off to Hollywood to meet with a producer who wants to develop a storyline. That's just a couple of weeks' commitments. Multiply that by the other 50 weeks in the year, then throw in programme design work, mapping out models, monitoring them, training the 'training team', trawling for foundation money, meeting potential donors, talking to surf companies about what they can do to maintain their support in times of a recession, helping launch a fundraiser in New York's Times Square at the Billabong flagship store, assisting with NZAID and AusAID and spending time out in the field with their auditors, staying on and doing some more training with the staff and helping them find high-risk families, then going back out to find more money to keep it all going, and you can understand why everything that follows or comes from Dave is nothing short of 100 per cent commitment to the organisation. What else can be done? Who can be talked to? How can SurfAid be improved? That's why the music CD SurfAid's recently released has really got him excited.

Radioworks have given them free advertising to help with its promotion. Next week, while in America, Dave's talking to some of the big players in the music industry, having made the contacts through the wide network of people he's developed over the years. By the time it's re-recorded with some bigger international acts, new posters are made, Australasia's biggest PR company gets behind it, and it becomes available in American music shops and on iTunes, the money it's already raised (around $40,000) will explode into the hundreds of thousands. 'It reflects there's goodwill, because while people aren't wealthy enough to donate money, they will buy an album instead, as a charity thing. We have a unique story, and it seems people like it.'

Dave doesn't get to surf as much as people might think. In the beginning, there was a lot of resistance to the concept of SurfAid, because people thought Dave and Steve and the rest of the original team were in it to go surfing. A group of waxheads scamming their way into getting paid to do what they loved. But the nay-sayers never realised that the group themselves were donating money to keep SurfAid afloat. 'We actually call it no-surf SurfAid. Staff can't swim, let alone surf. It's not a great leadership role to go past a break that's going off and say, let's hit it, while the non-surfers sit in the sun. In saying that, when we can do it we encourage it. While you have a moral obligation, you also have an obligation to look after yourself both physically and spiritually.' What role does surfing play in his life these days? 'To me, it's my meditation. I'll get up at five-thirty, do some yoga, then be the first to paddle out. It's about having conversations with nature. I'm not a religious person but we're all spiritual. If you were religious it would be described as having a conversation with God. As you get older, you start to appreciate that side more, you start to wonder what we're doing here. I'm certainly more proactive about that sort of stuff now. I try and observe the clouds and start living in the moment. It's physical, it's spiritual, and it's all done by eight-thirty, then I'm back in the office.'

Are we ever going to see Dr Dave back in New Zealand permanently? His reply is sharp; it's over when he dies and maybe not even then. In saying that, he acknowledges life has all sorts of ways of surprising you. He still loves New Zealand, and all his friends and family are here. He'd come back in a heartbeat. But his devotion, and stubbornness I'd say, is too powerful to just pull the pin and let someone else fill two rather large shoes. He keeps in touch with his homeland via the Internet and reads the news constantly. I'm curious to discover how he sees New Zealand and what he thinks of the direction we're heading. The biggest risk he can see is that we'll lose our individuality and character. 'There's so much good from our Kiwi character and the people who emerge from it. It's going to come down to how individuals, families and a nation juggle the incentive structures. We have to be internationally competitive, yet we don't want to have to lose our nature, so that we can't go to the beach and strike a conversation with anyone and invite them back for a beer.' You don't want to change that, he says. Our unique structure is one of our biggest advantages on the world stage, but what he sees rubbing off on us from other countries worries him. 'The challenge for New Zealand is to maintain its character and personality. Its links with conservation and nature are critical for us. As the world gets more polluted, people will be looking for sanctuaries, and we're living in one, whether we like it or not. We have to be careful not to destroy it. Living within our means, understanding and cherishing how incredibly great our place is, should be a source of satisfaction and happiness.'

After proving that good can come from a bunch of surfers in a garage band, what else can society take from the surfing ethos? 'If you regularly participate with a sense of awe with nature and a sense of camaraderie, then that combination is the building blocks of happiness. You're going to be richly rewarded. I think that's what surfing has to offer and people see that. I'm afraid that human beings won't capture the opportunity they have; they won't make progress to understand some basic principles, that we have to be compassionate in order to be happy. We know what it takes but we don't do it, we're striving for the wrong goals, it's so predictable they won't deliver. There is going to be high levels of dissatisfaction. Corrupt, deceitful businessmen; one of the reasons for the global recession is a direct result of the top one per cent screwing it up for the rest of us. I fear we will not fulfil our potential. This is what I always like to see, a potential to see a village be healthy, the potential for the ten million children dying in the world reduced to one through fundamental structural changes in the way we deliver aid. We make the wrong decisions, we don't learn, we lack wisdom . . . I fear that myself. That I won't be the full person I want to be.'

Acknowledgements

A book of this magnitude doesn't get written on its own, so I'd like to take the opportunity to acknowledge my sincere appreciation for Lorain, Tracey, Eva, Antoinette, and the rest of the HarperCollins team, who took a punt on a guy with no formal journalism training and only one book under his belt. Their enthusiasm for the vision made the project a pleasure from start to finish; in particular, being able to work closely with the always-positive Tracey. A special thank you also to Sue Page for overseeing the editorial role and making sure the original creation became a far more polished one.

Thank you to the contributors, who all fielded a strange phone call from a guy in Hawkes Bay claiming to be a surf writer, and then allowed him into their homes and lives. Every visit was a moment of inspiration for me and it's been an absolute privilege to be able to tell your stories. I look forward to catching up with you all again, in and out of the water.

A big thank you to my friend and mentor, Bob Harvey, who let me talk him into writing the introduction as we moved between the sixth and first floors of the Waitakere City Council building. I cherish every visit I make to the dynamic shores of his beloved Karekare, where I get to share a brew and yarn with him. His affinity with the ocean knows no bounds. Also, a special thanks to Piha's Craig Levers for being a constant source of information and support, and for putting me up in his sweet pad whenever I ventured north. It's a huge honour to call you a mate.

Thanks to my parents who gave me a boogie board and a set of waterproof markers when I was 11. They encouraged me to draw my own design on the board, then let me use the old man's giant orange spring suit so I could feel cool amongst the real surfers, despite looking like a stick figure with square clothes. My parents have been a massive source of inspiration to me over the years, and I was especially grateful for their moral support and understanding each time I went off on a 'research trip', when really they would've preferred to see their marketing guy at work in the family business.

On the subject of family and friends, thanks to the world's coolest in-laws, Ian and Helen, who at family functions told everyone that I wasn't there because

I was living the high life of a rock'n'roll surf journo, when really I was hiding away in their back room pushing keys. For all my immediate and extended whanau and friends who chipped in along the way with accommodation and contacts, I'm eternally grateful for your assistance.

A massive thanks to the photographers who have managed to capture the faces in the stories, bringing a splattering of colour into a book of black and white pages. They include Craig Levers, Cory Scott, Gisiele Alves, Miles Ratima, Brennan Thomas, Digga, Daisy Day, Brian Herlihy, Toi o Tahuna Gallery, and Bob Barker. While every effort has been made, my sincere apologies and full appreciation to any owners of images not recognised. Thanks also to the creative team at Adplus who gave me a coffee's worth of free brainstorming to eliminate potential book titles that were clichéd, boring, or just blatant plagiarism.

A very special thanks to my friends and agents, Chris and Barbara Else, for yet more wisdom, support, and guidance through this project.

Finally, the biggest thank you goes to my beautiful wife, Joanna, and our sons, Taylor and Toby. Despite my intending to use the book as an excuse for plenty of family trips away, most weekends turned into solo missions. Regardless, Jo threw enthusiasm in behind the project and shared my passion from start to end. I promise I'll never spend another summer inside watching you and the boys through a window again. Love you guys.